AF764245

Fiscal Decentralization and Budget Control

STUDIES IN FISCAL FEDERALISM AND STATE–LOCAL FINANCE

Series Editor: Wallace E. Oates, *Professor of Economics, University of Maryland, College Park and University Fellow, Resources for the Future, USA*

This important series is designed to make a significant contribution to the development of the principles and practices of state–local finance. It includes both theoretical and empirical work. International in scope, it addresses issues of current and future concern in both East and West and in developed and developing countries.

The main purpose of the series is to create a forum for the publication of high quality work and to show how economic analysis can make a contribution to understanding the role of local finance in fiscal federalism in the twenty-first century.

Titles in the series include:

The Political Economy of Financing Scottish Government
Considering a New Constitutional Settlement for Scotland
C. Paul Hallwood and Ronald MacDonald

Does Decentralization Enhance Service Delivery and Poverty Reduction?
Edited by Ehtisham Ahmad and Giorgio Brosio

State and Local Fiscal Policy
Thinking Outside the Box?
Edited by Sally Wallace

The Political Economy of Inter-Regional Fiscal Flows
Measurement, Determinants and Effects on Country Stability
Edited by Núria Bosch, Marta Espasa and Albert Solé Ollé

Decentralization in Developing Countries
Global Perspectives on the Obstacles to Fiscal Devolution
Edited by Jorge Martinez-Vazquez and François Vaillancourt

The Challenge of Local Government Sizes
Theoretical Perspectives, International Experience and Policy Reform
Edited by Santiago Lago-Peñas and Jorge Martinez-Vazquez

State and Local Financial Instruments
Policy Changes and Management
Craig L. Johnson, Martin J. Luby and Tima T. Moldogaziev

Taxation and Development: The Weakest Link?
Essays in Honor of Roy Bahl
Edited by Richard M. Bird and Jorge Martinez-Vazquez

Multi-level Finance and the Euro Crisis
Causes and Effects
Edited by Ehtisham Ahmad, Massimo Bordignon and Giorgio Brosio

Fiscal Decentralization and Budget Control
Laura von Daniels

Fiscal Decentralization and Budget Control

Laura von Daniels

Free University Berlin and German Institute for International and Security Affairs (SWP), Berlin, Germany

STUDIES IN FISCAL FEDERALISM AND STATE–LOCAL FINANCE

Edward Elgar
PUBLISHING

Cheltenham, UK • Northampton, MA, USA

© Laura von Daniels 2016

All rights reserved. No part of this publication may be reproduced, stored in a retrieval system or transmitted in any form or by any means, electronic, mechanical or photocopying, recording, or otherwise without the prior permission of the publisher.

Published by
Edward Elgar Publishing Limited
The Lypiatts
15 Lansdown Road
Cheltenham
Glos GL50 2JA
UK

Edward Elgar Publishing, Inc.
William Pratt House
9 Dewey Court
Northampton
Massachusetts 01060
USA

A catalogue record for this book
is available from the British Library

Library of Congress Control Number: 2015957857

This book is available electronically in the **Elgar**online
Social and Political Science subject collection
DOI 10.4337/9781783475957

MIX
Paper from
responsible sources
FSC® C013056

ISBN 978 1 78347 594 0 (cased)
ISBN 978 1 78347 595 7 (eBook)

Typeset by Servis Filmsetting Ltd, Stockport, Cheshire
Printed and bound in Great Britain by TJ International Ltd, Padstow

To Albert Ludwig Hermann Abbondio Müller

Contents

Figures

Tables

Acknowledgements

In this text I am concerned with government finances and the capacity of nation-states to balance historically grown cultural, political and economic diversity, all reflected in their degree of decentralization, with the desire to reach and keep macroeconomic stability. My main point is that we should aim for a more comprehensive perspective on stability in fiscally decentralized schemes, including the message that changing fiscal rules at the central government level might send to politicians at all levels of government. Over the course of writing and completing this book, I have acquired a number of significant debts. Many people have contributed to the success of this project. This book would not have been possible, however, without the willingness of my interview partners in Latin America to share their past crisis experience. Interviews with policy makers and economists from four countries (Argentina, Brazil, Ecuador and Uruguay) were invaluable to my understanding of economic policy making in the context of emerging markets. Talking to country experts at international institutions and private sector representatives in New York and Washington, DC further added to that understanding. I thank them all for their openness to my project. The book at hand presents work written at the Freie Universität Berlin and the Hertie School of Governance, and then completed during research stays at Princeton and Harvard Universities, continuing into my first academic position as visiting assistant professor at the Central European University Budapest. I thank Alex Pettifer and his team at Edward Elgar Publishing for their support and patience during the completion of the manuscript. Many people at these institutions offered help and advice, and I thank them all for their time and effort. All of the remaining errors are, of course, to be considered entirely my own.

I am also grateful for financial support for the research that led to this book. This was provided by the Deutsche Forschungsgemeinschaft under the research center 'Governance in Areas of Limited Statehood' (SFB 700). As a member of the research center, under the directorship of Thomas Risse and Ursula Lehmkuhl at the Freie Universität Berlin, I benefitted greatly from the intellectual environment and the administrative and financial support. I am also grateful for financial support from the German Academic Exchange Service (DAAD) and the Berlin Consortium for German Studies (BCGS) together with Princeton University. The Thyssen Foundation generously supported my research at Harvard University's Weatherhead Center for International Affairs through the Transatlantic Fellowship Initiative. At Harvard, I would like to thank Steve Bloomfield, the managing director of the Weatherhead Center for International Affairs, and also his staff for their untiring support. I am indebted to Karl Kaiser, longtime director of Harvard University's Program on Transatlantic Relations, for his help and guidance.

Without question, the most sustained debt is to Henrik Enderlein and Mark Hallerberg at the Hertie School of Governance in Berlin. As professor and academic advisor, Henrik had inspired me at an early stage of my academic career to work on topics in international political economy. To this day, Henrik continues to be a source of inspiration in so many ways and I consider myself very lucky to have had an opportunity to work alongside him for several years in his project on sovereign debt crises in emerging market economies. Mark Hallerberg agreed to become my second advisor almost the moment he arrived as professor at the Hertie School, and has served as an incredible source of intellectual inspiration, academic guidance and support to me. As a graduate student in Berlin, I benefitted from the exchange with many colleagues at the Hertie School and at the Freie Universität, in particular Christoph Trebesch from whom I have learned a great deal. I am deeply grateful also to two outstanding professors at the Freie Universität Berlin; to Tanja Börzel for her guidance and to Susanne Lütz for providing helpful academic advice. Many thanks also to Thomas Eimer.

Outside Berlin's educational institutions, I was strongly supported by a number of extraordinary people. At Princeton University, Dani Campello provided important help, reading and commenting extensively on my work. Robert Keohane and Helen Milner both provided crucial comments and pointed me to interesting historical cases. I am also grateful for the helpful comments and suggestions I received from members of Princeton University's Comparative Politics Seminar and Harvard University's Political Economy Seminar. At Harvard University, I am indebted to Jeffry Frieden for offering his invaluable academic advice and help in getting me in touch with other scholars in the Harvard community. Several colleagues stood ready to read my work and provide invaluable comments, including Gabi Spilker, Joachim Wehner, Daniel Mügge, Fabio Wasserfallen and Jorge I. Dominguez. Gabi, together with Mareike Kleine and Cornelia Woll, also turned out to be an impeccable source of moral support during the final writing phase of the manuscript. I am deeply grateful for their help. But I am also grateful for crucial support at the early stages of my research project. Pablo Pinto, who was my professor of political economy at Columbia University, provided me with important contacts in Argentina. Many thanks also to Daniela Ayoso and Vincente Albornoz for sharing valuable contacts with policy makers in Ecuador. I thank Caroline Silva-Garbade for lavishly sharing her contacts with crucial interview partners in Argentina and Brazil and for engaging me in inspiring discussions about (failed) economic policies for Latin America.

Over the course of writing this book, I was lucky to receive support from several dear friends and family. I thank Antje von Daniels for letting me draw on her creative mind, elevating my poor drawings to a much higher graphic level. Maria Ziegler and Michael Peters have been true friends and inexhaustible sources of fine advice. I am deeply thankful to Céline Küsters for being there, always and unconditionally. Also to Julia-Hannah Stahl and Lisa Julie Rauen for their cheering up when I needed it most. I am also deeply grateful to Britta Fischer and Herb Fox and their wonderful and inspiring family. I could always count on their help and moral support.

This book is dedicated to my father because I know that no one else would have been prouder to hold these pages in his hands. However, I feel greatly indebted to my whole family – the one I was born into as much as those who so generously accepted me as one of their own. Without the loving support and patience of my mother-in-law and father-in-law, this endeavor would hardly have been possible. Certainly, life would have been much less enjoyable. In the writing of the chapters of this book, many events, but more importantly people, were moving my life. Four of them are the most fantastic gift that anyone could hope to have in their lives: Justus, Lucie, Romy, and Franz. Their love carries me always.

1. Fiscal institutions and budget balances

> No one can be more appreciative of the advantages of the federal system than I. I see it as one of the most potent arrangements there is for making men prosperous and free. (Alexis de Tocqueville, *Democracy in America*, 2004, vol. 1, Part 1, Chapter 8, p. 192)

> In the democratic centuries that are about to begin, I think that individual independence and local liberties will always be a product of art. Centralization will be the natural form of government. (Alexis de Tocqueville, *Democracy in America*, 2004, vol. 2, Part 4, Chapter 3, p. 796)

By minimizing the role of local government, there will simply be less scope for locals to seek fiscal assistance; they will have less capacity to raid the fiscal commons. But this can amount to throwing the baby out with the bath water. Central governments, as we all know, can themselves exploit their monopoly position. (. . .) The challenge is rather one of determining the kinds of institutions that can accommodate fiscal decentralization so as to realize the political advantages and economic gains from local control, while avoiding the potentially distorting and destabilizing effects that can result from soft budget constraints. (Wallace Oates, *Toward A Second-Generation Theory of Fiscal Federalism*, 2005, p. 362)

1.1 MOTIVATION

Why are some countries struggling with fiscal crises while others maintain stable government finances? To understand the dynamics of today's fiscal and debt crises, it serves to go back to previous cases. One region where fiscal instability was a major obstacle to reaching overall macroeconomic stability in the past is Latin America. There is little argument that past crises in that region have, to a considerable extent, been home grown and that inefficient policy processes invited structural imbalances. Fiscal mismanagement became evident when the Latin American debt crisis broke out in 1982 and again, in a series of financial crises, during the late 1990s and early 2000s.

At the end of the 1980s, the international community made a large effort under the Brady Plan[1] to assist highly indebted countries (measured by the share of public debt in national income) in bringing down their debt levels. Yet, international crisis management was not sufficient as an instrument to get countries on a sustainable track. Domestic impediments to reaching macroeconomic stability remained in many countries. When the Mexican crisis spilled over to other Latin American countries in 1994, fiscal imbalances came to the fore once again, becoming a major concern for governments, among other reasons, because the International Monetary Fund (IMF) emphasized the importance of fiscal balance adjustments in continued consultations with debtor countries. Nevertheless, as is often the case, when times became better with growth rates resorting to pre-crisis levels soon after, structural problems became of less concern to governments. During the economic recovery of the following years, only a few governments made it their priority to address the remaining institutional problems and undertake reforms. When a second wave of external macroeconomic shocks reached the Southern Cone economies, after the Asian crisis in 1997 and the Russian default in 1998, the repercussions were soon felt across the region (Reinhart and Rogoff 2009).

Fiscal imbalances in Latin America figured prominently once more in the business pages of international newspapers at the end of the 1990s and the beginning of the 2000s after the region's two largest economies, Brazil and Argentina, experienced a toxic mixture of current account, currency and public financial crises. Throughout 2001, the year of the Argentine sovereign default, public debt ratios and government deficits in most of Latin America rose to alarming levels, threatening the stability of the region as a whole. However, not all countries were affected by the external shocks in the same way. While some countries suffered large-scale crises in government finances, bringing governments to (the brink of) default on external liabilities and leading them to abandon fixed exchange rate systems, others were less affected.

Compared to the situation in the mid-1990s, we see by the late 2000s profound improvements in government finances on average. Fiscal balances have been recovering for more than half a decade since 2003 and did not deteriorate to alarming levels throughout the Global Financial Crisis (GFC). Given the region's long history of pro-cyclical government finances, this may be seen as a success. Also, a large number of governments decided to use increasing tax revenue during the economic upswing of the 2000s to reduce public debt to more sustainable levels. Nevertheless, large cross-country differences remained in the Latin American and Caribbean region following the financial market crises of the early 2000s, considering that the gap between the country with the highest budget surplus, Chile, and the country with the highest deficit, Nicaragua, was roughly 12 percent of

GDP around the middle of the 2000s, according to the IMF's Government Finance Statistics (GFS). Figure 1.1 depicts how strongly Latin American countries differed in their average performance over the full period under consideration. Yet, as shown by the deficit data in Figure 1.1, there is also significant variation in performance within countries over time.

The different effects of macroeconomic shocks or, more precisely, the different capacities of Latin American governments to act on external shocks, open up an important research question. Given that countries experienced largely the same external macroeconomic shocks and financial conditions and followed similar policy recommendations by international organizations, why are they so different in their macroeconomic and, in particular, their fiscal performance? After the Asian crisis and the Russian default, emerging market economies were suffering from similar credit constraints following from the risk aversion of financial market participants. Likewise, they were affected by similar trade shocks resulting from a slowdown in international demand for their exports in 1999. If these macroeconomic factors cannot explain the differences in outcomes, it seems timely to consider some alternative institutional explanations.

One argument that immediately comes to mind is that governments were unable to adjust to external shocks in due time because they were too constrained by inflexible exchange rate regimes (currency pegs) (see e.g. Clark and Hallerberg 2000, Garrett 2000, Feldstein 2002, Calvo et al. 2003, de la Torre et al. 2003). Yet, the degree to which fiscal accounts were stabilized and brought back on a sustainable track differs even in countries that followed similar trends in exchange rate policies. For example, both Argentina and Brazil relied on fixed exchange rate regimes, aiming to stabilize their economies before this policy was changed in reaction to major economic shocks towards the end of the 1990s. In the course of economic recession and speculative attacks on their currency regimes, both countries were forced to abandon their pegs and shifted to a currency float. But they differed fundamentally in their approach to fiscal consolidation. In the end, they also differed in their macroeconomic performance.

If the answer is neither to be found in the realm of macroeconomic conditions nor in the area of exchange rate regimes, we may be best advised to look at other institutional and political determinants. In the present study, several of the 'usual suspects' drop out right away by logical reasoning. For example, differences in the regime type (presidentialism) and common distinctions between electoral systems (proportional representation versus majoritarian systems) cannot explain the variance depicted in Figure 1.1, given that they are more or less constant across the cases in my sample. In contrast, by looking at the difficulties with initiating macroeconomic reforms in Latin America in the past, we may find that veto players certainly

Average Nominal Budget Balance-to-GDP Ratios (1990–2006)

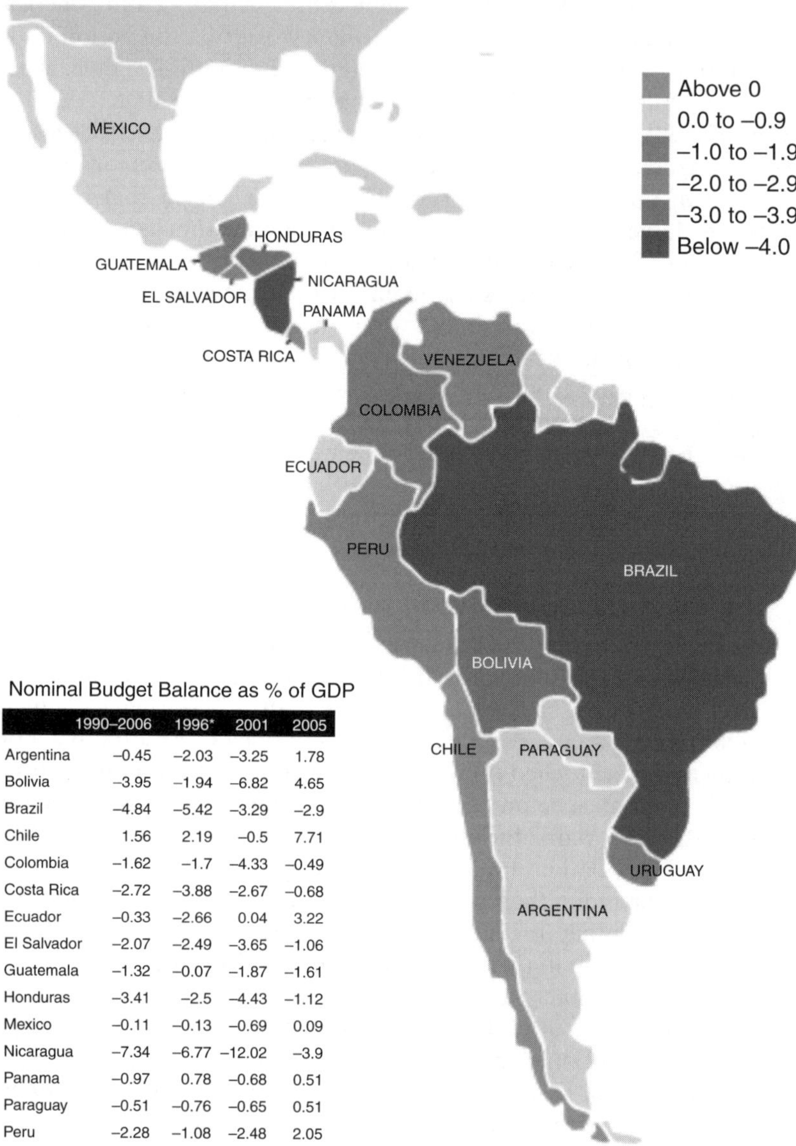

Nominal Budget Balance as % of GDP

	1990–2006	1996*	2001	2005
Argentina	–0.45	–2.03	–3.25	1.78
Bolivia	–3.95	–1.94	–6.82	4.65
Brazil	–4.84	–5.42	–3.29	–2.9
Chile	1.56	2.19	–0.5	7.71
Colombia	–1.62	–1.7	–4.33	–0.49
Costa Rica	–2.72	–3.88	–2.67	–0.68
Ecuador	–0.33	–2.66	0.04	3.22
El Salvador	–2.07	–2.49	–3.65	–1.06
Guatemala	–1.32	–0.07	–1.87	–1.61
Honduras	–3.41	–2.5	–4.43	–1.12
Mexico	–0.11	–0.13	–0.69	0.09
Nicaragua	–7.34	–6.77	–12.02	–3.9
Panama	–0.97	0.78	–0.68	0.51
Paraguay	–0.51	–0.76	–0.65	0.51
Peru	–2.28	–1.08	–2.48	2.05
Uruguay	–1.49	–1.46	–3.68	–0.57
Venezuela	–2.22	–3.98	–4.35	0.02

Data for the General Government, Sources IMF, country data as reported in IDU data base.
*If unavailable the next annual data point available is impaired.

Figure 1.1 Fiscal imbalance in Latin America

mattered. Indeed, veto player theory may serve scholars in understanding why and under what circumstances leaders were able to move from a 'negative' to a 'positive' fiscal policy equilibrium. However, acknowledging that the number of ideologically dispersed veto players affects leaders' ability to change their policy position does not provide a satisfactory answer as to why deficit financing and over-borrowing by public entities became so prevalent in the first place in some countries but not in others.

1.2 INSTITUTIONAL EXPLANATIONS OF FISCAL IMBALANCE

1.2.1 Fiscal Imbalance as a Common Pool Resource (CPR) Problem

The present study builds on previous political economy research in arguing that the incidents of extremely negative fiscal outcomes apparent in the data can best be understood as a consequence of a collective action problem – that is, the problem of coordinating fiscal policy among different rational, self-interested budget actors in a way that leads to optimal outcomes for the general public. Under the assumption that these budget actors are not constrained by any rules or other budget constraints, individual politicians are likely to succeed in maximizing their share of what constitutes the 'common pool resource', the national tax base, while keeping their contributions as low as possible. As a result, we often observe government spending bias and eventually growing budget deficits and unsustainable borrowing levels.

1.2.2 Budgetary Institutions

To solve the above-described problem, generally referred to as the common pool resource (CPR) problem, governments may choose to take measures leading to a 'hardening' of budget constraints. As was suggested by a significant amount of institutional literature in economics and political science, we may find that hard budget constraints by and large follow from a more hierarchical control by a 'central budget authority' with the clear objective to provide long-term stability of government finances (von Hagen 1992; for a comprehensive overview, see Persson and Tabellini 2000, and Hallerberg et al. 2009b). Next to hierarchical institutions, a large number of contributions discuss the value of implementing fiscal targets – also referred to as a 'statutory approach'– to harden budget constraints. Without doubt, the latter assumption would seem to depend on whether budget actors are able to credibly commit to a sanctioning mechanism, guaranteeing that fiscal rules are respected. In the budgetary institutions literature, the term 'centralization' is generally employed to describe a stronger coordination of fiscal policies, with the aim of reducing the negative externalities of individually rational free-riding behavior, whether this is achieved through implementing more 'hierarchical procedures' or through a 'statutory approach'. The more budget decisions are centralized in that sense, the more is government oversight over revenue and expenditure expected to improve. Ideally, this leads to reducing spending bias and a list of related problems, including the threat of growing fiscal deficits and public debt. As has been emphasized in a number of more recent contributions in that literature, for reforms of budgetary institutions to facilitate improved fiscal policy coordination, what may be more important than the distinction between delegation and statutory approaches is the way in which a specific approach harmonizes with the underlying characteristics of the political and electoral system (Hallerberg and von Hagen 1999, Hallerberg 2004, Hallerberg and Marier 2004, Hallerberg et al. 2009a, 2009b).

Critics of the above-described budgetary institutions approach often emphasize the difficulty of isolating the suggested independent effect of budgetary centralization on fiscal balances from the effect of other – unobserved – factors. When budgetary institutionalists point to recent cases of successful stabilization, such as Brazil since the early 2000s, questions immediately arise whether we can attribute the fiscal improvement to institutional reforms or whether it is best explained by favorable external economic conditions benefitting governments in the entire region (Izquierdo et al. 2008).[2] To be able to provide a more nuanced picture of the potential relationship between institutional reform and macroeconomic outcomes, more empirical analysis seems necessary. Before we get there, however, it may serve to look at some stylized facts from a historical example that will illustrate the theoretical meaning of hard budget constraints.

1.2.3 A Historical Example of Budget Process Centralization: Early 20th Century USA

Are institutional reforms that centralize fiscal authority in the hands of the executive an effective way of improving fiscal outcomes? If so, are there historical examples that allow us to evaluate the effect of institutional change over a longer time horizon, providing evidence that centralized institutions can successfully be 'locked in' and serve as binding constraints on budget policies long after they have been established?

To find out if reforms of fiscal institutions can lead to long-term improvements in fiscal outcomes, it may serve to look at an early 20th century example from the USA. With the founding of the Bureau of the Budget (BOB)[3] under the auspices of the Treasury Department through the Budget and Accounting Act of June 10, 1921, President Warren G. Harding (1921–1923) took a bold step to centralize fiscal authority.[4] President Harding's reform aimed at strengthening executive control over the previously less structured budget process, with the ultimate goal of reaching fiscal stability and taking control of the public debt that had risen to a historical peak following war-time military expenditure (Berman 1979, p. 3).[5] And so, the BOB was founded as a new agency with the authority to assemble, revise, reduce or increase the budget proposals of government departments and agencies. While reform proposals had circulated for at least a decade, the political window of opportunity to take action on fiscal matters opened suddenly during a short but harmful economic recession that lasted from the beginning of 1920 until mid-1921. Americans experienced the recession as a painful shock after the general economic upswing following the end of World War I. Given that, under the Gold Standard, the US government lacked the monetary instruments to react promptly to the upcoming recession in 1920, the government found itself in the uncomfortable position of having to control fiscal deficits or lose access to financial markets. Choosing the first option, the US government embarked on a path of fiscal consolidation. Following the new legislation, government expenditure fell from a peak of 29 percent of GDP in 1919 by more than 10 percentage points until 1922. From then on until the Great Depression in 1929, government size relative to GDP stabilized at around less than 12 percent. Looking at historical fiscal data, it becomes clear that the course of fiscal consolidation taken under Harding was followed by a significant improvement in the fiscal stance.[6] But was this policy sustainable?

Looking at the 1930s, we observe, at first, expansive fiscal policies, following increasing numbers of budgetary actors involved in household decisions as a consequence of the New Deal policies advanced during the presidency of Franklin D. Roosevelt (1933–1945). Although initially eager to create new government agencies with the objective of stimulating the economy, the Roosevelt administration soon tried to recentralize budget control. It was Roosevelt himself who tried in 1934 to recentralize government control over the budget process. To do so, he elevated the BOB to a cabinet-level agency, however kept under the auspices of the presidential office. These institutional changes were followed by several budget cuts, effective in 1935, 1937 and 1938. From a historical perspective, the founding of the BOB – later renamed the Office of Management and Budget – marks an important turning point for the USA. To date, the office remains an essential resource for presidents targeting areas where spending could be reduced and revenue raised.[7] While some may view the creation of the agency as 'original sin', allowing presidents to pass contested fiscal adjustment programs through Congress more readily, there is little doubt that the agency helped the US government to build a reputation over many decades as a sovereign debtor able to act on fiscal problems in due time when necessary, even in times of strong political polarization.

As shown in the historical example, centralizing a country's budget processes can inspire a virtuous cycle, leading to a significantly improved fiscal stance. A possible causal mechanism leads from institutional centralization to changed incentives for budget actors, facilitating fiscal policies that are oriented towards the long-term sustainability of government budgets. All things being equal, the strengthening of budget constraints, together with improved transparency, should therefore lead to improved fiscal stability.

There are also, of course, more critical accounts of increased centralization. What they have in common is a critical view of all-too-powerful central governments. To be able to control the latter, power needs to be checked not merely by distributing decision rights to other actors on the national level (i.e. power sharing between different branches of government), but also by dividing fiscal authority along the vertical axis, i.e. by providing subnational governments with fiscal authority.[8] For good reasons, these arguments have made their way into actual policy recommendations to developing countries by the World Bank and other international organizations (for an overview, see Tanzi 1996, World Bank 2000 and UNDP 2005). Based on such recommendations, governments have followed vertical decentralization policies in the transition to democracy. A concern is that governments may have followed such recommendations more or less blindly, at least with regard to the potentially negative budgetary consequences of allowing for more fiscal decentralization. Looking at the Latin American and Caribbean region, we observe, for instance, an increase in vertical decentralization – measured as subnational expenditure over total government expenditure – from an average of 13.1 percent in 1985 to 19.3 percent around the mid-2000s, according to research by the Inter-American Development Bank (Daughters and Harper 2007).[9]

1.2.4 Vertical Fiscal Decentralization and the CPR Problem

In the institutional literature, we find both proponents of fiscal federalism and critics that warn of potential destabilizing effects. In one branch of the literature, decentralizing fiscal authority along the vertical axis of government is described as beneficial for overall fiscal stability, for several reasons.[10] First, as pointed out by Brennan and Buchanan (1977, 1980) in their influential theoretical contribution, decentralization strengthens stability through its capacity to limit the exploitative fiscal policies of 'Leviathan' governments. Second, as was demonstrated by Oates (1972) in his 'decentralization theorem', vertical decentralization may improve allocative efficiency because subnational governments are better able to match the tastes of their constituencies with the public goods they provide. We should thus see less wasting of public resources under more decentralization. In the long run, this should enhance the stability of subnational finances and hence reduce the risk of fiscal imbalance on the aggregate level.[11]

According to Brennan and Buchanan's (1977) Leviathan model, which sees over-arching and intrusive central governments as a key impediment to stable government expenditure, a strategy that empowers decentralized budget actors allows the latter to control expenditure by the center. Beyond that effect, however, vertical decentralization may not only serve to control central government expenditure but also to control local-level government expenditure. Along the lines of Tiebout's (1956) earlier argument, competition among subnational governments may be seen as a viable mechanism for limiting the growth of government on the local level,[12] where local governments are under the scrutiny of local constituencies with an interest in fiscally responsible management of their local contributions. Although the empirical evidence for both hypotheses above remains mixed for industrial countries, the notion that decentralizing fiscal authority induces smaller government is taken up in several follow-up contributions focusing more on the developing and transition countries (see the discussion in Oates 1985, Rodden 2006, and Prohl and Schneider 2009).[13] For example, the argument that competition among vertically decentralized governments enhances fiscal stability at the local level is revived in the 'market-preserving federalism' literature (Qian and Weingast 1995, Weingast 1995). There, the central question is how economic innovation and growth can be stirred in an environment in which over-arching centralist governments, for example in the former Eastern Bloc countries, pose a major obstacle to allocative efficiency. In such a context, local budget authorities are ascribed a superior role in guaranteeing a better match between the tastes of constituencies and the provision of public goods. A related argument states that (vertical) decentralization of fiscal authority in low-income countries is crucial to ensuring that pro-poor policies actually reach the targeted groups and segments of the population (Pauly 1973, Bird and Vaillancourt 1998, World Bank 2000, UNDP 2005).[14]

Notwithstanding the popularity of decentralization policies, in particular among development scholars, a significant amount of research on the effects of fiscal federalism has questioned the notion of the predominantly welfare-improving effects of vertical fiscal decentralization. For example, Prud'homme (1995) warns of the potential dangers of decentralization, which increases the number of policy makers with incentives to exploit the 'fiscal commons'. In this scheme, subnational budget actors are likely to shift the burden of financing local spending programs to the central level.[15] This critique is taken up by a number of policy studies as well as in broader empirical analyses that have identified common pool resource problems on the subnational level, following from increased decentralization in expenditure and borrowing rights. Unless contained in due time, subnational CPR problems are found to pose a threat to the overall stability of government finances (Tanzi 1996, Ter-Minassian 1997a, Burki et al. 1999, Stein 1999, Treisman 2000, Wibbels 2000, Rodden 2002, 2003, 2006, Rodden and Wibbels 2002, Rodden et al. 2003).

An illustrative negative example is Argentina before the sovereign default in 2001, where fiscal profligacy on the part of the provinces repeatedly put overall government stability at risk (Braun 2006). Looking at the past history of subnational fiscal instability in Brazil, before the government of President Fernando Henrique Cardoso implemented institutional reforms at the end of the 1990s, we find similar evidence of subnationally induced fiscal imbalances at the national level. The same patterns of subnational CPR problems as drivers of both subnational and eventually central-level fiscal imbalance, were also identified in a series of cross-country studies by Rodden (2006). The latter represents a major contribution to the empirical literature on fiscal imbalance in the region and beyond, combining case studies with large N cross-country time-series analyses, looking at OECD and non-OECD countries over time. A main conclusion is that fiscal imbalance is most likely where subnational governments are simultaneously free to borrow and highly dependent on central-level transfers. Similar factors drive subnational and, subsequently, central-level deficits. These results are in line with other studies, pointing to the budget-undermining relationship between subnational fiscal indiscipline and increases in general government expenditure and debt (e.g. von Hagen and Eichengreen 1996, Treisman 2000, Wibbels 2000, Rodden 2002, 2003, Rodden and Wibbels 2002, Rodden and Eskeland 2003). The reason why the decentralization of budget control along the vertical axis leads to imbalances is generally seen in the increasing CPR problems following from a larger number of unconstrained budget actors drawing on the national tax base to finance local-level public goods. Although I side with Rodden (2006) on the potential fiscal destabilization following vertical fiscal decentralization, I come to a different conclusion on the mechanism that explains this outcome.

1.3 TOWARDS A NEW FRAMEWORK OF ANALYSIS

1.3.1 The Conditional Effect of Vertical Fiscal Decentralization, Depending on Horizontal Centralization

The institutional literature introduced above provides considerable evidence suggesting that by decentralizing fiscal authority on different levels, policy makers may have enhanced the risk of fiscal imbalance. This was explained in a parsimonious and convincing model – the so-called common pool resource (CPR) model. Accordingly, any move towards decentralizing fiscal authority increases the number of budget actors with incentives to free-ride on the national tax pool, leading to an overuse of the common tax pool. A number of follow-up problems, affecting overall stability, are likely to evolve. Contributions from the budgetary institutions strand of the literature show empirical links between decentralization of the budget process on the national level and fiscal performance indicators, including the size of government, deficits and public debt, both in absolute terms and relative to the economic strength of an economy. Budgetary institutions have been found to affect both levels of and changes in fiscal variables. Also, authors were able to show that the effectiveness of certain types of budgetary institutions depends on the ways in which they harmonize with underlying political institutions.

However, one aspect that has not yet received enough attention is the question of how budgetary institutions at the central level of government can help to reduce subnational-level free-riding on the common tax pool. Although it was argued by a significant body of fiscal federalism literature that vertical decentralization can create instability, affecting the central level in the long run, the budgetary institutions branch of the literature has, by and large, kept subnational budget actors out of the analysis. How can we explain that choice? Most authors are concerned primarily with fiscal instability in countries that are committed to a no-bailout doctrine with regard to subnational government units (e.g. the USA). Where no-bailout clauses are the norm and local governments are controlled by functioning markets for government debt, national-level policy makers should care less about the fiscal activities of subnational governments because the center cannot – and will not – be held responsible for subnational fiscal crises. However, as the more recent fiscal federalism literature has pointed out, the 'no-bailout assumption' may have to be relaxed in a context where subnational governments are highly dependent on transfers and where the latter have been – for a long time – free to finance their deficits by increasing borrowing (Rodden 2006). Such seems to be the reality in the countries analyzed here. Given that in these – and perhaps in other – cases, subnational budget making and fiscal responsibility are indeed connected to central government more strongly than is acknowledged in the budgetary institutions literature, it seems important to scrutinize how changes in central-level institutions influence subnational budgetary decisions.

This being said, we also find little mention of the role of central-level budget institutions in the fiscal federalism literature. Here, the focus is almost exclusively on local-level causes of instability. However, leaving the central-level institutional context out of the picture may bias results. My aim here is to propose a new way of thinking about the effects of decentralizing fiscal authority. Along the lines of both types of literature presented above, I argue that decentralization of fiscal authority along the vertical axis bears risks for overall fiscal stability. However, my point is that the extent to which vertically decentralized fiscal authority creates imbalances depends on the general strength of budgetary institutions at the central level.

A significant amount of research suggests that vertical decentralization can, under certain circumstances, reduce the stability of national government finances. The question is how or through what mechanism we should think that fiscal behavior on the subnational level turns into a risk for the overall fiscal stability of a nation. One obvious way in which subnational fiscal imbalance may affect overall stability is by creating liabilities for the nation as a whole. Subnational deficits and accumulated public debt at the lower levels of government may simply add to whatever fiscal problems exist on the national level, making central government the 'lender of last resort' for the undisciplined local budget actor. In the chapters below, I submit a different view of central–subnational fiscal relations. We should only see imbalances, stemming from subnational fiscal indiscipline, if budgetary institutions at the national level appear to be weak. Specifically, that means that where the national-level budget process is only weakly coordinated and lacking transparency, subnational fiscal actors are much more likely to over-spend and accumulate deficits. This is because soft budget constraints at the national level signal soft enforcement of fiscal discipline to the local level, affecting the political calculus of subnational leaders and, in much likelihood, their spending behavior. Hence, I expect the degree of budget process centralization at national level and the behavior of subnational budget actors under vertical fiscal decentralization to interact.

Figure 1.2 summarizes the potential causal mechanism that I have in mind. The first arrow leading from 'horizontal decentralization' to fiscal stability reflects my first hypothesis, arguing that a less coordinated horizontal-level budget process directly affects budget stability by shaping incentives for national-level budget actors to free-ride on the common

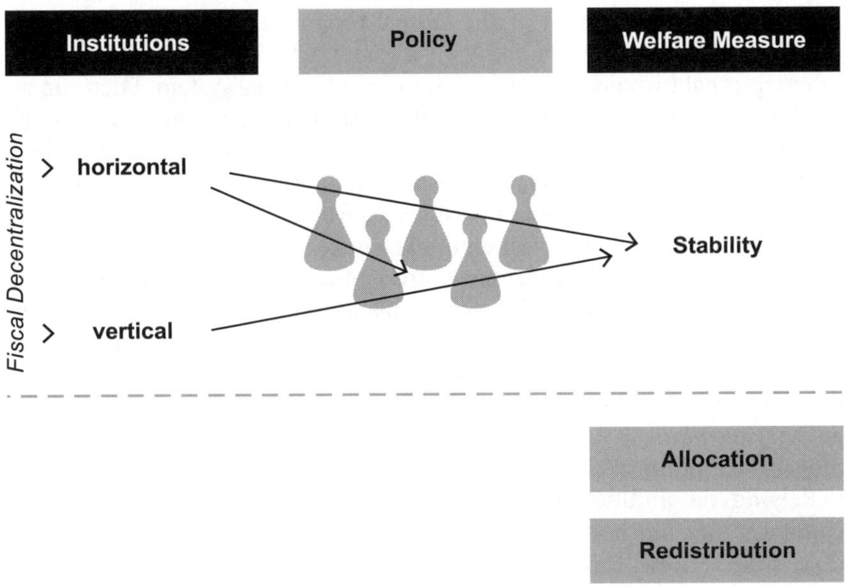

Figure 1.2 Horizontal and vertical fiscal decentralization of decision-making authority

tax pool. In addition to the direct effect, the two other arrows indicate that subnational fiscal behavior interacts with national budgetary institutions. Under vertical fiscal decentralization, subnational budget actors face stronger incentives to reap the benefits arising from local authority over-expenditure and 'export the costs' to the nation. However, I argue that central-level budgetary institutions are capable of conditioning this potentially destabilizing effect of vertical decentralization.

1.3.2 Methodological Approach

To the best of my knowledge, no study has tried to analyze vertical decentralization and national-level budgetary institutions in a single framework. Yet, a more comprehensive empirical approach, integrating both aspects, seems necessary to get to the roots of fiscal imbalance and macroeconomic instability, based on insights from previous research on budget imbalances in Latin America. In the empirical analysis below, I therefore start by analyzing the effects of horizontal decentralization on fiscal imbalance, relying on different research methods, combining graphical analysis of cross-country data with comparative case studies on institutional changes (or lack thereof) in Argentina and Brazil between 1990 and 2006. My analysis ends in 2006 at the advent of the Global Financial Crisis, beginning with the 'Subprime Crisis' in the USA a year later, which inaugurated a period of exceptional turbulence in the international financial system. Focusing on the Latin American region comes at the cost of building one's conclusions based on observations of a relatively small number of countries, especially given that the data availability narrows the sample size down to 15 countries. On the upside, this regional sample allows me to assume relative unit homogeneity as countries share a fair amount of historical experience and cultural norms. Another advantage is that I automatically control for a number of alternative political and institutional explanations of fiscal imbalance (e.g. democracy, presidentialism, electoral systems). With the graphical analysis of cross-sectional data, I aim to identify common patterns, regarding the effect of horizontal decentralization on fiscal stability. Extensive case study analysis allows me to focus on institutional change over time, bringing to the fore also the political circumstances of reform endeavors.

Relying on additional country- and subnational-level data for two countries that are not available for the larger sample, I highlight in the case studies how central government reforms and subnational fiscal behavior interact. The choice of the two countries follows from a most-similar systems design. Argentina and Brazil share largely similar country characteristics, regarding economic structure, the degree of openness in trade and of financial market integration. Furthermore, their political and institutional systems share many characteristics. Both are presidential democracies with a federalist tradition, including a high degree of vertical fiscal decentralization. Yet, both countries varied over the time period studied in the way they organized fiscal decision-making processes, on the national level and between the central and lower tiers of government. For my case studies, I draw on first-hand information gathered in over 30 semi-structured expert interviews with policy makers in Latin America. During research stays in Argentina and Brazil, I interviewed former members of those core economic teams that were in office during the governments of President Carlos Menem (1989–1999) and President Fernando de la Rua (1999–2001) in Argentina, and during the government of President Fernando Henrique Cardoso (1995–2002) in Brazil. Additional background information comes from interviews with country experts at the International Monetary Fund, the World Bank, the IADB and with private sector experts. Finally, I rely on archival data from the IMF and other academic sources on the fiscal and macroeconomic crises in both countries. Evidence from the case analysis allows me to develop my theoretical model further, incorporating new findings that may, as suggested by Lieberman (2005), allow me to engage in improved theory-driven large N analysis at later stages.

1.4 ALTERNATIVE EXPLANATIONS FOR BUDGET IMBALANCES

1.4.1 Fragmented Policy Making in Proportional Representation (PR) Systems

After laying out my own argument above, I proceed by reviewing some of the most widely discussed alternative explanations for fiscal imbalance in the political economy literature. First, there is a widely shared belief, going back to two influential articles by Roubini and Sachs (1989a, 1989b), that more fragmented (coalition) governments are more likely to be associated with fiscal imbalance than single-party governments because the former incur a greater risk of political instability. To support their claim, the authors initially presented their analysis of growth in government expenditure and in public debt, respectively, in OECD countries between 1960 and 1985, concluding that the difficulties that several developed countries faced in reducing high deficits in the post-Bretton-Woods era resulted from fiscal management problems under 'fractionalized' coalition governments. However, it should be noted that empirical evidence on the relationship between coalition government and fiscal instability does not clearly support the argument made by Roubini and Sachs.[16]

Coalition governments generally come about as a result of proportional representation (PR) electoral systems, whereas majoritarian voting rules are usually associated with single-party governments. Following a widely quoted article by Alesina and Drazen (1991), a broad literature revolves around the question of whether PR systems lead to more severe political gridlock, thereby incurring macroeconomic instability, including fiscal deficits. Alesina and Drazen (1991) refer to this as a 'war of attrition' game between governments and their political opponents. In these models, rational self-interested leaders postpone their decisions, waiting for the other side to move first. As a consequence, crucial policy decisions are likely to be delayed, worsening an already existing problem. Unlike the more general claim about coalition governments made earlier by Roubini and Sachs (1989a, 1989b), the 'war of attrition' model, pointing to the relationship between PR systems and fiscal instability, is supported by many empirical studies. However, this finding does not necessarily conflict with my argument that CPR problems are at the root of fiscal imbalance.[17] To be sure, all of the countries in my sample have electoral systems that involve some degree of PR. It may therefore seem rather implausible that proportional representation by itself could explain the – sometimes – considerable differences in fiscal stability between countries across the region at hand and across time.

1.4.2 Veto Players

Related to the first argument about macroeconomic imbalances under coalition governments, we may find that larger numbers of – ideologically dispersed – veto players explain why fiscal adjustment is often missing where and when it seems most needed. Following Tsebelis (1995, 2002), it could be argued that the larger the number of such veto players, the higher is the status quo bias and, hence, the potential for reform delay and, consequently, for fiscal instability. Empirically, this relationship seems to be rather robust.[18] Yet, while there is little doubt that higher numbers of ideologically dispersed veto players are likely to reduce the maneuvering space for a government, it is not self-evident that status quo bias leads to worse fiscal outcomes.[19] It could also serve to 'lock in' policies that are conducive to fiscal stability. Whether we actually observe instability due to a delay in necessary fiscal adjustment or quite to the contrary, a government's stern conviction to stick to adjustment thus depends on the status quo ante and needs to be determined on a case-by-case basis.

1.4.3 Electoral and Partisan Cycles

All of the different alternative explanations discussed so far focus on a 'policy delay' or 'gridlock' channel, providing reasons why fiscal restraint is not implemented. Other research has focused more on the failure to design budgetary institutions in such a way that 'vote-maximizing' politicians will face few incentives to over-exploit the common tax pool to begin with. To take a real-life example, we are, as political observers, well aware of the fact that, unless they are constrained by budget rules, politicians are likely to increase government expenditure on local public goods around election time, targeted at creating the support of certain groups of voters. Since Nordhaus' (1975) landmark contribution, economists and political scientists have stressed the importance of so-called political business cycles (PBCs) for public expenditure, deficits and debt.[20]

A different but related approach, advanced by Hibbs (1977) and Tufte (1978), states that fiscal imbalance is more likely to appear under left-wing party incumbency. So-called partisan cycles in government are thought to lead to spending increases, given the different redistributive priorities that are rooted in leftist political ideology. In these approaches, left-wing governments, as opposed to centrist or right-wing governments, are seen as more prone to increase public spending and less willing to apply fiscal cuts in transfer schemes. However compelling one may find the argument that partisan cycles explain large differences in fiscal outcomes, it appears that, empirically, there is no clear-cut support for the argument, neither in studies looking only at OECD countries nor in those drawing on larger samples, including non-OECD countries. Partisan cycles have not only been questioned by a range of empirical studies on OECD as well as non-OECD countries.[21] Clearly, the partisan-cycle argument would appear difficult to keep up in the context of Latin America in the past two decades, where left-wing governments are connected with all kinds of economic policy preferences and where the fiercest advocates of Washington-consensus-type macroeconomic reforms are to be found among leftist (or supposedly left-wing) governments (Campello 2015).

1.5 LOOKING AHEAD

In the chapters ahead, I start out by developing my theoretical approach to fiscal imbalance in emerging market nations, based on earlier insights from the institutional literature. Arguing that horizontal-level budget institutions interact with subnational fiscal behavior under different degrees of vertical fiscal decentralization, I proceed in several steps: in Chapter 2, I first return to the literature on budgetary institutions before I go deeper into fiscal federalism theory and review different predictions about the effects of decentralizing fiscal authority. Based on this review, I suggest a new model that combines previous approaches (Chapter 3).

In line with the previous literature, I submit that (a) decentralization of the budget process on the national level creates CPR problems, which are at the root of persistent fiscal deficits, and (b) the decentralization of budget authority along the vertical axis incurs additional CPR problems and fiscal indiscipline on the local level, creating liabilities for general government finances. However, I depart from the existing literature in the following way, providing novel insights on the interplay of subnational- and national-level fiscal discipline: according to my suggested theoretical framework, the negative effects of vertical fiscal decentralization depend to a large extent on a contextual factor, which is the degree of budget process decentralization on the national level or what I refer to as 'horizontal decentralization'. Thus, I suggest that vertical decentralization and horizontal decentralization interact, assuming that the decisions that subnational leaders make are influenced by institutional centralization on the central level. In Chapter 3, I discuss my argument in more detail and present the working hypotheses that serve as a guiding line for the two comparative case studies on Brazil and Argentina (chapters 5 and 6) and may eventually provide a basis for the future cross-sectional time-series analysis.

In Chapter 4, I analyze the fiscal imbalances in Latin American and

Caribbean countries between 1993 and 2006. Given the lack of comparable data for earlier periods, my graphical analysis is restricted to data from two waves of surveys on the strength of budget institutions in the region. In chapters 5 and 6, I discuss in detail how national-level institutional reforms (or lack thereof) in Brazil and Argentina changed incentives for policy makers, both on the national and subnational levels. In Chapter 7, I summarize my key findings from comparing both cases. The evidence that I find confirms to a large extent the patterns that I detect in the graphical analysis for the larger sample of Latin American and Caribbean countries. In both cases, I find strong support for my argument that subnational CPR problems lead to severe fiscal problems for the country, on condition of a loose central-level budget process and low transparency at the national level. However, the situation changed significantly over time in the case of Brazil where a gradual reform process, beginning in 1996/97, induced stronger budget coordination and enhanced transparency at the horizontal level. I argue that in both countries, governments initially relied on 'market discipline' to impose hard budget constraints on local governments. However, given that the ambitious no-bailout doctrine soon turned out to be incredible, inviting creditor 'moral hazard', the hoped-for market-disciplining effects were essentially undermined. In the case of Brazil, where subnational governments experienced in 1997 the third fiscal and debt crisis in under 10 years, the federal government engaged in reforms of its budgetary institutions, leading to a centralization of fiscal decision-making power at the national level, increasing budget transparency and strengthening controls over the borrowing activity of subnational governments and other government agencies. What we observe in Brazil at the end of the 1990s can be summarized as a shift from a strategy that relies mostly on 'market discipline' to a 'regulatory approach'. In Argentina, we observe no comparable shift to a long-term-oriented strengthening of budgetary institutions at the horizontal level. Subnational fiscal problems increase to worrisome levels after 1997, creating pressure on the federal government to provide a bailout. At a point in time when the financial markets (and international financial organizations) were becoming more and more sensitive to any signs of policy gridlock and political uncertainty, the federal government was strongly constrained in its ability to implement fiscal adjustment in the amount needed to stay on top of its mounting debt-servicing obligations. The government's inability to come up with a macroeconomic strategy to manage the growing sovereign debt problem, including a plan to reduce subnational deficits and stop subnational debt expansion, contributed significantly to the sovereign debt crisis, culminating in the default declaration in December 2001.

At the beginning of this chapter, I submitted that (fiscal) decentralization has important virtues and, as de Tocqueville (2004) noted early on, it seems well founded to say that it contributes crucially to democracy in America and elsewhere. Yet, as the same author argues in a later chapter of his treatment of political and economic life in the early USA, decentralized fiscal authority also carries risks for economic and political stability under democratic government. Much in line with Oates (2005), I argue that governments need to set up binding central constraints on budget actors in order to deliver the benefits of vertical decentralization. Ideally, such institutions deter the raiding of fiscal commons, both by politicians on the national and subnational levels of government. By implementing strong central-level budgetary institutions, governments commit to hard budget constraints and to more transparency of the budget process, fundamentally changing incentives for subnational budget actors. I will return to this point in the last chapter (8) and discuss it in light of my empirical results. In the latter sections of Chapter 8, I include a list of policy recommendations based on the analysis of fiscal institutions carried out below. As a social scientist, I am aware of the potential pitfalls of drawing conclusions from limited empirical samples. That is why my final remarks should be seen more as an endeavor to provide some 'rules of thumb' for political actors and decision makers, rather than as a (fruitless) attempt at any kind of prognosis as to where things are heading in certain regions or countries in the years to come.

NOTES

1. Since the outbreak of the Latin American debt crisis in 1982 in Mexico, following quickly rising interest rates combined with low commodities prices undermining many debtor countries' ability to service their liabilities, a series of debt negotiations with private creditors has taken place. For most countries, the negotiated debt rescheduling and restructuring agreements still fell short of providing governments with enough 'breathing space' to repay their outstanding debts. First implemented in 1989, the Brady Plan – as a coordinated debt restructuring framework – thus depended on a growing understanding among creditors that many of the loans provided to Latin American governments over the 1980s would never be entirely repaid, and that some form of substantial debt relief was necessary to allow countries to get back on track with regard to economic growth. To this end, the Brady Plan was designed to contain the following three elements: (1) an agreement between external private creditors and debtor governments that lenders would accept debt reduction in exchange for improved collateral; (2) government agreement to improve macroeconomic stability by implementing a set of crucial macroeconomic reforms; (3) new debt instruments to be introduced that improved the tradability of government debt in international financial markets (e.g. the so-called Brady bonds). Although each country's debt negotiations with its international creditors were held separately, leading to a unique debt agreement, each Brady restructuring included choices from a common 'menu of options', leading to a debt reduction involving similar debt instruments, such as the exchange of bank loans for bonds of equal face amount with fixed, below-market interest rates (par bonds) or loans

for lower face-value bonds with market-level, floating interest (discount bonds). The Brady Plan, judged by most financial experts as a successful policy solution, enabling many countries to regain access to international capital markets, lasted from 1989 – with the onset of negotiations on Mexico's sovereign debt – until 1994 when the last agreement, between Brazil and its external creditors, became operational. Eighteen countries signed a Brady agreement with their creditors over that period. According to Cline (1995), the typical Brady deal led to a reduction of 30–35 percent of a country's debt.

2. Giambiagi and Ronci (2004), taking a mid-way position regarding fiscal improvement in Brazil, argue that while the fiscal adjustment in the second half of the 1990s was possible due to an increase in revenue rather than through a reduction in expenditure, the fiscal responsibility legislation (FRL) and the implementation of fiscal constraints were necessary to preserve fiscal stability. Alston et al. (2009, p. 77) come to a similar conclusion, pointing to the disciplining effect of the FRL in Brazil, which they find to extend beyond the national level, arguing that the FRL in Brazil 'does in fact constrain the behavior of the state governments, contributing greatly to achieving and maintaining fiscal sustainability'.
3. The Bureau of the Budget (BOB) was, later on, under the presidency of Richard Nixon (1969–1974), renamed the Office of Management and Budget and granted further autonomy.
4. Kiewiet and McCubbins (1991, p. 166) note that while the Budget and Accounting Act built largely on 'practices that had already been implemented' prior to World War I, it sufficiently 'redelegated the authority to formulate appropriations requests and compile the budgetary data to the newly created Bureau'.
5. At the same time, however, the simultaneous creation of the Independent Audit Office under the same Act was to assure us that presidential control over government finances was monitored by an independent agency outside of government.
6. According to historical data series available through Proquest Statistical Insight, the US government secured rapidly growing budget surpluses until the end of the 1920s, with the budget outcome growing by 46 percent between 1921, the year of the Budget and Accounting Act, and 1927 when a turning point was reached.
7. Pfiffner (1979, quoted in Kiewiet and McCubbins 1991, p. 166) notes that the creation of the Bureau of the Budget marks the 'beginning of the domination of the budgetary process by the institutionalized presidency'.
8. One obvious starting point for these approaches is the following: while the centralization of decisions increases fiscal stability, it very likely has effects on two other main functions of fiscal policy that are not, for practical reasons, covered to the necessary extent in the study at hand and that have been identified by Musgrave (1959) as effective allocation and redistribution functions. This means that I forgo a more detailed discussion of the allocative function at this point and will only make reference to approaches in that literature where an argument can be made that determinants of allocative efficiency are also likely to have an impact on stability. Likewise, I leave the general discussion on redistributive concerns, summarized by Beramandi (2007), among others, to future research.
9. Daughters and Harper (2007) report that the median for expenditure decentralization in Latin American and Caribbean countries was 8.3 percent in 1985, compared to 13.7 percent in 2004. Based on their data, the largest increase in expenditure decentralization took place between the early and mid-1990s, indicated by a shift in the sample median of 3 percent.
10. For a recent discussion on the effects of vertical fiscal decentralization on all three separate policy objectives – stabilization, allocation and redistribution – defined earlier by Musgrave (1959), see e.g. Fedelino and Ter-Minassian (2010, part 1).
11. Tiebout (1956) had advanced a similar proposition, however, based on the more restrictive assumption that in a world of freely moving households, tax payers would choose among different packages of public goods offered by communities, essentially allowing the latter to constrain local governments through a 'vote by the feet'. Based on these

conceptions, we would likely see more accordance between revenue and expenditure, meaning that rather than posing a threat to overall stability, the latter should be improved through vertical decentralization.

12. In the following, I use the terms subnational government and local government interchangeably with reference to executives of the state or provincial-level executives and the local or community level.
13. One reason why the empirical evidence on the effect of vertical fiscal decentralization may be ambiguous, as Rodden (2003) notes, is that researchers were not using the 'right' empirical indicators, failing to control for a set of variables that may otherwise obscure the hypothesized relationship.
14. Comparing these arguments to the reality in developing countries, Bahl and Linn (1992) argue that allocation efficiency, described by Tiebout (1956) and Oates (1972), is likely to be conditional on a country's ability to reach a certain 'threshold of development'. In other words, before we think about how to better guarantee a perfect match of tastes and public goods, it would seem advisable to think about ways to guarantee some degree of economic development. On a more critical note, Wibbels (2000) presents strong empirical evidence that questions the welfare-enhancing effects predicted by Weingast (1995) and others in the context of developing countries that lack crucial economic and institutional pre-conditions for 'market discipline'. Wibbels (2000) concludes that greater vertical fiscal decentralization in non-OECD countries is more likely to significantly reduce governments' ability to adjust economically, as it increases domestic collective action problems. Tommasi (2006) finds the success of vertical decentralization to depend on an accountability that guarantees that electorates have control over public good provision by local governments, while Blanchard and Shleifer (2001), among others, point to the danger that a weak center could more easily be 'captured' by revenue-maximizing local leaders, undermining attempts to redistribute income to poorer parts of the population.
15. Earlier, Scharpf (1979, 1988) also emphasized the downside of multi-tiered (fiscal) governance in developed countries when it comes to changing the status quo of government finances and re-organizing fiscal relations between the center and its constituent units.
16. To be sure, several follow-up studies, using the same 'fractionalization' index, did not reach the same conclusions and largely rejected the empirical relationship presented by those authors. For an overview, see de Haan and Sturm (1997).
17. Persson and Tabellini (2000) provide an overview of theoretical models of the war-of-attrition type that are concerned with the failure to react to fiscal distress promptly, while Persson and Tabellini (2003) discuss an array of empirical contributions on the link between proportional representation (PR) systems and macroeconomic outcomes, concluding that PR systems are linked to larger government expenditure and deficits. In a comprehensive cross-country time-series analysis using data for 88 countries, the authors conclude that 'majority elections induce smaller governments, less welfare state spending, and smaller deficits than proportional elections' (Persson and Tabellini 2003, p. 215). In a panel analysis of OECD countries (1970–1995), Kontopoulos and Perotti (1999) find confirming empirical evidence for the gridlock hypothesis.
18. Franzese (2002), in a comprehensive analysis of 21 OECD countries (1948–1997), provides robust empirical evidence confirming a negative relationship between the number of veto players and fiscal deficits.
19. As Franzese (2002, p. 48) points out, '(f)ractionalization and polarization produce inaction, and the impact of inaction depends on what would have happened under the status quo'. Indeed, if the relationship between the number of veto players and fiscal imbalance depends on the status quo ante, high fiscal deficits should only appear where public expenditure was high in the first place and where increasing veto players led to a preservation of high spending levels, even after the macroeconomic circumstances deteriorated. In a similar vein, with regard to inflation outcomes, Treisman (2000) argues 'that additional veto players may "lock in" existing patterns of monetary policy – whether inflationary or strict'. Hence, by saying that higher numbers of veto players

cause policy inertia, it is not said that the outcome is higher inflation (fiscal deficit) but only that whatever the status quo ante looked like will prevail.

20. See Persson and Tabellini (2000) for an overview of theoretical models following Nordhaus (1975); Brender and Drazen (2005) and Kaplan (2013) provide more recent overviews. Recent empirical evidence on the effect of PBCs remains quite mixed, with some contributions questioning the role of political cycles in industrialized countries under increased financial globalization (Helleiner 1994, Mosley 2000, 2003). When we shift the focus to non-OECD countries, the evidence seems to be more supportive of the PBC hypothesis (Leblang 2002, Block and Vaaler 2004). However, regarding Latin America results are similarly mixed. Here, Nieto-Parra and Santiso (2009) find that general elections are associated with much greater changes to fiscal policy in Latin America than in high-income countries. They submit that the average primary balance declines by almost 0.7 percent of GDP during an election year, looking at a sample of 28 OECD and 19 Latin American countries between 1990 and 2006. Kaplan (2009), who looks at PBCs around 122 elections in 16 Latin American countries between 1961 and 2006, concludes that under the condition of increased financial opening and countries' prior shock experience with hyperinflation during the 1980s, incumbents in the post-1990s era rely on inflationary manipulation of the economy much less frequently than before. Hence, Kaplan (2009) attributes the 'demise of the PBC' largely to the fact that politicians in crisis-ridden Latin American countries not only react to market pressure but also to the changed macroeconomic priorities of constituencies.
21. Franzese and Jusko (2006, p. 13) show, in a meta-study of the empirical literature, including OECD and non-OECD countries, that partisan cycles have a significant impact on several macroeconomic outcome variables, with the strongest effects present in studies of the size of government, revenue and spending policies. To be sure, however, Franzese and Jusko (2006, p. 14) also emphasize that 'naive left-deficit, right-surplus arguments (. . .) have least support' of empirical data. This finding is in line with several recent empirical studies providing evidence that markets remain sensitive to left-wing electoral victories, particularly in emerging market economies that are characterized by high political uncertainty (Leblang and Bernhard 2000, Leblang 2002, Martínez and Santiso 2003, Block and Vaaler 2004, Vaaler et al. 2006). Campello (2008) provides a model of optimal taxation under capital mobility that accommodates both (left-wing) divergence and convergence hypotheses. Accordingly, investors tend to flee a country when a left-wing government with a redistributive agenda replaces a right-wing government. Changes from right- to left-wing government evoke strong investor reactions, particularly in emerging economies. However, in anticipating increased capital flight during elections, left-wing incumbents in an unstable environment are likely to back down on their initial redistributive agenda, particularly in countries that have recently experienced a currency crisis. The empirical analysis of portfolio investors' behavior during 125 elections, both in industrialized and low-income countries, largely confirms the predictions of the model that investors are sensitive to information about redistribution (Campello 2008). Furthermore, Campello shows, in data for 89 Latin American elections between 1982 and 2006, that left-wing candidates in countries experiencing currency crises prior to the election campaign, are those most likely to back down from their initial redistributive agenda.

2. Overview: institutional approaches to fiscal imbalance and public indebtedness

2.1 INTRODUCTION

In this chapter, I discuss the literature in political science and public economics concerned with the effects of decentralized budget decision making on fiscal performance. Above, I sketched out my theoretical approach, which is based on the assumption that institutions are of crucial importance for fiscal outcomes because they set policy incentives for rational self-interested politicians. Hence, I focus on the role of institutions. In doing so, I order the literature along conceptual lines. First, I concentrate on the budgetary institutions literature, which, by and large, argues that stronger centralization of decision-making processes at the national level and binding fiscal rules, together with improved transparency and a credible enforcement mechanism, enhance fiscal stability. Second, I provide an overview of the fiscal federalism literature that deals with the consequences of decentralizing budget-making authority along the vertical axis. In this literature, the decentralization of budget decisions is often thought to invite subnational CPR problems, posing a threat to overall fiscal stability over time. The purpose of the review is hence to present key concepts from both branches of literature that have evolved largely independent of one another, before I propose and test a new model (chapters 3 and 4).

In a widely quoted contribution, von Hagen (1992) embarks on a common pool resource (CPR) model of fiscal imbalance. Accordingly, budget actors fail to coordinate on sustainable fiscal policies because the existing institutions set the wrong policy incentives. If public expenditure is financed out of a common tax pool, the benefits of government spending programs are likely to be concentrated while costs are diffuse. The CPR problem is hence a particular type of a collective action problem, assuming that (increasing numbers of) self-interested rational budget actors draw on a common tax base. In the absence of a hard budget constraint, individual policy makers are encouraged to bargain for a larger share of the budget as they internalize only part of the costs. Under soft budget constraints, budget actors face strong incentives to take policy decisions that increase their own utility (i.e. higher expenditure on local public goods), rather than to consider the negative externalities of their actions. Hence, one may argue that the CPR problem follows from the underlying, flawed fiscal institutional structure that invites spending bias and stands in the way of the long-term stability of government finances. To solve the CPR problem, policy makers need to think of ways to introduce binding budget constraints that force individual budget actors to consider the long-term costs of their spending decisions.

A large amount of research over the past three decades has identified institutions that effectively centralize the budget process, improving fiscal discipline in the context of both OECD and non-OECD countries.[1] More recently, researchers have taken an important step forward towards analyzing the effect of budgetary institutions, depending on the characteristics of the underlying political systems and policy decision-making process (Hallerberg and von Hagen 1999, Hallerberg 2004, Hallerberg et al. 2009b). In what follows, I refer to these contributions as the ‘horizontal decentralization’ branch because their main concern is with the effect of budgetary veto players that are located at the national level, i.e. line ministries and legislatures. In the following sections, I present some main concepts and solutions to the national-level CPR problem, as discussed in the literature. Afterwards, I go on to discuss the findings of the fiscal federalism and public choice literature that are concerned with the effects of decentralizing budget authority along the vertical axis of government. Before concluding, I present contributions that take an approach similar to my own, i.e. studies that make statements about the effects of vertical fiscal decentralization, depending on the institutional strength of the central government (sections 2.3.3 and 2.3.4).

2.2 CPR PROBLEMS ON THE NATIONAL LEVEL: BUDGET PROCESS DECENTRALIZATION

As a first crucial assertion, the budgetary institutions literature states that stronger centralization of the budget decision-making process at the national level serves as a solution to the CPR problem, arising under soft budget constraints on line ministries and legislatures. Researchers study which budgetary institutional arrangements show a potential to improve fiscal discipline by changing the incentive structures of those budget actors with the highest potential to maximize their own short-term utility without considering the longer-term effects for the general tax payer (for recent overviews, see Hallerberg et al. 2009b and Wehner 2010). Two main focus areas are the budget-making process within the executive – i.e. between the ministers – and the approval phase in which executives and legislatures interact. While authors generally agree that stronger centralization of budgetary institutions during both phases of the budget process improves fiscal outcomes, they initially differed quite a bit in their recommendations on how to achieve stronger centralization or more effective policy coordination.[2]

In a widely quoted contribution, von Hagen (1992) suggested that by increasing the degree of hierarchy in the budget process, political actors would be forced to choose more sustainable spending levels instead of maximizing short-term gains from increased expenditure. To be able to test his propositions, von Hagen (1992) introduced a 'Structural Index', capturing different institutional aspects of the budgetary process: the structure of negotiations within the cabinet, the structure of the parliamentary process, the flexibility of budget execution, and the presence of a long-term planning constraint. In a quantitative analysis of European Community (EC) member countries during the 1980s, he showed that centralization was associated with more fiscal discipline. A large number of contributions following von Hagen's (1992) approach, looking at different regions and time periods, similarly concluded that increasing decision-making hierarchies leads to more budget discipline (see Hallerberg et al. 2009b, Chapter 2). However, next to these 'delegation approaches', another branch of research evolved around the idea that a 'statutory approach' can equally serve to constrain budget actors. Fiscal contract between coalition partners, defining expenditure (revenue) targets and debt ceilings as well as fiscal deficit laws, (constitutional) debt ceilings, and public spending targets, are thought to improve fiscal stability by changing the incentives of relevant budget actors. As will be shown below, there is merit to both approaches – delegation and constitutory – confirming their usefulness as a constraining device for different budget actors, under certain circumstances.[3]

2.2.1 Strong Finance Ministers and Delegation

Approaches that advocate a delegation of budgetary powers follow the basic intuition of the CPR model that higher numbers of budgetary veto players lead to spending bias. Increasing the hierarchy in the budget process is thought to improve fiscal stability because it provides the one budget actor with the highest incentives to reach stable budgets and debt levels with veto power over other budget actors that try to maximize short-term gains from increased expenditure (lower taxes).[4]

To prevent negative externalities, some research suggests delegating final decision powers to one 'central budget authority', a position that is generally filled by the prime minister or finance minister in parliamentary set-ups and by the president or finance minister in presidential systems (Wildavsky 1975, von Hagen 1992). For the delegation hypothesis to be supported, of course, finance ministers or presidents must be more austere than other budget actors. The literature hints at several reasons justifying this assumption (e.g. von Hagen and Harden 1995, Hallerberg and von Hagen 1999). First, we can reasonably assume that finance ministers try to keep a reputation as successful policy makers, which in their position – more than for others – depends on their ability to safeguard macroeconomic stability. Turnover rates for finance ministry appointees, in particular in times of financial distress, are much higher than for their colleagues (Moser 2008). Second, finance ministers have a better overview of the overall state of government finances, given that their ministry constantly receives and keeps information on revenue expenditure, on on- and off-budget funds as well as on the level of the public debt, maturity structures and scheduled debt interest payments. Third, and related to the second argument, finance ministers are the most likely candidates within the cabinet to have the required educational background, and possibly also technical experience, allowing them to process the aforementioned information and to manage complex budget and debt matters. If not personally competent (enough), finance ministers can rely among their staff on the largest human resource pool with skills required for solving budgetary problems. Taken together, these three factors make it much more likely for the finance minister to consider the (long-term) stability effects of fiscal policies than other actors involved. Delegating decision-making power to the one budget actor with the highest probability of keeping budgets balanced should hence improve the fiscal stance.

2.2.2 Fiscal Targets and Statutory Approaches

Rather than by delegating decision powers, fiscal stability could also be achieved by setting objective fiscal targets that would force budget actors to prioritize important spending arrears, for instance by setting expenditure limits or making expenditure dependent on current revenue. The main advantage compared to a discretionary approach, stating that fiscal stabilization would best be reached by regular fiscal policies, is time consistency (Kopits and Symansky, 1998, p. 22). Without fiscal rules, the short-term preferences of democratically elected politicians seem more likely to dominate over what is preferable in the long run. Such binding fiscal rules can take the form of global targets, such as rules demanding a reduction in nominal government deficits. A more elaborate approach may be the introduction of a concrete target for the primary budget balance, i.e. the government's budget balance net of debt payments. Additionally, fiscal rules can be extended to the area of borrowing, introducing certain conditionality on borrowing by national and subnational government units and government agencies. Although they are using similar concepts, contributions in the 'fiscal targets' branch of the literature fall roughly into three different groups with a different scope of analysis: (1) looking at the relevance of fiscal targets and balanced budget rules on the subnational level (e.g. US states); (2) focusing on the national-level budget process (e.g. OECD countries); and (3) discussing the relevance of fiscal rules in the context of the common European market (literature on Maastricht and the Stability on Growth Pact).[5]

In the first group, which is mostly concerned with the US context, the empirical evidence on the relevance of state-level fiscal rules remains mixed. Initially, ex ante controls were attributed only limited relevance for reducing fiscal imbalances and debt levels, although in recent years there seems to be more evidence that such rules may have indirect effects on stability through their effect on financial markets because bond raters and investors seem to care about them. While Eichengreen (1990) finds a negative relationship between fiscal rules and debt levels at the state level in the USA, this view is contested by von Hagen (1991), looking at a broader range of public debt instruments in a sample of US states between 1975 and 1985, and concluding that ex ante fiscal rules are not an efficient way of reducing the likelihood of extreme outcomes in fiscal performance. Von Hagen (1991) explains this by arguing that often spending and debt reductions take place only on paper, for example when state governments in the USA substitute non-restricted for restricted debt instruments. Yet, the continuously increasing real default probabilities give little support to the notion that fiscal targets lead to substantial changes in the ways budgets are made. Nevertheless, there are several contributions arguing that fiscal rules are important for credit risk perceptions. For example, Johnson and Kriz (2005) suggest in their analysis of yields on General Obligation (GO) bonds of US states between 1990 and 1997 that bond raters incorporate information on fiscal institutions in their assessment of state government credit quality. While the study failed to find a direct effect of state fiscal rules on bond spreads, it provides significant evidence for an indirect effect through bond ratings. Expenditure limits, stricter balanced budget rules and restrictions on state debt issuance were found to lead to higher credit ratings, thereby reducing borrowing costs. Looking at fiscal rules and sovereign bond spreads on US states, Poterba and Rueben (2001) find that the sudden appearance of unexpected deficits is positively correlated with higher state bond yields, however this effect is smaller for states with tight anti-deficit rules compared to states that lack similar rules.

Turning to the literature on country-level fiscal rules in the OECD and non-OECD context, a large number of contributions find confirming evidence that fiscal institutions, including rules defining transparency standards, have a significant impact, both on budget and debt outcomes and on market sentiment about the state of public finances and default risk. Von Hagen and Harden (1995) find that budgetary laws and debt ceilings lead to significantly improved budget outcomes and debt levels in EU countries before the introduction of the euro by reducing the 'fiscal illusion' of voters.[6] However, the general argument that fiscal rules improve fiscal outcomes is qualified in later contributions arguing that the stabilizing effect of fiscal rules is largely dependent on how well these rules fit with the underlying political system (Hallerberg and von Hagen 1999, Hallerberg 2004, Hallerberg et al. 2009b). Going back to the debate on whether hierarchical approaches are more effective than contractual approaches in reducing fiscal imbalances, Hallerberg and von Hagen (1999) argue that either approach to recentralizing the budget process may be suitable, depending on the particular type of political system and the type of government that comes as a result of different electoral rules. Based on an empirical investigation of fiscal performance in 15 EU countries between 1981 and 1994, these authors conclude that delegation may be the best approach for majoritarian systems leading to single-party governments, while contracts may work better for coalition governments in proportional representation (PR) systems. That means that different political systems are correlated with different 'ideal forms' of budgetary institutions, leading to similar (positive) outcomes. Hallerberg (2004), who addresses endogeneity concerns with institutional explanations for fiscal outcomes, investigates what political factors stand behind the different budgetary institutions we find in EU countries before the currency union and EU Eastern enlargement. In Chapter 2 of the book, Hallerberg (2004) shows how veto players affect the type of fiscal institutions that we find today.[7] To account for the relevant underlying political differences between countries, Hallerberg et al. (2009b) employ a new index capturing 'ideal-type fiscal institutions' in their empirical analyses of 15 EU countries between 1985 and 2004, and EU accession countries since 1990. The authors provide robust evidence that, indeed, countries that have adopted institutions close to their ideal type are associated with fiscal discipline, while highly decentralized ('fiefdom') systems are linked with higher expenditure growth, deficits and public debt. With regard to the Latin American countries that I focus on below, the above findings would suggest that a fiscal rules-based approach is preferable for controlling CPR problems because they are proportional representation systems. Looking at Table 4.1 in Chapter 4, we observe that most reform activity regarding budgetary institutions between 1990 and mid-2006 indeed took place in the area of fiscal rules.

Another major concern in the debate about the potential effects of fiscal rules remains around the transparency of the budget process (Alesina et al. 1996, Tanzi and Schuknecht 2000, Ch. 8, Milesi-Feretti 2003, Alt and Lassen 2006).[8] Fiscal institutions are unlikely to be perceived as a credible commitment to fiscal discipline by all actors involved if the budget-making process generally lacks transparency. This is because non-transparent budget processes allow budget politicians to engage in various forms of 'creative accounting'. To account for the negative effects of non-transparent budget decision making, two consecutive studies on the effects of budgetary institutions on fiscal stability in Latin America have therefore added a 'transparency' component to the aggregate measure of the degree of centralization of country-level budget institutions (Alesina et al. 1999 and, more recently, Filc and Scartascini 2004, 2007). Both studies employ an Index of Budgetary Institutions (IBI) that is based on the von Hagen Index and the literature that followed, concluding that not only do both forms of fiscal constraint – hierarchy and delegation – equally matter for improving budget stability, but the effects of increasing decision-making hierarchies and introducing objective fiscal targets also turn out to be much stronger where transparency is higher.[9]

Filc and Scartascini (2007) analyze the effects of their aggregate Index of Budgetary Institutions (IBI) on fiscal balances and public debt in a cross-section of 19 Latin American and Caribbean countries, finding that budget procedures and fiscal rules have a significant effect on government balances before interests. Moreover, these effects seem to be economically meaningful. Based on their results, Filc and Scartascini (2007, p. 274) note that 'those Latin American countries within the highest quartile of the composite index of fiscal rules, hierarchical and transparent procedures would have an average more positive fiscal balance of approximately 2.3 percentage points of GDP than those countries in the lowest quartile of the index'. Extending their tests to a larger sample including OECD countries, the authors report largely similar effects, allowing the conclusion that what they capture is not driven by any regional idiosyncrasies.

Next to the mentioned benefits, an important problem of statutory approaches remains, in the national context and even more so in the international context discussed below – policy flexibility under fiscal targets. Several authors have argued that legal constraints come at the potentially high cost of reduced government flexibility in reacting to 'transitory shocks' (e.g. Corsetti and Roubini 1992, Eichengreen and Bayoumi 1994, and Manasse 2005). As these studies argue, for fiscal rules to be credible sanctions and to fulfill a stabilizing function, governments need to retain a certain degree of flexibility. Manasse (2005) shows in a theoretical contribution that limits on deficit-to-output ratios may be sufficient to induce countercyclical policies only in very good and very bad times. When the economy is in intermediate states, Manasse argues, budget rules provide incentives to implement pro-cyclical policies. Furthermore, according to the model, the disciplining effect on governments only holds when limits are tight and expected sanctions are high. Even if this is the case, targets could incur a relatively large welfare cost. The implications of the model have not been tested on data, however they serve to remind researchers of the pitfalls in assuming that ex ante institutional reforms automatically improve fiscal performance.

Moving the focus from national-level fiscal rules that can be enforced by national governments to the supra-national level, researchers are generally less confident about the impact of fiscal rules. Naturally, the recent debt and fiscal crises in the Euro Area and European Union revive an old debate: how viable are contractual approaches, including the Stability and Growth Pact (SGP) in the Maastricht Treaty of the European Union, in a context where a central-level enforcement mechanism is missing? Much of the current debate centers on questions similar to those raised by Manasse (2005) (a) how to design fiscal rules that are binding, and (b) how to keep them sufficiently flexible (compare also Buti et al. 2003, Bearce 2009). Nevertheless, there is also robust empirical evidence that EU countries with fiscal institutions that effectively centralize the budget process, show better fiscal outcomes and are generally more stable.[10] Furthermore, Schuknecht et al. (2007) and Eichengreen (2007) find that a no-bailout commitment and fiscal targets for national governments in the Maastricht Treaty are significantly correlated with sovereign risk perceptions.[11]

Looking at quarterly data on political risk premia on 10-year government bonds over German government bonds in 10 EU member states between 1993 and 2005, Hallerberg and Wolff (2008) provide significant evidence supporting their hypothesis that bond investors are directly concerned with the quality of budgetary institutions in different EMU member countries. More decentralized institutions correlate with significantly higher risk premia. To measure centralization, the authors use, among other things, a new centralization index that is better suited to determine the degree of executive control over the budget process, depending on the underlying electoral system and type of government.[12] Next to the direct effects of institutional centralization, Hallerberg and Wolff (2008) find that conditional effects matter. Sovereign bond spreads over German bonds are regressed both on the difference in the budget deficit between country i and Germany, and on the difference in the public debt/GDP ratio between country i and Germany. The authors provide evidence for 10 EU countries that market concerns over temporal swings in deficit and debt differentials were muted by the degree to which budget processes were effectively centralized. Hence, deficits and debt levels turn out to be significantly less important for sovereign bond pricing decisions than the quality of budgetary institutions. This finding is in line with earlier research on fiscal rules and sovereign bond spreads on US states (e.g. Poterba and Rueben 2001).

In response to the current European debt crisis, several contributions suggest reforming the SGP by introducing more flexible fiscal rules, while others focus on sanctioning mechanisms. Contributions in the first category suggest new variants of a 'golden rule', aiming at improving adherence with budgetary rules without destroying economic growth (Fitoussi and Creel 2002, Blanchard and Giavazzi 2004).[13] However, the approaches stop short of including rules on expenditure, which, in combination with more global deficit rules, seem to have worked most successfully in reducing imbalances in OECD countries (Joumard et al. 2005).[14] Enforcement through new financial sanctioning mechanisms is part of the European Union's 'Fiscal Compact' that was agreed on by the European Council on March 2, 2012. EU member states are now required to introduce an automatic correction mechanism into their national legal systems at statutory or higher level, in case the annual structural deficit exceeds 0.5 percent of GDP.[15] In case of non-compliance, the EU's highest court can fine a country, and a financial penalty, equivalent to up to 0.1 percent of GDP, can be enforced. The treaty also foresees that, as soon as a member state is recognized to be in breach of the 3 percent deficit ceiling, the European Commission submits a proposal of counter-measures. These can include recommendations that affect the size and the time frame of adjustment measures. However, by a qualified majority of member states these proposals can be rejected.[16] Without doubt, the current discussion on fiscal rules in the E(M)U reinforces how relevant political forces are for successful reform implementation. The most effective way of constraining fiscally irresponsible behavior is reducing the autonomy of previously unconstrained budget actors, naturally evoking opposition. I will return to endogeneity concerns in Chapter 4 and in the country case studies. For now, it serves to note that a significant amount of empirical evidence suggests that once fiscal targets are introduced on the country level, in a sufficiently transparent policy environment, they are likely to change the behavior of budgetary actors, leading to more stable budget outcomes.

All in all, the literature on horizontal decentralization provides important conclusions on the types of fiscal rules and institutions that are likely to affect fiscal performance under certain political institutional circumstances. A significant amount of empirical research suggests that both hierarchies and fiscal targets matter when they match the characteristics of the underlying political system. Where governments rely on a rules-based approach, we have learned from the empirical literature concerned with budgetary institutions in the EU and the USA that specific expenditure targets seem to outperform more general deficit and debt targets, in particular where they are embedded in more long-term-oriented fiscal management strategies. For budgetary institutions to work, however, the literature points us to three crucial pre-conditions: (1) the budget process needs to fulfill minimum transparency requirements; (2) fiscal rules have to allow for a certain degree of flexibility; and (3) the enforcement of rules by a party that has been delegated the power to sanction transgressions of the rules is essential.

2.3 CPR PROBLEMS ON THE SUBNATIONAL LEVEL: VERTICAL FISCAL DECENTRALIZATION

Decentralization of fiscal authority to subnational levels of government is a recurrent topic in the public choice and the political economy literature on fiscal stability. Depending on the point of view, vertical fiscal decentralization is associated with more and less fiscal stability. On the one hand, vertical fiscal decentralization can lead to significant CPR problems on the subnational level, followed by overuse of the common tax base, as local executives over-rely on transfers and grants to finance local public goods. On the other hand, decentralization could be beneficial based on the assumption that it reduces allocative inefficiency on the subnational (and national) level and increases competition, which could have disciplining effects on local budget actors.

A significant amount of research in political science has emphasized the first view, providing evidence that vertical decentralization increases spending pressure due to the enhanced 'over-fishing' of the national tax pool. Over time, subnational fiscal imbalance may also grow into a serious budget problem for the general fiscal stability of a country (see e.g. discussions in Ter-Minassian 1997a and Rodden et al. 2003). Moreover, as several contributions have argued, the inability of national governments to control subnational government finances and borrowing activities can backfire because grave fiscal problems on the subnational level often require bailouts at the federal level, followed by tremendous increases in public debt held by the central government (Burki et al. 1999, Braun 2006, Facchini and Testa 2008). Both the more policy-oriented contributions and the academic literature relying on comparative case studies and large N empirical studies point to such dynamics. Indeed, decentralized spending has been shown to be correlated with higher government expenditure, deficits and higher levels of public debt, leading researchers to conclude that the more spending is assigned to subnational levels, the higher public spending is to be expected (Wallis 1991, Prud'homme 1995, Tanzi 1996, Fornisari et al. 1998, Burki et al. 1999, Stein 1999, Rodden et al. 2003).

A different but related branch of the political economy literature has pointed to the risk that under decentralized expenditure schemes, self-interested rational representatives in the national legislature face incentives to bargain for higher government expenditure on their local districts, in an effort to externalize their expected 're-election costs'.[17]

In contrast, public choice theories and 'second-generation fiscal federalism' approaches emphasize the positive role of vertical fiscal decentralization. In a widely quoted contribution, Oates (1972) posits that vertical fiscal decentralization should improve allocative efficiency, thereby contributing to subnational fiscal discipline. Moreover, subnational governments could provide an important check on overall public expenditure and the budget decisions of central governments (Brennan and Buchanan 1977). The latter argument, which is widely known as the 'Leviathan' hypothesis, requires that subnational governments reach a certain degree of fiscal sovereignty, meaning that they are able to raise a significant share of their revenue and are responsible for a balance between local expenditure and own-source revenue.[18] Otherwise, central governments run the risk that local electorates tolerate irrationally high levels of expenditure on local public goods.[19] In the next few sections, I explore these arguments further, focusing on what the literature predicts to be the effects of different categories of vertical fiscal decentralization, i.e. expenditure and revenue. Furthermore, I summarize what was said about cases where these two categories were strongly imbalanced.

2.3.1 Expenditure Decentralization

From a CPR problem approach, vertical fiscal decentralization in expenditure should lead to spending increases and a higher likelihood of deficits because it increases the number of budget actors with incentives to free-ride on the common national tax base. A similar logic applies at the subnational level as the one identified in the CPR problem literature that focused on the national level. That is, after delegating expenditure decisions to a large number of budget actors on the subnational level, we would expect 'office-seeking' local politicians to engage in spending increases, while trying to keep local contributions to the common tax pool as low as possible. Empirically, there is evidence that subnational budget makers are indeed more likely to engage in spending sprees after they have been given more authority over expenditure in the context of emerging market economies (Bomfim and Shah 1994, Dillinger and Webb 1999, Rodden 2002).

Another reason why expenditure decentralization increases overall fiscal instability could be that subnational budget actors become crucial veto players that can block any attempts by central government to implement fiscal adjustments during crises. In a theoretical contribution, Sanguinetti (1994) argues that after decentralization governments face stronger policy coordination problems, given the higher number of potential veto players opposing fiscal adjustment policies.[20] Does this mean that subnational fiscal indiscipline aggregates to national-level imbalances? A straightforward answer is difficult here given the mixed empirical evidence. Several empirical analyses suggest an outright increasing effect of expenditure decentralizing on overall government expenditure and deficits due to policy coordination failure (Grossman 1989, Bank 1997, Burki et al. 1999, Shadbegian 1999, Stein 1999, Plekhanov and Singh 2007, Fedelino and Ter-Minassian 2010). Yet, other contributions conclude that the negative effect of vertical decentralization in expenditure depends on additional factors, for example the degree to which subnational governments are dependent on central-level transfers.[21] These findings contrast with empirical contributions which argue that expenditure decentralization either has no effect at all or the opposite (negative) effect on total government expenditure and deficits to that expected under the CPR problem approach.[22] Yet, both views seem commensurable once we take into account that the way in which the delegation of expenditure authority plays out may be dependent on other contextual factors.

2.3.2 Revenue Decentralization

In the public choice and the fiscal federalism literature, it is often argued that subnational fiscal discipline can be enhanced by increasing the revenue autonomy of subnational governments, to the extent that revenue is in balance with local spending. Given what was said before about the potentially destabilizing effects of expenditure decentralization under high subnational dependence on central government transfers, we would expect that both subnational and aggregate government spending is reduced and fiscal performance improved, once we increase the revenue-raising capacities of subnational governments (Rodden 2002, 2003, 2006, Rodden and Wibbels 2002). There are basically two reasons why this may be the case: (1) competitive pressures among subnational governments; and (2) checks on central government expenditure.

First, based on Oates' (1972) decentralization theorem revenue, decentralization should reduce public expenditure as it enhances competition between local governments. Accordingly, fiscal decentralization has the potential to reduce public spending by increasing the public's 'recognition of the cost of public programs'. This can be achieved if public spending on a particular level of government corresponds to taxation at the same level. Under competition for tax payers, local administrations then have incentives to show that they keep a good balance between revenue and expenditure. Second, as claimed by Brennan and Buchanan (1977, 1980), the increased taxation autonomy of subnational governments could serve to reduce spending bias and fiscal instability at the central government level. In a widely quoted article in which they propose what became known as the 'Leviathan hypothesis', Brennan and Buchanan (1977) argue that increasing the taxation autonomy (along with the spending autonomy) of local governments serves as a check on what they describe as a revenue-maximizing, over-arching and highly intrusive central government. Revenue decentralization could efficiently slow down the growth of the size of government because local budget actors would be empowered to stand against the attempts of central government to increase expenditure (and taxes). Empirically, however, the evidence for the Leviathan hypothesis remains mixed at best. Several tests carried out on large N samples were either unable to confirm the expenditure-reducing effect of increased vertical decentralization or came to the opposite conclusion, that it was followed by higher imbalances (Oates 1985, 1989; see also Prohl and Schneider 2009 for an overview of the debate). On the other hand, several studies have found that a greater revenue autonomy of subnational governments significantly reduces the size of government. For example, Rodden (2003), who looked at data for a broader world sample, including OECD and non-OECD countries (1978–1996), found that a higher ratio of subnational own-source revenue to total government revenue (a proxy for subnational taxation autonomy) reduced the size of central government expenditure to GDP significantly.[23] Additionally, the author provides robust evidence that a higher ratio of government grants to GDP significantly increases both subnational and central government expenditure. For the sub-sample of OECD countries, Rodden (2003) shows that by increasing the share of own-source revenue in total government revenue, the size of government (the share of government expenditure in GDP) grows more slowly. Looking at the interaction of vertical fiscal decentralization, he finds, for the subsample of OECD countries, significant evidence that decentralization reduced the size of government when funded primarily by autonomous local taxation.[24] However, when funded by transfers or centrally regulated taxation, a larger government seems to be the result.

Rather than advocating vertical fiscal decentralization as a 'simple solution' to subnational fiscal imbalance, Rodden (2003) therefore argues that it is essential that the delegation of expenditure authority is in parallel to the increasing revenue-raising responsibility of subnational governments, in particular where the latter are free to borrow on the financial markets.

2.3.3 Transfer Dependence under (Un)constrained Borrowing

Given the above findings, the question may come up as to why central governments are not simply increasing the degree of revenue autonomy of subnational government units, as this would allow for financial market control of fiscally 'quasi-sovereign' subnational governments. In this section, I point to certain historically grown impediments to improving subnational fiscal discipline through market controls.

A relatively new branch of the literature posits that spending decentralization is not per se problematic but may be a potential driver of imbalances if subnational governments face soft budget constraints, i.e. when they are at the same time highly dependent on central transfers and/or free to borrow on capital markets to finance their deficits. For various historical reasons, we often find local governments to enjoy large borrowing autonomy (Rodden 2006). If the barriers for subnational borrowing are low and subnational governments are transfer dependent, subnational governments have incentives to finance high (and increasing) public expenditure through borrowing and/or continued bargaining with the central level over increases in transfers.[25] Likewise, it could be argued that a high degree of transfer dependence comes as a consequence of a historical bargaining over the distribution of (taxing) power between regional leaders and a newly formed central government (Congleton 2006, Rodden 2006). In the case of Latin American countries, the current state and design of transfer systems look to be contingent on the democratic transformation process, which took place towards the end of the 1980s (Diaz-Cayeros 2006). While most authors agree on the destabilizing effects of transfer dependence, it is also obvious that changing existing transfer systems and levels is politically very difficult (Rodden 2003, 2006, Rodden et al. 2003).[26] So-called 'automatic transfers' that are distributed to subnational governments through a transfer system are often 'hard-wired' into the new constitutions (or amendments) that were agreed upon during the democratic transformation. Certain political groups were rewarded by the new democratic leaders for their allegiance with side payments, among others, taking the form of future access to government revenue via automatic transfers. Given the historically grown high level of involvement of central governments in the financing of constituent unit expenditure, it becomes very difficult for governments to credibly commit to no-bailout policies.[27] A follow-up problem of such difficulties in committing to a non-bailout rule often turns out to be, as in the case of several financial crises in Latin America, creditor 'moral hazard'. In other words, 'market discipline' as a constraint on subnational government deficit-making has failed in several cases because market participants expected central governments to bail them out.[28] A case in point for that is Brazil, where central government provided three consecutive bailouts for its states in less than a decade after the democratic constitution of 1988 (Ter-Minassian 1997a, b, Rodden 2006).

2.3.4 Subnational CPR Problems and Indiscipline under Central-level Controls

Few authors have studied the potential interactions between central-level institutions and subnational fiscal discipline. Rodden (2006) follows – to some extent – the assumption that the scope of subnational fiscal indiscipline depends on the strength of centrally imposed borrowing rules. He looks at determinants of subnational and aggregate fiscal performance in 43 countries (1978/1986–1996) and finds a significant impact of subnational transfer dependence on both levels of government, depending on the degree to which subnational governments are free to borrow in financial markets. Rodden's contribution stands out because it first provides crucial new insights into the determinants of subnational fiscal imbalance in federal and unitary states before it also links these determinants to imbalances at the central level. Relying on expenditure and revenue data for total, state and municipal governments, he arrives at showing how subnational transfer dependence first affects subnational fiscal performance and second, total government deficits and changes in the budget relative to expenditure. A major conclusion of Rodden's (2006) book is that subnational CPR problems, driven by transfer dependence, only turn into a significant instability problem when the central level imposes a loss of control over subnational budget actors. However, at levels of borrowing autonomy, subnational fiscal indiscipline is not found to have a significant impact on total government fiscal results.[29]

While these findings build a basis for the interaction argument I present above, Rodden's (2006) analysis is focused on borrowing rules, leaving other types of centrally imposed budget constraints out of the picture. However, it seems reasonable to assume that borrowing rules only work if they are imbedded in a broader set of fiscal rules. Plekhanov and Singh (2007) argue that in the context of emerging market economies, borrowing constraints are only efficient if central governments also guarantee that international budget transparency and management standards are observed. In a recent empirical analysis of government budget balances in 43 OECD and non-OECD countries (1982–2000), Plekhanov and Singh (2007) go beyond Rodden's (2006) approach, adding an important aspect. In their analysis of the determinants of subnational government fiscal budget balances in 43 OECD and non-OECD countries between 1982 and 2000, they look at the role central government plays in constraining subnational indiscipline. Based on their assumption that 'subnational governments also tend to be more disciplined in countries with more disciplined central government', Plekhanov and Singh (2007, p. 437) look at the effects of borrowing constraints on subnational governments, conditional on the presence of common financial reporting and budgeting standards at national government level.[30] Specifically, they use a measure for Common Standards of Public Expenditure Management (PEM) employed by von Hagen and Harden (1995) and Poterba and von Hagen (1999), to study the possible interaction effects of this national-level institutional variable on vertical decentralization. They find significant and robust empirical evidence that the marginal effect of borrowing constraints is significantly higher in countries that have better national-level budgeting standards in place. Where these institutions are weaker, the only type of borrowing constraint that significantly affects fiscal balances seems to be centrally imposed rules. In their study, the interaction of national-level budget institutions and borrowing constraints has a stronger effect on subnational fiscal outcomes in non-OECD countries. With regard to subnational-level CPR problems, Plekanov and Singh (2007, p. 440) conclude that, 'in emerging market economies that tend to have weaker institutions, fiscal discipline at the subnational level may also be weaker'. In other words, we are likely to find that the fiscal discipline of subnational governments in less developed and transition countries, depends largely on the strength of central-level budgeting capacities and transparency.

2.4 CONCLUSIONS FROM THE LITERATURE

Above, I have presented an overview of different institutional explanations for the persistence of fiscal imbalance. Authors have approached the problems of growing public expenditure, deficits and debt accumulation from different angles. A common threat is that fiscal imbalances are thought to be a consequence of CPR problems, following from an increase in the number of potential veto players over final budget decisions. Unless there is a hard budget constraint, delegating more fiscal power to larger numbers of budget actors is likely to increase CPR problems, given that each and every politician has incentives to draw extensively on the national tax base while keeping their own contributions as low as possible.

As was shown, this kind of 'over-fishing' can occur on different levels of government, though to very similar effects. First, there is a certain risk in giving too much decision-making power to budget actors within government (line ministers) and in allowing the legislature to amend the budget bill presented by the government without setting a hard budget constraint. Second, we are reminded by the fiscal federalism literature that increasing the fiscal decision-making authority of budget actors on the subnational level carries the risk that they, too, will engage in spending sprees and deficit financing unless there is a hard budget constraint. The negative consequences of vertically decentralized fiscal authority, under certain circumstances, seem likely to outweigh the potential benefits emphasized by the earlier public choice and second-generation fiscal federalism literature (e.g. improved allocative efficiency and subnational government competition for tax payers). Where budget constraints on local leaders remain soft and borrowing controls are weak, fiscal indiscipline on the subnational level can create major liabilities for overall government fiscal accounts.

Looking for existing work on the determinants of fiscal instability in decentralized systems, it turns out that the approaches of Rodden (2006) and Plekhanov and Singh (2007) are closest to my own approach. Both studies point to the finding that subnational CPR problems, depending on the institutional context at the central level, can translate into significantly different subnational fiscal outcomes. The main difference in my approach is that I propose a broader range of central-level budgetary institutions than previously identified to alter subnational fiscal behavior. What is needed to arrive at a credible institutional constraint is likely to go beyond borrowing controls. To predict the center's capacity to contain subnational instability, it seems important to consider the general degree of control over the budget process, at the formulation stage – within the executive – and during the approval and implementation stages.

To solve such CPR problems, the literature generally identifies two alternatives regarding how to harden the budget constraint on local governments. The first option consists of increasing local governments' capacity to raise their own taxes, allowing them to borrow on financial markets to finance additional expenditure. Following this approach, policy makers leave it to financial markets to impose fiscal discipline on subnational governments. In contrast, the second option suggests a central-level regulation of borrowing and local budget decisions by introducing specific fiscal targets and strengthening decision-making hierarchies. As laid out above, the empirical reality in post-transition Latin American countries raises at least some concern about the viability of a pure 'market discipline' approach. Below, I therefore propose a regulatory model, in which central governments constrain local budget decisions by centralizing national-level budgetary institutions, signaling to the local level that fiscal stability is a priority and that budget constraints have been strengthened. That being said, I find this approach to be compatible with arguments in the fiscal federalism literature, such as Rodden and Eskeland (2003), who suggest combining hierarchical control with market discipline, allowing the latter more weight over time.

NOTES

1. A comprehensive overview of CPR models is presented in Persson and Tabellini (2000). For an updated discussion of theoretical and empirical contributions, see Hallerberg et al. (2009b) and Franzese (2010).
2. The empirical link between budget process centralization and fiscal imbalance has been confirmed in an array of studies covering different geographical regions and including countries at different levels of economic development. They include studies for European Union countries (discussed in Hallerberg et al. 2009b), OECD countries (e.g. Kontopoulos and Perotti 1999, Hallerberg 2004), Central and Eastern Europe (Gleich 2003, Ylaeoutinen 2004, Hallerberg and Ylaeoutinen 2010), Asia (Lao-Araya 1998) and the Latin American and Caribbean countries (Alesina et al. 1996, 1999, Stein 1999, Hallerberg and Marier 2004, Filc and Scartascini 2007, Hallerberg et al. 2009a).
3. Von Hagen (1991) and von Hagen and Eichengreen (1996) initially questioned the notion that fiscal rules can equally serve as a commitment device in the way that delegation would. However, in later contributions both authors acknowledge that contractual approaches can be useful, depending on the underlying political institutions (see e.g. Hallerberg and von Hagen 1999, Eichengreen 2007, Hallerberg et al. 2009b).
4. Another possible approach would be the creation of independent 'fiscal councils', as suggested by Eichengreen et al. (1999). However, empirical validation of the effect of such councils is hard to achieve at this point, given that there is little data on them to be used in quantitative analyses.
5. As Hallerberg et al. (2009b) point out in a comprehensive review of the literature, studies on the impact of fiscal rules were for a long time looking only at fiscal rules applying to subnational governments.
6. This approach stands somewhat in contrast to the earlier finding in von Hagen (1991), regarding the (missing) link between fiscal rules and budget outcomes in US states. Von Hagen and Harden (1995) explore the 'fiscal illusion' argument, which puts emphasis on the role of information on budget decisions for voter control of potentially profligate governments. By making the (negative) consequences of increasing expenditure and excessive borrowing explicit to the (uninformed) public through publicly discussed targets, the pressure on governments to 'put their fiscal house in order' is increased.
7. A crucial point advanced in Hallerberg (2004) is the finding that budgetary institutions need to be adjusted – moving either towards a more contractual or a more delegative approach – in order for them to continue to produce stable outcomes as soon as the number of veto players or the ideological distance in a government coalition changes. In other words, there is no one-and-for-all budgetary institutional solution for each country but institutions would need to be flexible enough to adjust to the type of government.
8. Alt and Lassen (2006) show using data on 19 OECD countries that a higher degree of fiscal transparency is associated with lower public debt and deficits, even after

controlling for alternative explanations, including the competitiveness of the political system.

9. Alesina et al. (1999) find that in regression analyses of the determinants of fiscal deficits and public debt that include as independent variables all three sub-indicators of the Index of Budgetary Institutions, typically only the 'hierarchy' and 'fiscal rule' indicators turn out to have individually significant coefficients. 'Transparency' seems to increase the effect of both other indicators, rather than being individually significant. Also, high measurement error, in particular in the case of the transparency measure, is a concern and a source of potential bias in the results reported.
10. Hallerberg (2004) combines cross-country and detailed case study evidence on 15 European Union countries (1973–2000), supporting the view that budget performance in the EU converged towards greater fiscal discipline because states either improved or maintained certain fiscal institutions that helped them to solve CPR problems. He relies on a theoretical model showing that fiscal institutions vary on a continuum between decentralized forms of fiscal governance dubbed 'fiefdom governance' and centralization of budget processes through two 'ideal types' of budgetary institutions – 'delegation' or 'commitment'. Each country's fiscal institutions are a function of the type of government (majoritarian vs minority), the characteristics of the party system (two-party vs multiparty, ideologically distant systems) and the level of electoral competition. Evidence from both the quantitative and qualitative analyses presented in Hallerberg (2004) strongly confirms that countries adapting fiscal institutions that match their political institutions are able to control deficits, and that effect is independent of the introduction of the 'Maastricht rule' (i.e. 3 percent deficit rule). Where 'fiefdom governance' persisted, fiscal outcomes continued to be suboptimal despite the Maastricht rule. Fiscal accounting 'tricks' may have worked to achieve temporal improvements in the fiscal stance, however fiscal outcomes soon deteriorated again. Beetsma et al. (2009) show for a panel of 14 EU countries between 1999 and 2007 that countries with tighter fiscal constraints at the national level faced fewer problems in implementing planned fiscal consolidation. Hallerberg and Wolff (2008) provide cross-country time-series evidence for 10 EU countries (1993–2005), showing that better institutions affect credit risk perceptions (bond spreads) directly. This is in line with Eichengreen (2007) who provides evidence that fiscal institutions had a strong and significant impact on sovereign bond ratings for 10 EU member states (1991–2005) by the three major rating agencies (Standard and Poor's, Moody's and Fitch). Moreover, Hallerberg and Wolff (2008), using quarterly data, are able to show that the short-term fiscal position of a country is likely to interact with the overall quality of budgetary institutions, such that among the countries that experience (temporary) swings in their fiscal and debt position, political risk turns out to be significantly lower for those countries that are characterized by more centralized budgetary institutions. Hence, deficits and debt levels turn out to be significantly less important for sovereign bond spreads than the quality of budgetary institutions. This finding is in line with earlier research on fiscal rules and sovereign bond spreads on US states (e.g. Poterba and Rueben 2001).
11. With regard to subnational fiscal and debt dynamics, Schuknecht et al. (2007) find that market discipline on German subnational debtors was strengthened under the European Monetary Union (EMU) as German Länder were for the first time forced to pay risk premia related to their individual fiscal performance rather than to overall government balances.
12. The new 'index ideal' employed by Hallerberg and Wolff (2008) builds on and develops further earlier measurement approaches (e.g. von Hagen 1992, Hallerberg and von Hagen 1999), taking into account that efficient centralization can take place either through the delegation of fiscal powers to a single budget authority or through a contractual (or what Hallerberg (2004) calls 'commitment') approach. Accordingly, the 'ideal' way to centralize the budget process depends on the type of government in an individual country, which is largely a consequence of the underlying electoral system. The 'index ideal' thus includes measures of 'delegation' for states where delegation

institutions are expected to be optimal, which are countries where the ideological distance among coalition partners is zero or small. For states where the ideological distance is large, the variable 'target' is used instead. This includes the sum of four measures of the use of multi-annual fiscal targets.

13. The core idea is that over the cycle, government borrowing should not exceed net government capital formation. Current expenditure should only be financed out of current receipts (Creel and Saraceno 2010). These contributions aim at reaching a (cyclically adjusted) 'net-of-public-investment deficit' golden rule to exclude the negative consequences of prescribing deficit goals, allowing for needed policy flexibility in the future (e.g. when countries cut investments in infrastructure or education to bring down capital expenditure).
14. Hauptmeier et al. (2010, p. 5) note, by way of example, that implementing such fiscal rules could have made a real difference to those European countries that are now experiencing the worst fiscal and debt crises – Ireland, Greece, Portugal and Spain. These authors use simulation methods, predicting the effects of different types of fiscal rules on government expenditure in EMU countries between 1999 and 2009, finding that 'Public debt ratios in the euro area would not have been much above 60 percent and in the macro-imbalances countries near or below 60% at the end of 2009 if a neutral expenditure stance had been pursued'. For further discussion of the relevance of different types of budget and expenditure rules in the EU context, see also Wierts (2008) and Creel and Saraceno (2010); for a detailed account of subnational-level fiscal rules in OECD countries, see Joumard et al. (2005).
15. An exception is granted to countries with government debt levels significantly below 60 percent. There, the structural deficit is allowed to reach up to 1 percent of GDP.
16. The 'Fiscal Compact' (Treaty on Stability, Coordination and Governance in the Economic and Monetary Union) is an intergovernmental treaty, which was signed by 25 of – at the time – 27 member states of the European Union (with the exception of the Czech Republic and the UK) on March 2, 2012. The treaty entered into full effect for all 19 members of the Euro Area and is implemented with exceptions in the other EU member states.
17. The classic text is Weingast et al. (1981). Regarding Latin American countries, Hallerberg and Marier (2004) make a similar argument, while introducing a set of conditions under which rent-seeking by legislators becomes more or less feasible, depending on the characteristics of the electoral system and party-disciplining mechanisms.
18. For a related argument regarding subnational governments as borrowers in private credit markets, see von Hagen and Eichengreen (1996).
19. A similar argument, put forth by Buchanan and Wagner (1977), points to the problem that unless local electorates are aware of the source of revenue for financing local expenditure, they can easily fall victim to 'fiscal illusion'. As a consequence, local incumbents remain in office despite bad fiscal performance (see also von Hagen and Harden 1995).
20. Sanguinetti (1994) provides a theoretical model showing how expenditure decentralization can increase spending bias, thereby affecting government balances over time. The author shows that in federal–subnational fiscal bargaining, non-cooperative strategies lead to spending increases, both at the local and central levels. The theoretical model is applied by the author to the case of provincial–federal relations in Argentina (1970–1987), arguing that decentralization in expenditure, combined with a strong reliance on grant financing, leads to inefficient public goods provision, both at the subnational and central government levels. The author suggests a solution where the federal government pre-commits some of its key fiscal instruments. However, the validity of this suggestion is not tested in the article.
21. Stein (1999) carries out an explorative empirical analysis, studying the relationship between different vertical decentralization variables, borrowing constraints and total government expenditure as a share of GDP (1990–1995 averages) in a cross-section of Latin American and OECD countries. His particular concern is how different areas

of decentralized fiscal activity interact. He reports on a strong and significant positive effect of expenditure decentralization on the size of government. Moreover, this effect seems to be stronger the more subnational governments rely on transfers from the center to finance local expenditure and also the freer they are to borrow on private capital markets, either directly or through state-owned banks. De Mello (2000) finds similar results for a panel of 17 OECD and 13 non-OECD countries. Rodden and Wibbels (2002) find that expenditure decentralization only drives deficits on the national level in cases where subnational governments are highly dependent on central-level grants for financing their expenditure. Jin and Zou (2002), looking at panel data from 32 OECD countries between 1980 and 1994, equally find that expenditure decentralization drives public expenditure when subnational units are highly transfer-dependent.

22. For example, Oates (1985, 1989), who initially assumed that expenditure decentralization would lead to smaller government expenditure, famously claimed to find no significant relationship between the variables, based on evidence from both a time-series analysis of the USA and in a cross-section of 43 countries. In a recent contribution, Prohl and Schneider (2009) report that increasing expenditure decentralization is linked with a lower growth in government expenditure in a sample of 29 OECD and non-OECD countries (1978–2003). However, these effects turn out to be much smaller in the sub-group of non-OECD countries.
23. Jin and Zou (2002), looking at 32 OECD countries (1980–1994), equally find that increasing the revenue autonomy of subnational governments has strong negative effects on aggregate public expenditure as a share of GDP.
24. To be fair, this is a point that is hard to make given the scarceness of reliable data on 'autonomous' subnational tax revenue in non-OECD countries. See Rodden (2004) for a discussion of data issues.
25. Early contributions by Eichengreen and von Hagen (1996) and Stein (1999) noted that in order to capture the size of the subnational CPR problem, it serves to look at the product of vertical fiscal imbalance or, in other words, the degree to which subnational governments depend on the central government, and the degree of borrowing autonomy these governments enjoy. Both studies find that the product of transfer dependence and unconstrained borrowing seems to be linked to higher fiscal imbalances on the national level. Several consecutive cross-country time-series studies, including Rodden (2002, 2003, 2006) and Rodden and Wibbels (2002), reconfirm that higher transfer dependence, in particular when subnational governments are free to borrow, contributes to fiscal imbalance, both on the subnational and national levels. Further evidence from case studies points in the same direction (e.g. von Hagen et al. 2000, Webb 2003). Over the past two decades, governments in Latin America seem to have acknowledged the potential dangers of loose borrowing constraints. As data on subnational borrowing autonomy from the World Bank's Qualitative Decentralization Indicators database shows, most countries in the region now have borrowing controls on subnational governments in place, which, however, was not the case two decades ago (compare with Alesina et al. 1999 and Filc and Scartascini 2007).
26. A somewhat contradicting argument is presented by de Mello (2000), who finds that having more dependence on intergovernmental transfers may improve fiscal performance by strengthening central control over the spending decisions of the lower tiers of government. De Mello (2000, p. 367) adds that to the extent that subnational governments rely on revenue-sharing transfers, conditionality on how sharable funds are to be spent is likely to reduce actual fiscal management autonomy, in which case expenditure decentralization would be little more than 'mere delegation', turning local executives into the 'spending agents of higher levels of government with limited decision-making autonomy'. However, based on the literature, we would still assume that as long as subnational budget actors remain free to borrow in private markets, the leverage of the central level remains relatively small. Regarding the potentially destabilizing effects of leaving 'too much' subnational autonomy in expenditure and revenue to the subnational level, Brazil seems to match the argument. Historically, the Brazilian states have

possessed strong autonomy over their revenue, not quite in the range of the US states but clearly going beyond the norm in the Latin American region, as well as in OECD countries like France and Germany, among others (Rodden 2002). As the discussion of fiscal institutions and macroeconomic instabilities in Brazil (Chapter 5) shows in detail, in the past three decades the economically strongest states have placed a heavy toll on general government balances on several occasions. When the federal government of Fernando Henrique Cardoso launched its plans for a major reform of fiscal institutions targeted at fulfilling austerity goals, the governors of the most powerful and economically independent and fiscally autonomous states signaled their opposition, making them a major obstacle to reaching any kind of reform. In this situation, a growing subnational debt crisis played into the hands of the president who now had greater leverage over subnational leaders requesting federal financial rescue measures. The very least that the story of continued federal bailouts in Brazil suggests is that high degrees of revenue autonomy of subnational government should not generally be seen as a 'cure' from fiscal indiscipline. Instead, fiscal and borrowing decisions of highly independent state governments may at times turn into a very real threat for the stability of a fiscal union. Higher financial leverage of the center over subnational budget actors can serve as a disciplining device.

27. This compares quite well to the likely problems of a potential European fiscal union, sketched out in an early contribution by von Hagen and Eichengreen (1996).
28. Lane (1993) points to four necessary conditions for financial markets to 'discipline' subnational borrowing effectively: (1) markets should be free and open, with no regulation of financial intermediaries that could place subnational governments in a privileged borrower position (e.g. portfolio composition requirements); (2) relevant information on the borrower's outstanding debt and repayment capacity needs to be disclosed to potential lenders; (3) central governments must refrain from giving any kind of bailout guarantee (explicit or implicit) to subnational governments; and (4) borrower governments need to have institutional tools at their disposal that allow a reaction to market signals.
29. Clearly, Rodden's (2006) conclusions differ from my suggestions. While he emphasizes that transfer dependence is only problematic under unconstrained borrowing, his suggestion is not that the central government should take more constraining measures. Rather, he advocates an increase in autonomous revenue-raising by subnational governments. Accordingly, by decreasing transfer dependence, subnational governments become less likely to exert pressure on central governments to bail them out, which contributes to a stabilizing of overall government fiscal results in the longer run.
30. Another important new aspect of the study by Plekhanov and Singh (2007) is that they account for different types of borrowing autonomy, allowing us to differentiate between self-imposed borrowing rules, cooperative borrowing and centrally imposed rules. Prior to that, research was more generally concerned with the question of whether the presence of any kind of borrowing rule made a difference or whether having more borrowing constraints was better than having fewer.

3. Fiscal institutions and their effects on public households

3.1 VERTICAL DECENTRALIZATION, BUDGETARY INSTITUTIONS AND FISCAL IMBALANCE

In this chapter, I develop an argument about the effects of decentralized fiscal authority, drawing mainly on two branches of literature discussed in Chapter 2 – the budgetary institutions and the fiscal federalism literature. In the existing academic literature, authors generally treat the effects of vertical fiscal decentralization and decentralization of the budget process on the national – horizontal – level as separate problems. Expanding on these contributions, I suggest a different approach to budgetary policy making in a fiscally federal context. My goal is to arrive at a model that allows me to treat the consequences of decentralized budget making – both at the national and subnational levels – in a single analytical framework.

First, I start from the premise that vertical fiscal decentralization destabilizes overall government fiscal outcomes under certain circumstances. In line with much of the fiscal federalism literature, I assume decentralization to exert destabilizing effects, as long as there are no hard budget constraints on subcentral budget actors. Without budget constraints on local politicians, a decision to delegate more authority to subnational governments in expenditure sets incentives for local budget actors to draw on the common national tax base to capitalize on it politically, in the local political arena, without bearing the costs of rising public expenditure and debt. One way to solve such *common pool resource problems* would consist in installing local-level budget constraints. Such an approach seems reasonable in certain political and institutional contexts. However, here I try to make a case that for the countries at hand such hard budget constraints are best stemming from budgetary institutions that are located at the national (central) level. In general, constraining budgetary institutions in a fiscal-federal set-up could of course be located either on the subnational or national level of government or both. There could be a combination of budgetary institutions and fiscal rules on different levels of government, as is the case in larger political federations like the USA or Germany. In the present study, however, I focus on emerging market nations and attempt to explain what type of fiscal arrangements are most likely to achieve fiscal stability in those countries. Below, I will explain in more detail why the distinction between more and less economically and institutionally advanced countries may be of importance for designing fiscal institutions. For now, I assume that the group of countries under scrutiny here are substantially different from OECD country cases, in particular regarding their ability to implement binding fiscal constraints. It seems well founded to assume that for this group of advanced countries, characterized not only by their superior macroeconomic performance, but also by their level of financial market development, decentralized budget constraints are the best option to ensure fiscal stability at the local level. The arguments for this are well known and discussed at length in several landmark contributions in the literature (e.g. Rodden 2006). However, there are at least two important ways in which emerging market economies differ from more advanced economies. First, they show less macroeconomic stability. Second, they are characterized by less efficient financial markets, often failing to serve as a check on public finances. For these reasons, I assume that the best policy option to constrain subnational budget actors should be seen in policy tools that allow the central government to intervene and enforce fiscal stability where necessary.

While the decentralization of expenditure may well be commensurable with fiscal stability under a strongly coordinated national-level budget process, it seems much more likely that it leads to fiscally irresponsible decisions on the local level, once we observe that a central government has only weak control over the budget process and fails to abandon off-budgeting and other procedures that undermine budget transparency and fiscal discipline. Instead, loose national-level budgetary institutions signal to local budget actors that they can increase the level of expenditure on local public goods while passing on the costs to the nation.

Subnational budget making is hardly a stand-alone decision-making process in a political vacuum. On the contrary, it seems more plausible to assume that national-level budget processes have a signaling effect on subnational politicians. Therefore, it is argued here that subnational fiscal discipline could be conditional on the degree of budget process centralization and transparency on the national level. Subnational budgetary actors may be seen as strategic politicians, taking budgetary choices dependent on what they observe on the national level. When subnational actors are observing a loosely structured national budget process, lacking transparency as a precondition for evaluating achieved, and projecting future, budget results, we are more likely to see subnational fiscal profligacy.

Given their historical experience with political centralization, which has left its mark on the political decision culture in the countries at hand, we are likely to find that local-level politicians turn to their national-level peers to see 'how far they can go'. Is it legal and politically opportune to 'privatize' public resources and 'socialize the costs' for individual political campaigns? To find answers, local political strongmen are thought to take a look up the 'chain of command' in their respective parties and up the ladder of political office holders. However revealing of the lack of political freedom and sovereignty of local leaders, this strong sense of hierarchy may not be for the worst for constituencies. If a government chooses to change the budget process to a more transparent and structured political decision-making process, this should have positive effects on subnational-level fiscal discipline. More structured and transparent budget processes on the national level could set the right incentives, not only for national but also for local budget actors, to join a 'coalition' for fiscal stability. In other words, I suspect that the consequences of loose central-level budgetary institutions in Latin American countries could be twofold. First, it seems likely that loose subnational fiscal control, encouraged by loose central-level control, creates liabilities for the general government budget. Over time, the lack of hard budget constraints is likely to undermine overall fiscal stability. At the very least, we may expect that central government liabilities will combine with accumulated subnational liabilities to form large overall public debts. Second, the lack of control over subnational budget actors may turn out to be particularly costly in times of economic downturn and financial distress when central governments find it even harder to implement swift fiscal adjustment measures. In short, the overall fiscal crisis will be greater.

Adding the subnational level to the discussion of how to improve fiscal stability therefore seems important because, as we have seen – for instance, during continuous sovereign debt crises in Brazil and Argentina – a subnational spending bias and soft borrowing constraints can create severe financing problems for a country as a whole. A country that is unable to control subnational debt crises potentially also carries a greater contagion risk for other countries in the region.

Both the budgetary institutions and the fiscal federalism literature point to a coordination failure among decentralized budget actors under persistently soft budget constraints as a crucial source of fiscal instability. In both types of literature, unconstrained decentralization of fiscal authority is often seen to be at the root of instability because it increases the number of budget actors with incentives to raid the national fiscal commons without being forced to bear long-term costs. As was discussed above, the budgetary institutions literature focused on the national (horizontal) level of government, finding that a stronger centralization of budget processes leads to a 'hardening' of budget constraints. This can best be achieved either through a delegation of budgetary powers to a single budget authority or through a statutory approach, depending on the underlying characteristics of the political system (Hallerberg and von Hagen 1999, Hallerberg 2004, Hallerberg et al. 2009).

Looking at decentralized budget authority from a different angle, the fiscal federalism literature identifies familiar problems of decentralization, showing that dividing fiscal decision rights along the vertical axis leads to larger numbers of unconstrained budget actors. What Prud'homme (1995), Eichengreen and von Hagen (1996) and Stein (1999), among others, have argued and what has been further established by empirical findings presented by Jonathan Rodden – in single-authored contributions and in joint work with several colleagues – is the notion that in the absence of an equivalence between subnational expenditure and revenue, fiscal discipline depends crucially on the 'hardness' of fiscal institutions, including fiscal targets and borrowing limits (Rodden 2002, 2003, 2004, 2006, Rodden and Wibbels 2002, Rodden et al. 2003). Central governments are the best equipped to impose hard budget constraints through conditionality in central–subnational fiscal relations. Central governments have the power to make their fiscal transfers to subnational governments dependent on efforts to establish fiscal stability. Central governments can furthermore contribute to the fiscal stability of subnational governments by committing to a credible no-bailout rule, allowing financial markets to take over the role of the disciplinarian. Finally, central governments can take control of subnational fiscal activities by constraining borrowing activities. Indeed, loose control over subnational borrowing correlates strongly with subnational debt accumulation. Leaving subnational budget actors – as well as their creditors – with the impression that they can borrow 'cost-free' to finance local public goods, seems like weaving moral hazard into the very fabric of fiscal-federal relations. This problem seems to be enhanced by the fact that subnational governments are often highly dependent on fiscal transfers to carry out their own fiscal activities (Rodden 2002, 2004, 2006).

In the political context of the Latin American countries under scrutiny here, where central governments face difficulties in credibly committing to no-bailout rules because subnational governments are, for various (historical) reasons, dependent on central transfers and revenue-sharing schemes to provide even basic local public goods, relying on 'market discipline' as the only constraining mechanism seems fundamentally problematic. Given the widespread problem of moral hazard, nurtured by continuous government bailouts of subnational governments and public enterprises in many of the countries at hand, it seems hard to believe that financial market control of subnational government fiscal behavior should be the most viable solution. Instead, I argue that countries aiming for a more permanent stabilization of public finances may be better off when they successfully implement borrowing constraints and fiscal rules at the central level, allowing them to resolve CPR problems linked to vertical decentralization.

Specifically, I argue that government budgets can best be stabilized through the implementation of limits on deficits and public spending in certain areas. However, for such fiscal rules to be efficient they need to blend into a broader fiscal consolidation plan, ideally defining specific goals and responsibilities for all branches and levels of government, formulating transparency standards and, even more importantly, identifying enforcement mechanisms. As sketched out above, I assume two ways in which central-level budgetary institutions may help to reach fiscal stability:

1. National-level institutions affect central government outcomes directly.
2. Central institutions may also condition the way vertical decentralization of fiscal authority affects subnational fiscal activities.

In what follows below, I try to explain in several steps the relevant explanatory variables in my model of fiscal imbalance and the relationships between them. First, I discuss in more detail why we are likely to find that institutional decentralization at the national level – from here on referred to as 'horizontal decentralization' – leads to worse budget outcomes in Latin American countries. Second, I explain the potential effects that vertical fiscal decentralization may exert on budgets, not only at the subnational but eventually also at the general government level. Finally, I develop my argument that vertical fiscal decentralization can lead to different positive or negative 'policy equilibria', depending on the strength of a given country's budgetary institutions.

3.2 PREDICTIONS ABOUT HORIZONTAL INSTITUTIONAL (DE-)CENTRALIZATION

Building on the existing budgetary institutions literature, I argue that higher degrees of budgetary process decentralization and lower transparency should negatively affect fiscal stability in a given country. In contrast, higher degrees of budget process centralization – whether achieved through a delegation of decision-making powers to a central budget authority, through a contractual approach or some combination of both – should help to reduce spending bias. Following the CPR problem logic, we may expect improved fiscal outcomes because the centralization of budgetary institutions introduces – ceteris paribus – a hard budget constraint on the government.

At this point, it is important to discuss the scope of my analysis and to define the terms 'horizontal decentralization' and 'vertical decentralization', which I find to be crucial explanatory factors for fiscal imbalance. As for scope, I constrain my current analysis to presidential democracies in Latin America since the late 1980s. In these cases, we can expect a constitutionally guaranteed minimum degree of shared decision making over the budget. That means that I only consider cases in which there is at least a minimum amount of democratic decision making within the cabinet and in which the legislature is entitled to vote on the budget presented by the executive and to request amendments. Naturally, the degree to which a president is forced to share decision rights with other budgetary actors – in the cabinet, the legislature or elsewhere – varies between different presidential systems. Decentralization of budget decision making is thought to vary on a continuum reaching from a very centralized and transparent budget decision-making process to highly unstructured decision procedures that lack transparency. Along the lines of the budgetary institutions literature, I define a budget process to be centralized (decentralized) when the following criteria apply (are lacking):

- either budget decisions are delegated to a central budget authority (the president or the finance minister), keeping a final veto on all spending requests from line ministries and government agencies or budgets are constrained by a contract between different partners of a ruling coalition or a binding fiscal law, spelling out expenditure, deficit and debt targets (or a combination of delegation and fiscal contracts/laws);
- the executive holds agenda-setting powers in the legislative budget approval process and has a veto over budget amendments from the legislature;
- the central budget authority retains the right to withhold expenditure in economic downturns and may even be entitled to put a hold on particular budget items after they have been approved and allocated to certain units. This means that the central budget authority, or a third party entitled to this right, can effectively sanction the violation of fiscal rules by putting a hold on financial transactions;
- the executive works towards full transparency of the budget process, with an assurance that international accounting standards are being met (e.g. in one unified consolidated account, prohibiting off-budget accounts). Furthermore, the government commits to observing international standards regarding information dissemination on government expenditure, revenue and borrowing, serving as an

important pre-condition for fiscally sustainable budget planning, implementation and auditing;
- the central budget authority has control over all borrowing activities of public agencies, including subnational governments, and can sanction transgressions of borrowing rules.

To be able to differentiate this form of decentralized decision making on the national political level from another form of decentralization, i.e. decentralization in budget decision rights along the vertical axis (fiscal federalism), I will from here on refer to the former as *horizontal* decentralization, with the latter referred to as *vertical* decentralization. By horizontal decentralization, I mean a decentralized budget process on the national level. This includes budget decisions taken within the executive (at the cabinet level) as well as negotiations between the executive and the legislature, and other branches of government.

In sum, it seems that under more centralized budget control, governments in emerging market nations should find themselves in a better position to contain spending pressure and take decisive steps to reduce deficits and public debt levels. In contrast, governments that lack such institutional provisions are constrained in their capacity to control fiscal imbalance and high public indebtedness as a consequence. In line with several other empirical approaches, claiming a positive relationship between institutional strength and public accounts in countries in the Latin American and Caribbean region in earlier periods (Alesina et al. 1999, Stein 1999, Filc and Scartascini 2007), as well as a number of studies stressing the benefits of centralized budget making in advanced countries, I assume the following to be true for the relationship between horizontal decentralization and a nation's fiscal stance:

Hypothesis 1: Higher levels of budget process decentralization on the national level increase the risk of fiscal imbalance.

3.3 VERTICAL FISCAL DECENTRALIZATION AS A THREAT TO OVERALL FISCAL BALANCE

To arrive at a more comprehensive picture of the effects of decentralized budget making on the fiscal stance of a country, it seems appropriate to consider a broader range of decentralization decisions. Both the budgetary institutions and the fiscal federalism literature made significant contributions to our understanding of CPR problems lurking behind fiscal imbalance. However, they have each described the consequences of decentralized decision making on a particular level of government, largely in isolation of what is happening on other levels. Below, I suggest a combined view of decentralization effects. As a point of departure, let us consider a political system that is exposed to a higher risk of fiscal imbalance due to a lack of stringent horizontal-level budgetary institutions and a general lack of transparency of the budget process. Due to changing preferences for decentralized political control, our country experiences an increase in the fiscal decision-making authority of subnational governments. Notwithstanding the potential advantages of such a decision for the establishment and further implementation of democratic decision structures in our country, what would such a decision mean for overall fiscal stability? Based on what we know from the fiscal federalism literature, decentralization of budget control along the vertical axis is likely to be followed by fiscal imbalance, unless governments can credibly implement hard budget constraints. For simplicity, let us rely here on a definition of vertical fiscal decentralization, defined as the ratio of decentralized spending to total government expenditure.[1] In reality, fiscal-federal relations are often much more complicated, involving the subnational level right to collect (and keep) revenue, as well as schemes for redistributing revenue from the center to the subnational level and/or between subnational governments. Here, I will only consider the potential (negative) effects of allowing subnational governments to take their own expenditure, independent of the question of whether there are other fiscal-federal institutions and political obligations tying them together. By delegating fiscal decision-making authority to local-level budget actors, central governments run the risk of increasing coordination problems and making fiscal adjustment more difficult than under centralization. This is because decentralization increases the number of rational budget actors with incentives to draw on the common pool resource, the national tax pool, while trying to contribute as little as possible. Unless local budget actors are facing hard budget constraints, decentralizing budget authority to the local level increases spending on local public goods. Over a longer time period, such spending bias seems likely to give rise to other problems, including accumulated fiscal deficits and deficit financing through increased borrowing.

Standard ways of ensuring subnational fiscal discipline include, on the one hand, subnational-level budget institutions (fiscal and debt targets) and, on the other hand, market-based control of fiscal deficits through financial investors. State-level budget institutions, specifically fiscal rules, in US fiscal and debt crises after the mid-19th century, are probably the most widely known example of such subnational-level self-regulation. Opponents of centralized budgetary constraints often refer to the US case to stress that states are capable of keeping their fiscal house in order without federal interference in local budget decisions. A crucial mechanism forcing subnational governments into fiscal discipline are self-imposed balanced-budget or 'golden' rules, requiring that governments come up with sufficient own-source revenue to balance any additional spending on local public goods.

Notwithstanding the virtue of the US example, for the present analysis, I largely exclude the possibility of credible, self-imposed subnational constraints. Instead, I will focus here on the role of central-level controls instead. Why this objection to subcentral self-regulation? First, as scholars of the US fiscal rules are well aware, it is not merely through self-imposed subnational fiscal rules that state governments feel pressured to balance their budgets. In the absence of any developed and well-functioning markets for state debts, it seems hard to believe that subnational governments in the USA would feel 'constrained enough' by a set of self-imposed rules. Such rules could be changed through state-level legislation without the consent of other states or the federal union. A general concern with self-imposed fiscal rules is that they may not work due to the lack of a central enforcement agency. In good times, subnational governments may praise themselves for following their own budget and debt rules, but under increasing economic pressure, for how long are states going to obey rules that can more or less easily be changed within their own legislatures? Delegating fiscal control to a budget authority, external to the state-level political process, therefore seems like a more viable solution. Such authority could generally be taken on by a fiscal stability board or some other form of budgetary authority that keeps track of subnational budgets. However, to be taken as credible hard budget constraints such an authority needs to be equipped with the power to sanction transgressions of the fiscal rules. For any subnational-level fiscal authority, similar concerns arise about the credibility of sanctioning powers, as in the case of subnational governments.

Coming back to the example of the US states since the mid-19th century, one may find that doubting incredible state-level sanctioning mechanisms is a negligible concern. Vertical fiscal decentralization remains commensurable with fiscal discipline as long as markets exert the expected disciplining effect. Indeed, proponents of 'market discipline' will find it superior to any kind of government intervention due to the expected lower market distortions. However compelling in theory, 'market discipline' still rests on the assumption that the federation commits to a no-bailout rule – an assumption that cannot easily be made in the case of the emerging market nations at hand. Due to the US government's commitment to a no-bailout doctrine since the 1840s, financial markets today cannot expect to be compensated by the union for potential losses. Market participants thus price in the respective default risk of each state based on fiscal performance indicators.[2] Given the US government's stern commitment to not bailing out subnational governments in previous crises, concerns about 'moral hazard' have thus been shown to be unfounded. As a result, if we base our judgment only on the US experience, 'market discipline' seems to be a viable alternative to the central-level enforcement of fiscal discipline.

Looking beyond the US case, however, to consider the Latin American emerging market context, it would seem like a more risky bet to rely merely on 'market discipline' to contain public deficits and debt. In the wake of recurrent financial crises, financial markets have been shown to drastically underestimate the credit risk of subnational governments (e.g. in Brazil and Argentina). Relying on central-level regulation therefore seems like a more promising solution in situations where the market control of government fiscal management either fails or is simply not available, for instance due to a low degree of financial integration in international markets. Another impediment to functioning market discipline in the cases at hand is often a general lack of reliable information about institutions and government policies. To date, subnational governments in the region are far from being considered as either fully or 'quasi' fiscal sovereigns. Indeed, if they were fully – fiscally – sovereign there would be little reason for them to stay in a union with weak states (Wildasin 1997; see von Hagen 2000 for an opposing view). At the same time, national governments to date are unlikely to let subnational governments fail and stay committed to no-bailout resolutions. Consequently, subnational governments seem unlikely to stay committed to their own budgetary targets over time, at least not as long as there is no central enforcement mechanism.[3]

Coming back to our example of a country that is already characterized by weak national-level budget constraints and in which it is decided that (greater) fiscal autonomy should be delegated to the subnational level, its prospects for fiscal stability after vertical decentralization seem more negative than before. Instead, we would expect fiscal deficits to accumulate on the local level, adding to the high expected deficits on the central government level. Based on this reasoning, the following hypothesis on the relationship between risks of fiscal imbalance incurred on both levels of government should hold:

Hypothesis 2: In countries that are characterized by loose central-level budget control, the risk of incurring high fiscal imbalance increases with higher degrees of vertical fiscal decentralization, due to the added negative budgetary effects of opportunistic subnational and central government spending decisions.

3.4 POTENTIAL INTERDEPENDENCE OF SUBNATIONAL AND CENTRAL-LEVEL FISCAL INSTITUTIONS

In this section, I introduce an argument about the interrelation between national-level and subnational-level fiscal decision making. It goes beyond the existing literature, trying to expand our thinking about the impact of budgetary institutions on subnational budget actors in a fiscal-federal framework. Above, I argued along the lines of the existing scholarship in fiscal federalism that vertical fiscal decentralization bears significant risks for overall fiscal stability. In a context where markets insufficiently constrain subnational budget actors and in the absence of credible subnational-level budget constraints, subnational governments face strong incentives to overspend. Rising subnational deficits and public debt then contribute to overall government deficits and debt accumulation. This is a well-known problem and has already received attention in the fiscal federalism literature discussed in previous chapters. Going beyond this 'additive effect' of vertical fiscal imbalance on general government balance, I submit here that subnational fiscal behavior under vertical fiscal decentralization may interact with the institutional framework on the central level. In other words, I assume that subnational fiscal decisions depend on the degree of budgetary institutional centralization on the national level.

We have already discussed that under vertical fiscal decentralization, rational subnational budgetary actors face incentives to draw on the available common pool tax resources to increase their own local political capital. This effect would – in theory – be eliminated by hard budget constraints – enforced either through market discipline or through credible, local-level budgetary constraints. As I have stated above, both types of budget constraints seem likely to break down in the emerging market context in Latin America. Instead of 'fearing' the private financial markets or paying attention to subnational-level budgetary rules, I assume local budget makers to be looking at the central government level to inform their own fiscal strategies. Given a tradition of centrally imposed political decisions in those countries, subnational politicians seem likely to expect constraints – as much as financial rescue – to come from the political center. As a consequence, we would expect local leaders to turn to the central level for policy signals, indicating either tight or less stringent budget control.

If a country decides to allow for more fiscal policy autonomy of the lower levels of government, subnational fiscal discipline is likely to depend on national-level budget institutions for several reasons. First, it can be argued that rational local politicians adapt to the changing tide in national-level budget politics. In the absence of any hard budget constraints, local politicians face strong incentives to draw on the common national tax pool, exploiting the latter for their own local political purposes. Changing the way budgets are negotiated and sanctioned at the central level is likely to impact on local fiscal behavior. Once the center reforms budgetary institutions to achieve greater transparency and stringency of the budget process, for example by delegating budget power to a budget authority conservative in its spending and/or by setting numerical fiscal targets with the aim of improving long-term fiscal stability, this may initiate a re-orienting of local politicians. Institutional centralization should alter national politicians' fiscal behavior. As they observe changing national-level fiscal behavior, local budget actors seem likely to change their own budget policies accordingly.

Second, a strengthening of the national-level budgetary institutions in the ways described above would allow subnational governments to 'tie their hands' vis-à-vis their local constituencies. Central enforcement may help the lower tiers of government to contain the political risk associated with implementing fiscal discipline because local politicians can easily shift the blame to the central level.

Third, it seems plausible that once 'windfall gains' from improved fiscal stability are starting to materialize, to the benefit of local constituencies, local leaders may be able to capitalize on a reputation as 'fiscally responsible' leaders. As shown in the case of Brazil after 1998, local politicians can indeed benefit from fiscal compliance with central-level rules and prudent policies, when they establish a new image as members of a powerful, nationwide 'coalition for stability'. Hence, local politicians may increase their political capital by stabilizing local budgets. At the same time, all local calls for an end to 'austerity politics' and a softening of budgetary institutions would bounce off local budget actors as such decisions are not (or no longer) entirely in their hands. In sum, implementing a set of centrally imposed fiscal rules that include but go beyond mere borrowing controls on lower tiers of government, is likely to constrain subnational budget makers. By strengthening the budget constraint and by changing incentives for budget actors on the national level, stronger national-level budgetary institutions are likely to affect fiscal discipline on all levels of government.

To be sure, I am not arguing here that decentralizing fiscal authority in the context of a relatively recent transition to democracy and opening of markets is generally incommensurable with fiscal and overall macroeconomic stability. Countries that allow their subnational governments, for well-deserved political reasons, greater independence in taking spending decisions, are not doomed to end up in a fiscal and public debt crisis. Even in the absence of functioning market controls on subnational governments, and in the absence of any credible subnational fiscal constraints, governments can retain overall fiscal stability. What it takes, I argue, are tighter central-level budget constraints, together with high standards on transparency of the budget process. In countries that allow for stronger vertical fiscal decentralization, meanwhile failing to establish strong national-level budget institutions, the expected fiscal costs may go beyond the added effects of subnational and central government deficits. This is because loose horizontal budget processes are thought to invite further subnational fiscal indiscipline. This leads me to suggest the following hypothesis on the relationship between budgetary institutions and fiscal stability:

Hypothesis 3: Higher degrees of vertical expenditure decentralization increase the risk of nationwide fiscal imbalance, depending on the strength of national-level budgetary institutions.

3.5 SOME PREDICTIONS ABOUT THE EFFECTS OF BUDGETARY INSTITUTIONS ON FISCAL BALANCES

Following the discussion in the two prior sections, it appears that fiscal stability in a fiscal-federal system may depend on different institutional constraints, depending on our theoretical priors about what drives subnational fiscal behavior. Table 3.1 summarizes the predicted likelihood of fiscal imbalance based on the second hypothesis, claiming a simple additive effect of what I have dubbed 'horizontal' and 'vertical' fiscal decentralization. The second table (Table 3.2) indicates the expected likelihood of

Table 3.1 Predictions: added effects of vertical and horizontal decentralization

		Horizontal decentralization	
		low	high
Vertical decentralization*	low	*Type 1* no fiscal imbalance	*Type 3* intermediate-high risk of imbalance
	high	*Type 2* intermediate-high risk of imbalance	*Type 4* high risk

Note: * SNG expenditures/total government expenditures

Table 3.2 Predictions: interaction effects

		Horizontal decentralization	
		low	high
Vertical decentralization*	low	*Type 1* no imbalance	*Type 3* intermediate-high risk of imbalance
	high	*Type 2* low risk of imbalance	*Type 4* very high risk

Note: * SNG expenditures/total government expenditures

public financial crises, assuming that subnational fiscal decision making interacts with the strength of budgetary institutions on the central level.

3.5.1 Additive Effect of Fiscal Decentralization

In this study, my goal is to get to a more comprehensive understanding of potential CPR problems following decentralizing fiscal decision making on the level of the central government and in a fiscal-federal scheme, within a single analytical framework. Looking at the added effects of fiscal-federal decentralization and loose national-level budgetary coordination therefore appeared as a natural point of departure. Table 3.1 indicates the assumed predicted risks of fiscal imbalance under different institutional conditions. To allow me to evaluate the potential fiscal risks of decentralized fiscal control in a parsimonious model, I suggest here thinking of vertical fiscal decentralization as a decentralization of spending rights. Horizontal decentralization refers to a loosening of budget control of the central fiscal authority (president or finance minister) over different line ministries represented in the government and other public enterprises, as well as a lack of transparency and control over legislative spending amendments in the budget process. Table 3.1 presents four 'ideal types' of countries with varying degrees of horizontal and vertical fiscal decentralization. The first two types (upper and lower left hand) include cases that show a strong degree of horizontal centralization, meaning that there generally exist strong budget constraints on national-level budgetary actors and suggesting that the governments work towards ensuring a transparent budget process. Given these favorable institutional conditions on the central level, Type 1 or Type 2 cases seem safe from accumulating central government-level fiscal deficits. Unlike Type 1 cases, that also show a high degree of central control over subnational expenditure, Type 2 cases have much more autonomy in making spending decisions. Accordingly, I expect them to carry a higher risk of subnational fiscal imbalance. This is because local-level budget actors face incentives to overexploit the common tax pool and to raise local expenditure to an unsustainable level at the cost of the general public.

Given that we assume simple additive effects in the present model, Type 3 cases should carry an equal risk of accumulating fiscal deficits as Type 2 cases. While we expect none or very little negative impact of the subnational fiscal stance on overall government finances, loose national-level budget institutions expose Type 3 cases to an enhanced risk of central government deficits. Such risk naturally appears to be highest for Type 4 cases characterized by an accumulation of negative impacts, both from vertical fiscal decentralization and horizontal decentralization.

Looking at the suggested typology (Table 3.1), it should be noted that it incorporates only the added effects of vertical decentralization and a loose national-level budget process. Such a framework allows us to get closer to the overall fiscal costs of allowing decentralized decision-making processes. However, it constrains our thinking of budget politics to a world in which individual leaders are acting in a sort of 'political vacuum', independent of fiscal decisions or trends observed on other levels of government. In order to arrive at a more realistic model of budget decisions and their potential effects in a fiscal-federal framework, I suggest in the next section a new model that goes beyond the additive example presented above.

3.5.2 Assumed Interaction of Vertical and Horizontal Fiscal Decentralization

In this section, I consider the potential effects of vertical fiscal decentralization on overall government fiscal balances, depending on the degree of horizontal decentralization. My assumption here is that subnational fiscal behavior interacts with institutional characteristics at the central government level. Accounting for this potential interaction leads to new predictions about the risk of fiscal imbalance.

As before, we would expect to see a high degree of fiscal stability for Type 1 cases (upper-left quadrant), given a highly coordinated national-level budget process and few expected fiscal pressures from the subnational level (e.g. Chile). However, compared to the additive model above (Table 3.1), we now arrive at a different prediction for Type 2 cases. Above, we expected the higher degree of vertical fiscal decentralization to expose such cases to a slightly higher overall fiscal imbalance risk due to potentially accumulating subnational deficits. Under vertically decentralized fiscal decision making, there are more budget actors with incentives to reap the fiscal commons than before. However, as was explained above, in the interdependence scenario, we also expect subnational budget actors to adapt their fiscal strategies to what they observe on the national level. If they observe fiscal discipline due to strengthened budget constraints on the central level, subnational politicians appear more likely to interpret this as a signal of the government's commitment to impose fiscal discipline. The new central-level commitment tells local politicians something about the central government's resolve to achieve fiscal stability. With an increasing risk of the federal level reining in local budgetary decisions, subnational budget actors may prefer to take action against increasing fiscal deficits earlier on. Local politicians are well aware of several constraining measures that central governments may rely on to achieve their goal. These include: (a) reducing central-level transfers, and (b) enforcing (strengthening) budget and borrowing limits on subnational governments. Politically, local leaders may even capitalize on joining a broader 'coalition for stability'. For these reasons, we would expect the potentially negative effects of increased vertical fiscal decentralization to be mitigated by stronger horizontal-level budget institutions.

Compared to the former two categories, cases falling in the third and fourth quadrants (Types 3 and 4) carry a significantly higher risk of running high deficits. Given the low degree of coordination and transparency of the budget (high horizontal decentralization), we would expect that CPR problems lead to increasing government expenditure, and over time, to higher deficits. We would therefore expect an enhanced likelihood of fiscal imbalance, even if vertical fiscal decentralization is absent or low (Type 3). This is because, in the absence of any hard budget constraints, national-level CPR problems are sufficient to generate spending increases and deficits. While my prediction for Type 3 cases resembles the earlier prediction in the additive framework, I arrive at a different prediction for Type 4 cases. Going beyond the existing literature, I argue that we are likely to see an even higher proneness to deficits where national-level budget institutions are weak and where subnational governments have been delegated substantial spending authority (Type 4).

Why is the national-level budget process so important for creating hard budget constraints on the subnational levels of government? Again, the main reason may be seen in a signaling effect of strengthened national budget institutions on local-level politicians. Through centralized budgetary institutions, central governments pre-commit (and limit) their resources. Additionally, they show their resolve to set limits on budget actors at all levels of government, including the subnational level. Such precommitment can take the form of fiscal and debt targets, allowing central government to prioritize more easily in the following decision-making process. For example, in a horizontal, highly centralized case, annual budget bills are designed to fit into a medium-term fiscal framework, which identifies certain revenue and expenditure targets that have to be met for balanced fiscal accounts and for containing the growth of public debt. The mid-term as well as the annual fiscal plans would have to be in order with more fundamental fiscal and debt rules, defined, for example, by the constitution or a special law. Once legislators agree on certain budget goals, the executive can refer subnational politicians to the binding budget constraint. In combination with threats of imposing spending and borrowing constraints on subnational governments, the central level can force subnational governments to stabilize deficits and debts. To assure compliance, central government is in a position to start a set of financial and non-financial sanctions. On these premises, we would expect it to be less difficult for national governments to control deficits and the growth of public debt, even under strong vertical fiscal decentralization.

3.6 HISTORICAL EXPLANATIONS AND THE PROBLEM OF ENDOGENEITY

Ignoring how fiscal institutions came into existence yields a potential bias due to endogeneity. The political process by which present-day fiscal institutions were installed, reflecting the position of the involved political decision makers and the interests they represent, could explain certain 'pathologies' or success stories in fiscal and debt management. Hence, any argument about the potential relationship between fiscal decentralization and budget outcomes comes at the risk of being endogenous on important omitted variables.

Throughout the analysis, I am primarily concerned with the potential effects of budgetary institutions. Furthermore, I stated that subnational budget politics may be interacting with central-level budget institutions. For the time being, I take the degree of horizontal fiscal (de-)centralization as exogenously given and try to investigate its direct and conditional effects without engaging in the broader discussion of how it becomes possible for such budgetary institutions to be changed over time. To date, there is little theoretical guidance as to why certain countries engage in reforming their budgetary institutions while others do not. Nor can we rely on a model explaining why reforms are successful in some countries but not in others. One notable exception is Hallerberg et al. (2009b, Ch. 5), addressing the question of why EU countries adopt certain fiscal institutions. These authors consider the role of fiscal crises as focal points or moments in time where populations receive a great amount of information about the negative consequences of institutional decentralization. Countries with 'histories of fiscal crises have adopted more robust fiscal institutions', the authors claim (p. 9). And by robust, the authors mean that countries have chosen the types of budgetary institutions that best match the underlying political system characteristics (Hallerberg et al. 2009b). Given the crisis-induced, 'custom-made' design of budgetary institutions, they are thought to be much more likely to improve outcomes. Although the present study falls short of providing a full-blown analysis of the above argument, I will return to it in the in-depth case analysis in chapters 5 and 6. Specifically, I will return to the question of how institutional reforms, leading to significant improvements in the fiscal stance, were implemented in two crisis-ridden countries in Latin America. In extensive case studies of Brazil and Argentina, I investigate what role previous fiscal crises may have played in reform initiatives.

A related problem appears in using the degree of vertical fiscal decentralization as an explanatory variable. Before we can answer the questions of if and how decentralized spending schemes affect fiscal performance, we may first be inclined to ask why we find that certain countries decide to delegate (more) fiscal authority to the subnational level while others remain largely centralized. Congleton (2006) argues that fiscal-federal decentralization is the result of ongoing negotiations over the distribution of policy-making authority between regional leaders and a newly evolving central government. Accordingly, the initial bargaining could have led to largely different outcomes, depending on the conditions at the time when the (fiscal) constitution was written. In a similar vein, Enderlein (2009) points to path dependence in the design of different present-day fiscal-federal regimes, taking a historical-institutionalist perspective.[4]

One obvious determinant of subnational government fiscal independence that Congleton (2006) points out consists in the power of local leaders when they congregate to form the federal government. In places where the revenue-raising capacities of local elites are strong (providing them with strong political powers) at the birth of a federation, central governments may later find it hard to change the status quo of fiscal-federal institutions, including the degree of expenditure and revenue decentralization and the specifics of transfer systems.[5] One way to deal with endogeneity problems in large N empirical studies would be to search for an appropriate 'instrumental variable' to be included in regression analyses, investigating the unbiased effect of fiscal institutions on performance indicators. The purpose of such an instrumental variable would be to account for the possibility that fiscal bargains prior to the writing of present-day fiscal-federal frameworks explain fiscal performance.

NOTES

1. In the empirical investigation that follows in the chapters below, I equally rely on this expenditure-based definition of vertical fiscal decentralization. The measurement approach follows previous studies by Marlow (1988), Treisman (2000) and Rodden (2004) that rely on a definition of expenditure decentralization as the share of state and local government expenditure in total consolidated government expenditure (state + local government total expenditure)/(consolidated central government total expenditure + state + local government total expenditure).
2. Eichengreen and von Hagen (1996) and von Hagen and Eichengreen (1996) argue that in a monetary union, fiscal stability is better achieved through increasing (maintaining) the revenue-raising independence of member states than by imposing borrowing constraints on them. In a similar vein, Rodden (2006) indulges in the idea of miniature sovereigns that are less likely to put pressure on the central level for tax smoothing and public investment. Accordingly, central governments would be more likely to stick to no-bailout policies. Additionally, the financial markets would serve as a check on the fiscal discipline of subnational miniature sovereigns. State governments in the USA come very close to the suggested idea of 'miniature sovereigns' that are subject to 'market discipline' from investors in highly developed financial markets for subnational debt.
3. An empirical assessment of the actual role of subnational fiscal rules depends strongly on additional empirical evidence, taking into account a longer time horizon than is currently possible. Latin American governments only started to introduce subnational fiscal and borrowing constraints at the beginning of the 2000s. While a judgment based on cross-country studies at this point seems premature, a possible way to explore the role of fiscal rules is by focusing on the potential effects of subnational-level self-imposed fiscal rules by looking at a single case, for example in Brazil, which was the first country in the Latin American region to introduce such rules in the latest wave of institutional reforms (e.g. Webb 2003).
4. Enderlein (2009, p. 6) argues that historical 'institutional inertia (often constitutionally anchored in a unanimity requirement on changing the terms of the trade-off) and the high switching costs keep the regime static'.
5. A case in point would be the Brazilian situation between 1997 and 1999. As a consequence of significant revenue losses from trade after the Mexican 'tequila crisis' and due to fiscal mismanagement and large debt accumulation, the Brazilian state governments entered a deep fiscal crisis in 1997, requiring the third federal bailout within a single decade. To put an end to subnational fiscal mismanagement, the government of President Fernando Henrique Cardoso took bold steps to constrain subnational borrowing, including shutdowns of loss-making state banks and public enterprises that had facilitated the growth in subnational debt, and legal action against private creditors that had been neglecting credibility standards in their contracts with subnational governments. By the end of the 1990s, subnational governments were in a weak financial position and their continued fiscal autonomy was partly at stake. The federal government, in fact, charged subnational governments a significant amount for continued access to financial markets. Federal assistance was made conditional on a series of new fiscal constraints fixed in the debt contracts between the federal government and the bailout candidates that were implemented with the objective of reducing imbalances of revenue and expenditure in the future. In Chapter 5, I describe the Brazilian case in much more detail.

4. Fiscal imbalance in Latin America and the Caribbean

4.1 INTRODUCTION

This chapter presents a discussion of my three initial working hypotheses on the effect of budget process decentralization (Chapter 3) in light of the available empirical data for Latin American and Caribbean emerging market nations. A number of previous empirical studies, relying on data for economically advanced countries, found a negative empirical relationship between the decentralization of national-level budget processes and fiscal outcomes (see e.g. Hallerberg et al. 2009 for an overview). A lack of transparency in the budget process was also found to be associated with an increase in public debt. Looking beyond advanced countries, a few empirical studies focusing specifically on Latin American and Caribbean countries came to similar conclusions about the role of budget institutions (Alesina et al. 1999, Filc and Scartascini 2007). Taking their findings as a point of departure, I argue that increases in budget process centralization and improvements in transparency in the past few decades have had a positive effect on fiscal accounts in the countries at hand. To explain why we observe this beneficial effect of strengthening national-level budget institutions, I suggest a multi-level theoretical approach. Going beyond the above-mentioned studies, my approach incorporates institutional effects on budget actors at different levels of government. As suggested in Chapter 3, the effect on general government balances may be twofold. First, in line with the above studies, we would expect a stabilizing effect of strengthened budget institutions on the central government fiscal account. Second, strong and transparent budget institutions at the central level may contain negative effects of vertical fiscal decentralization on subnational fiscal budgets. By inhibiting unwanted subnational budget effects, central-level institutions help to improve general government fiscal outcomes. Numerous data constraints, particularly where subnational institutional, fiscal and other economic data are concerned, keep me from engaging in a multi-level empirical analysis at this point, including rigorous statistical testing of my key theoretical arguments, and presenting a series of robustness checks to back up my results. What I am able to and will present below therefore resembles more an empirical plausibility examination. That is, I try to evaluate my theoretical approach, drawing on macroeconomic, financial and institutional data, where available, allowing me to assess my arguments. Beyond that, primary data were gathered from more than 30 expert interviews that I carried out with policy makers. Below, I start with a section describing the development of fiscal imbalance in Latin American and Caribbean countries since the return to democracy following the Third Wave of Democratization in the late 1980s. Afterwards, I will go on to show developments in those institutions that are of most interest to me here: national-level budget institutions and fiscal-federal institutions, respectively.

My aim is to find out to what extent, and how, institutional decentralization affected fiscal stability in the region since the transition to democracy. My choice of explanatory variables comes at the cost of reducing the number of countries in the Latin American and Caribbean region with available institutional data to a total of 15.[1] Clearly, for the countries at hand a major obstacle is to find reliable sources on vertical decentralization. Following those sections that are meant to provide readers with a general overview, the final section of this chapter provides an outline of the comparative case analysis carried out in the next two chapters. Before we look at the in-depth case studies on Brazil and Argentina (chapters 5 and 6 respectively), section 4.6 explains the selection method for my case analysis. Finally, in the last section (4.7) I present a view of what a full-blown quantitative assessment of my multi-layered theoretical approach could achieve, once we are able to overcome the existing data constraints.

4.2 FISCAL IMBALANCE IN LATIN AMERICA

Before we get to the data on fiscal imbalance in Latin America and the Caribbean, a word on measurement seems warranted. In the literature, fiscal performance has been measured in various different ways, often depending on the specific research interest followed or the region studied. However, none of these approaches stands without critique for their lack of precision (see Bleher and Cheasty 1991 or Tanzi and Schuknecht 2000 for an extensive discussion). In the past, authors have often relied on central government deficit data for cross-country analysis, given that it is the most widely available measure. This can be problematic – as pointed out, among others, in a study by William Easterly and colleagues (1994) – because it excludes the part of fiscal deficits created by other public sector entities, including subnational governments. Following earlier studies on the Latin American and Caribbean region (Alesina et al. 1999, Filc and

Scartascini 2007), I employ data for the general government budget result defined as the difference between the total of government expenditure and its current revenue, relative to the size of the economy. The nominal general government balance is sometimes referred to as the 'conventional balance' as it remains the principal fiscal indicator in the design and monitoring of most IMF programs (Ize 1991).[2] For comparability it is often expressed relative to GDP. Below, I rely on data on the general government balance to GDP ratio coming from the Economist Intelligence Unit (EIU), beginning in 1990. The EIU data set, which relies on national government statistics provided by the Economy Ministry and data from the IMF's Government Finance Statistics (GFS) Yearbook, is also the most comprehensive available source on budget balances in Latin American countries since the early 1990s, providing yearly data on budget outcomes (scaled by GDP), allowing for comparison across countries and time.

Based on the nominal budget balance data available from the IMF and additional country sources combined in the EIU data set, it can be said that average fiscal performance in the Latin American and Caribbean region improved significantly in the early 2000s, after a strong decline during the 1990s that was followed by a period of volatility at the turn of that decade (see Figure 4.1, comparing average nominal and primary deficits

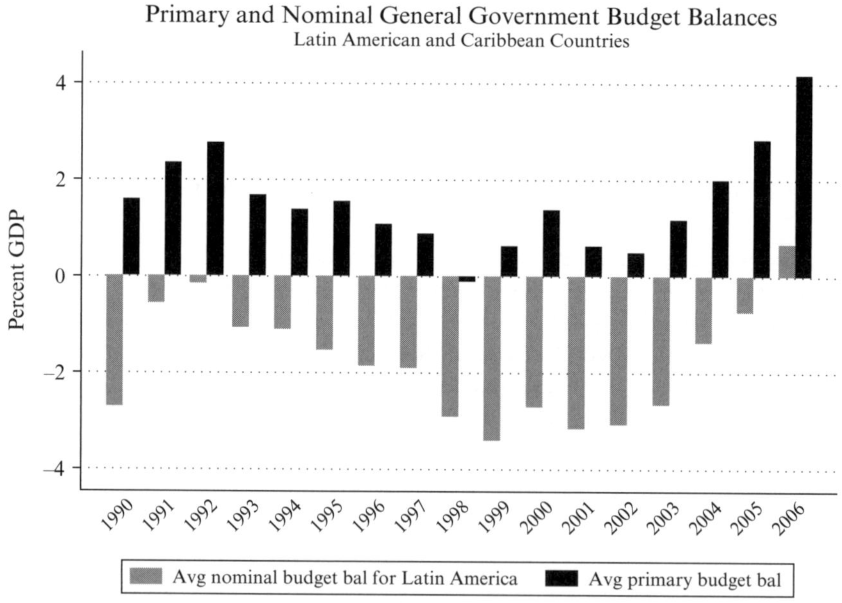

Figure 4.1 Nominal and primary budget balances, Latin America

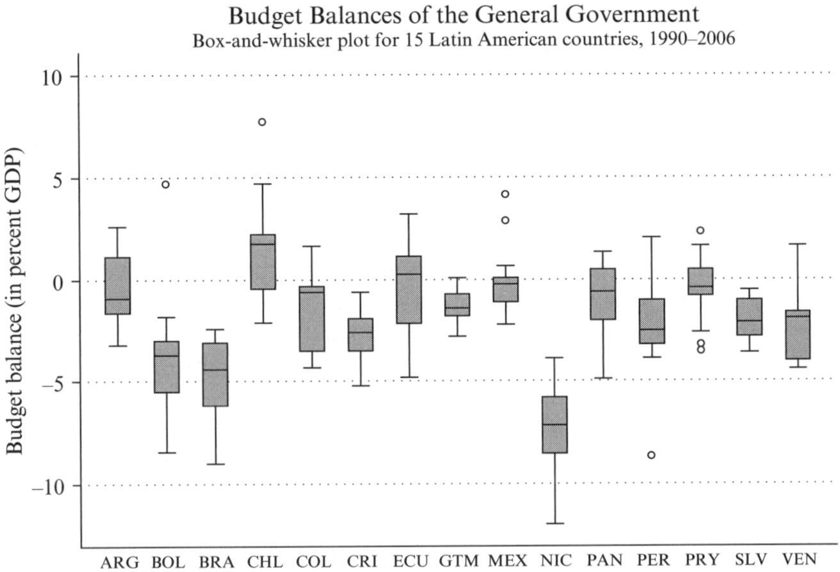

Figure 4.2 Budget balances in Latin American countries, 1990–2006

for the region between 1990 and 2006). Beginning in 2002, Latin American budget balances have seen a very strong improvement, with the average nominal budget balance increasing from −2.69 percent of GDP in 2002 to 0.65 percent in 2006.

High interest burden in several countries during financial market crises can explain the difference between nominal budget balances and primary budget balances visible in Figure 4.1 (e.g. Argentina 2001, Brazil 1998, 2002).[3] Figure 4.2, showing nominal budget balances in each country over the sample period (1990–2006), points to remarkable differences between countries in the Latin American region.[4]

4.3 DEVELOPMENTS IN HORIZONTAL DECENTRALIZATION

As a first institutional explanation, I consider the effect of horizontal decentralization. To measure decentralization on the national government level, I employ a scaled and inverted version of the Index of Budgetary Institutions (IBI) provided by the Inter-American Development Bank (IADB). The data come from two surveys on the state of budgetary institutions conducted by IADB researchers among finance and economy ministries, the presidential offices and central banks in Latin American and Caribbean countries since 1980 (Alesina et al. 1999, Filc and Scartascini 2004). The first survey, carried out by a research team around Alberto Alesina at the Inter-American Development Bank (Alesina et al. 1999), covers the degree of budget process centralization in 20 Latin American and Caribbean countries over the years 1980–1992. The second wave of data stems from the most recent survey carried out by researchers at the Inter-American Development Bank (Filc and Scartascini 2007), completed between 2000 and 2002. The second study covers one less country than the original survey, however, providing additional information on the budget process in each country.[5] Both data sets are generally commensurable, allowing for joint analysis (Filc and Scartascini 2004).

The IADB's Index of Budgetary Institutions consists of indicators capturing decentralization of the budget process on the national level, i.e. the degree of decentralized budget decision making within the government and between the government and the legislature. Specifically, the IADB index is constructed as an aggregate measure consisting of three sub-indices: (1) Fiscal Rules, (2) Hierarchical Rules, and (3) Transparency Rules.[6] The 'Fiscal Rules' sub-index includes information on fiscal limits imposed by the government, consistent medium-term fiscal framework documents, and the provision of sufficient reserve funds to meet unforeseen expenditure. Next, the 'Hierarchical Rules' sub-index picks up theoretical insights on the strength of finance ministers with (great) powers over line ministers and the legislature. Neither type of institution – rules nor delegation – is likely to reduce deficit financing and debt accumulation if budget actors can circumvent written rules in a policy environment that lacks transparency, making it difficult to monitor compliance with written rules.[7] To account for the role of transparency in the budget process, the IADB researchers decided to incorporate a third sub-index for 'Transparency Rules' (Alesina et al. 1999). This was included to correct for existing discrepancies between written rules and policy implementation. It consists of three indicators capturing how far the final budget bill can be undermined by certain budget practices (Alesina et al. 1996, Appendix A). Tables 4.4 and 4.5, at the end of this chapter, present details on the survey questions related to each sub-index and their weighting.

Table 4.1 indicates the sample average for the composite IBI Index as well as for the three sub-indices. If we look at the average changes across the two periods, we observe that most institutional change took place in the area of fiscal rules (including borrowing constraints on subnational governments). However, a strengthening of fiscal decision-making

Table 4.1 Budgetary institutional indices

Index of Budgetary Institutions and Sub-Indices				
	1990–2006	1996	2004	Change
Aggregate Index of Budgetary Institutions (IBI) (0–100 Scale)	56.37	57.04	59.7	2.66
Weighted Sub-Indicators				
Hierarchy Subindex (0–30 Scale)	13.27	11.62	14.91	3.29
Fiscal Rules Subindex (0–40 Scale)	20.17	16.17	24.16	8.02
Transparency Subindex (0–30 Scale)	23.93	25.45	22.41	1.65

Sources: Alesina et al. (1999), Filc and Scartascini (2004)

hierarchies is also apparent. Regarding the transparency sub-index, we observe a (small) deterioration on average for the region over the time period studied.

In the early version of the IBI, the aggregate index varied on a scale from 0 to 100, with higher values indicating a higher degree of budget process centralization, while the most recent edition employs a 0–10 scale. To be able to show institutional change within countries over time, I rescaled the index values of all countries included in the sample.

4.4 HORIZONTAL DECENTRALIZATION AND FISCAL IMBALANCE

Hypothesis 1 in Chapter 3 states that higher degrees of decentralized budget decision making (horizontal decentralization) increase the likelihood of fiscal imbalance. This is thought to be the case because horizontal decentralization enhances the CPR problem on the national level. Under more decentralized budget institutions, rational self-interested budget actors face stronger incentives to raid the fiscal commons. In the absence of hard budget constraints, these actors are likely to increase pressure on the government to fulfill their spending demands by increasing expenditure and borrowing. As a consequence, we are more likely to observe imbalances than we would under hard budget constraints. Figure 4.3 depicts the distribution of horizontal decentralization in my sample.

I argued above that centralizing the budget process on the national level provides a solution to the CPR problem. By centralization I mean a change in budgetary institutions that leads to delegation of more fiscal decision-making power to a single budget authority within the

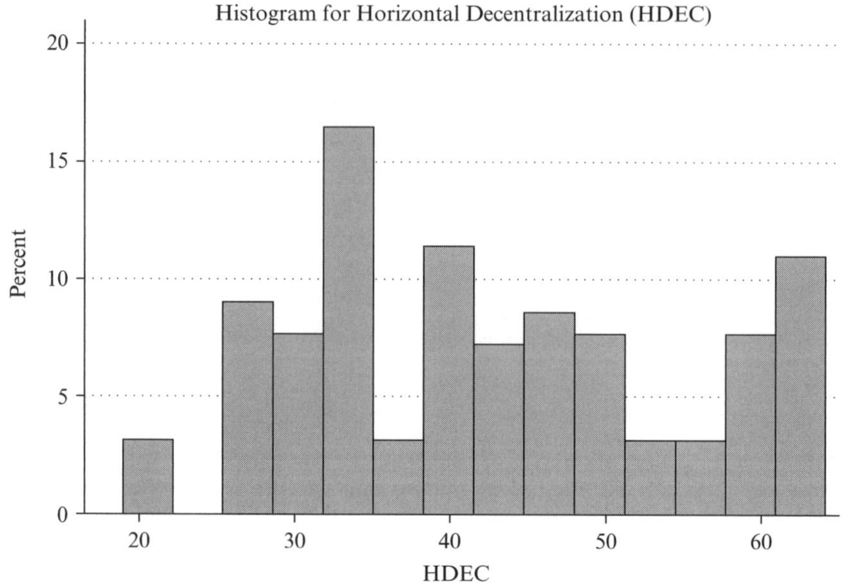

Figure 4.3 Distribution of horizontal decentralization in 15 Latin American countries

government, most commonly the finance ministry or presidency (delegation approach). Second, budget process centralization can take the shape of implementing fiscal targets that aim at stabilizing budgetary accounts over the business cycle (statutory approach). Both forms, the delegation and the statutory approaches, are seen as effective ways of centralizing the budget process and increasing fiscal discipline. Measures that improve transparency also count towards a higher score for 'institutional strength'.

Figure 4.4 indicates a negative relationship between the degree of horizontal institutional decentralization[8] and nominal budget outcomes for the countries in my sample in 1995 and in 2002 – those years with the highest completion rate of the IADB institutional surveys, thus including values for the largest number of countries. What we observe in both plots is a relatively strong and significant correlation (−0.54/−0.49), before controlling for any other variables. That means that for the countries in my sample, it appears that higher values on the aggregate horizontal decentralization measure correspond to significantly lower nominal budget outcomes. Looking at the broader picture for Latin America, the empirical evidence thus supports the view that more (or less) transparent and

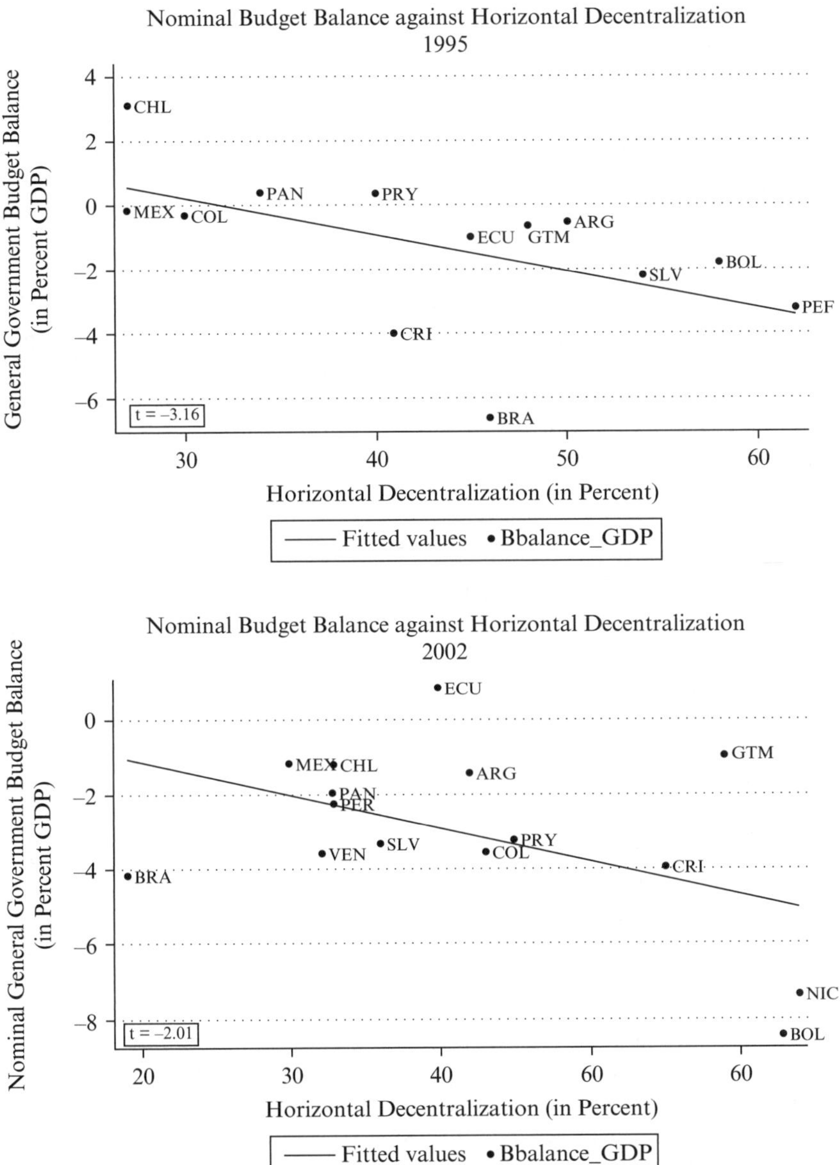

Figure 4.4 Decentralization of budgetary institutions and fiscal imbalance in Latin America

stringent budget processes at the central government level correspond to improvements (or deteriorations) in fiscal outcomes in the region. With a view to budget outcomes in Argentina and Brazil, we observe a reduction in the size of the nominal budget deficits in the latter and a small deterioration in the former country. On one hand, these changes correspond to a strengthening of national-level budget institutions in Brazil and a decrease in overall budget process centralization and transparency in Argentina over the time period. On the other hand, Argentina's fiscal performance, measured here in terms of the nominal fiscal balance relative to GDP, looks better than expected given the institutional design. In the in-depth case studies (chapters 5 and 6), I will return to the relationship between institutional reforms (or lack thereof) and fiscal outcomes, taking into account a broader range of indicators of the fiscal 'health' of each country, discussing also longer-term effects that are not well captured in Figure 4.4.

4.5 DEVELOPMENTS IN VERTICAL FISCAL DECENTRALIZATION

In previous chapters, I suggested that countries that decided to decentralize fiscal control along the vertical axis of government (fiscal federalism) carry a higher risk of overall fiscal imbalance. To explain this, I juxtaposed two potential explanations for the increase in fiscal risk. Following hypothesis 2, we would expect negative budgetary effects of vertical decentralization on subnational government balances to add on to the negative effects of a decentralized budget process on the central government level, leaving a country with a higher overall risk of incurring general government deficits. Hypothesis 3, in contrast, suggests an interaction effect of vertical fiscal decentralization and the strength of central-level budget institutions. Whether imbalances follow from an added model or an interactive model of institutional decentralization, what needs to be shown first is that vertical fiscal decentralization qualifies as an explanatory variable for any kind of variation in fiscal outcomes. That is, we need to see if vertical fiscal decentralization indeed varies across different countries in my sample and also across time. As a first indicator of vertical fiscal decentralization, I look at decentralization in government expenditure, following a widely used approach suggested earlier by Marlow (1988) and Rodden (2002). Expenditure decentralization is defined as the ratio of state and local expenditure to total government (central + state + local) expenditure in a given year. Data come from the IMF's Government Finance Statistics (GFS) data set for the years between 1990 and 2006.

Table 4.2 Expenditure decentralization in Latin America

Subnational Expenditures/Total Government Expenditures, 1990–2006				
Country	Mean	SD	Min.	Max.
All countries	21.49	12.30	2.36	41.46
Argentina	40.02	1.33	37.42	41.46
Bolivia	19.88	5.70	11	27
Brazil	36.39	4.53	31.51	40.45
Colombia	27.47	3.04	23.1	31.22
Costa Rica	3.58	1.38	2.62	6.01
El Salvador	5.7	2.48	3.23	8.7
Guatemala	5.07	0.718	4.44	5.99
Mexico	27.98	3.17	23.97	31.83
Nicaragua	2.93	–	2.93	2.93
Panama	2.49	0.11	2.41	2.57
Paraguay	8.39	0.523	8.02	8.76
Peru	18.40	1.75	15.48	21.41
Venezuela	2.36	–	2.36	2.36

Source: IMF/GFS-Data

Table 4.2 provides information on the distribution of expenditure decentralization (ED) in each country (1990–2006). As an interesting comparative, it may be said that the sample averages for the degree of ED in Latin American countries are significantly lower than those reported for OECD countries during a similar time frame (Daughters and Harper 2007). Looking at the full period (1990–2006), the average degree of ED in my sample of Latin American countries remains relatively low (at 21 percent). However, it should be noted that ED increased, in particular during the half-decade between 1993 and 1998. Even in small countries with little prior experience of political and fiscal decentralization (e.g. Bolivia, Caribbean countries), vertical fiscal decentralization increased after the return to democracy. Two countries with a long tradition of fiscal federalism, Argentina and Brazil, stick out as those with the highest degree of ED, with a period average of 40 percent and 36 percent decentralization in expenditure, respectively. They are closely followed by Mexico (28 percent) and Colombia (27 percent), the latter being a unitary country and a relative newcomer to any kind of vertical fiscal decentralization. Next to Colombia, two other non-federal countries have reached relatively high levels of vertical decentralization – Bolivia (20 percent) and Peru (18 percent). This finding raises the question of whether formal political institutions of federalism are a strong predictor of the degree of

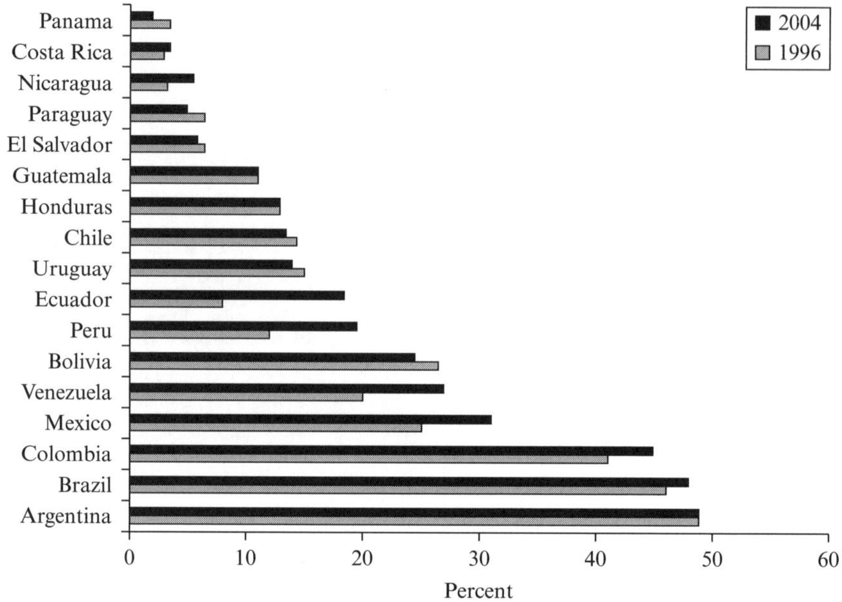

Source: Inter-American Development Bank (Daughters and Harper 2007)

Figure 4.5 Expenditure decentralization in Latin America, 1996 and 2004

vertical decentralization. Given the weak relationship suggested for the countries at hand, political federalism by itself appears unlikely to be a causal factor behind fiscal imbalance.

Figure 4.5 shows the evolution of decentralization in expenditure over time. For comparison, the figure also depicts the percentage share of subnational (state + local) own-source revenue in total government revenue, as reported in the IMF GFS database. We observe a strong increase in ED between the early 1990s and the end of that decade that was marked by grave fiscal crises in several countries. The years of financial distress and economic downturn (1998–2002) coincide with relatively strong reductions in ED in the region. Although ED picks up once more after the series of crises, it never fully returns to pre-crisis levels. Revenue-raising autonomy shows a much more unsteady evolution compared with ED, making it relatively unlikely to be a determining factor for fiscal stability in the cases at hand. Generally, we observe that in post-crisis years – that is, after 1995 (Mexico) and after 2002 (Argentina) – the revenue autonomy of subnational governments trends upward. However, after the most recent crisis episodes in several countries in the region, subnational governments were not granted the same degree of revenue autonomy. Since 2004, the average autonomy has even dropped to a level unseen since the beginning of the 1990s.

To sum up, it is apparent that vertical fiscal decentralization varies not only across the countries in my sample but also over time. Expenditure decentralization – which due to data constraints with regard to other decentralization measures still appears to be the most reliable indicator – reached its highest levels in time periods just before the outbreak of economic crises. As will be shown in the case studies (chapters 5 and 6), ED was particularly problematic in Argentina and Brazil, which were also struggling with subnational government insolvency. In both countries, the central governments were essentially forced into providing bailouts for subnational governments, creating follow-up problems including moral hazard. This being said, the role of revenue decentralization is less clear from the observed data (Figure 4.6). What we do observe is an increase in revenue decentralization following crises in several countries. This may be due to the (bad) tactics of government leaders, inviting the next subnational fiscal crisis as they over-burden local governments with raising sufficient revenue to finance local expenditure without the long-term perspective of new (stable) local sources of revenue.

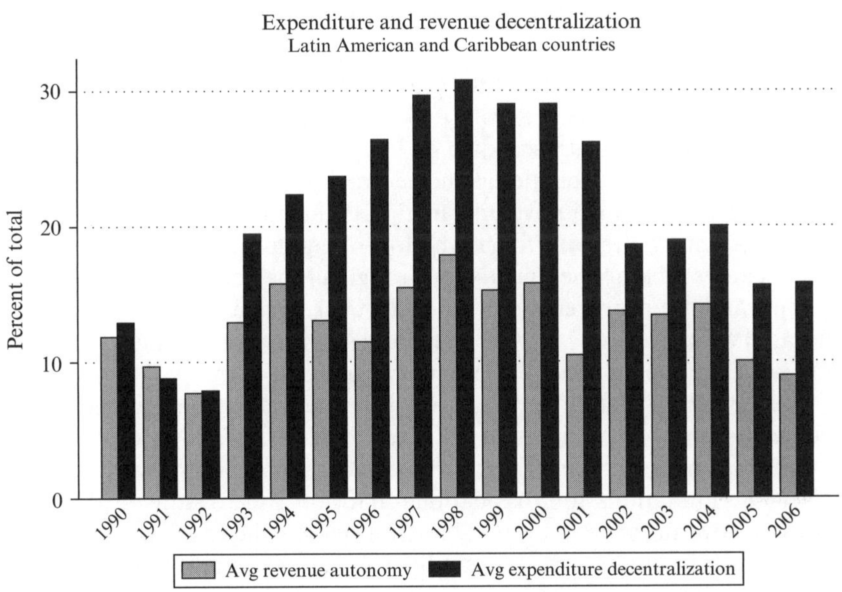

Figure 4.6 Vertical decentralization in Latin American countries over time

The sections above provide a first general overview of the evolution of fiscal imbalance and the strengths and weaknesses of fiscal institutions in the region since the return to democracy in the early 1990s. Data on budget institutions from two waves of surveys give a first impression of variation across countries and time. Given the relatively strong correlations between centralized budget institutions and fiscal results, approaches emphasizing the benefits of institutional strength and the transparency of budget processes in reining in budget deficits seem to have a point. To be able to analyze the role of vertical fiscal decentralization in creating fiscal instability systematically, more and better data are needed, including data on subnational fiscal balances for a large number of countries. Although data constraints stand in the way of cross-country analyses at this point, this does not prevent us from thinking about what such an 'ideal analysis' should include (see section 4.7). In the remainder of this book, I will rely on case comparison as an alternative empirical method. Before exploring the cases, I will explain in the next section why this approach appears best suited to finding out more about different institutional effects and outcomes. This includes a description of the criteria for selecting cases for the comparative analysis.

4.6 COMPARATIVE CASE ANALYSIS

In chapters 5 and 6, I evaluate the plausibility of my theoretical claims in light of additional evidence from two in-depth case studies. Next to discussing the available statistical data on budget outcomes and the quality of institutions for both subnational and central governments, the case studies present additional qualitative information gathered in standardized, semi-structured interviews with former high-ranking government officials. For those readers lacking the time to go through all the details on institutional reforms and their repercussions for budgets in Argentina and Brazil since the late 1980s, Chapter 7 provides a helpful summary of the main facts and findings from the qualitative comparative analysis.

The empirical data for 15 Latin American countries presented in section 4.4 support the view that the strength of national-level budget institutions co-varies with general government fiscal outcomes (hypothesis 1). Given the limitations to cross-national data on fiscal results at different levels of government and on fiscal institutions for the cases in my sample, I make use of comparative case study analysis to gain additional insights. In the comparative case analysis, I draw on information that is not available for the broader sample. For example, one important factor that is considered in much more depth in the case studies is the degree to which subnational governments hold own-source revenue-raising powers. Hence, the studies provide important additional, more nuanced evidence, with the potential to guide future large N analysis (Lieberman 2005).

My main objective in the case studies is to consider the broader picture of fiscal institutional reforms (or lack thereof) and their effect on budget results in Brazil and Argentina, including changes in vertical fiscal decentralization over the full time period (1990–2006). My description of fiscal institutions and budget results begins after the return to democracy and it ends just before the recent international financial crisis swept over to emerging markets, following the financial meltdown during the Subprime Crisis in the USA. How did budgetary institutions on the horizontal level affect fiscal and debt outcomes? And how did the effect of vertical decentralization in expenditure play out under different degrees of horizontal decentralization, both with regard to subnational and overall fiscal stability? To answer these questions, I compare in chapters 5 and 6 developments within both countries over time, using additional data on subnational governments that are not readily available for the larger set of Latin American and Caribbean countries.

The two cases were chosen due to their similar systems design. Both Argentina and Brazil show similar political characteristics, being presidential democracies with a long federal tradition and, most importantly for the purpose of this analysis, resembling each other in terms of vertical fiscal decentralization (see Figure 4.5). The two countries also have a similar macroeconomic environment, being major exporting countries and sharing similar experience with financial market liberalization and inflows of foreign investment capital. The two are also comparable in terms of their experience of major financial and sovereign debt crisis, as well as of subnational debt problems. Yet, they differ substantially in their approach to balancing government finances during their most recent crises. A look at how macroeconomic variables evolved after the return to democracy (Table 4.3) indicates that Argentina and Brazil differed tremendously in their capacity to stabilize important variables once their respective economies had suffered from external shocks during these events.

In the comparative conclusion at the end of Chapter 7, I come back to discussing differences in institutional reform across both countries. Below, I show how they diverged in the way that budgetary institutions were reformed. Differences in the types of fiscal rules implemented, and in the ways in which transgressions of the rules were sanctioned, stick out. I argued above that the interaction of horizontal and vertical decentralization should be more problematic for overall fiscal stability if the budget process at the national level is uncoordinated, signaling soft budget

Table 4.3 Overview of macroeconomic conditions: Argentina and Brazil

Overview on Macroeconomic Indicators, Argentina and Brazil (1995–2006)												
	1995	1996	1997	1998	1999	2000	2001	2002	2003	2004	2005	2006
Argentina												
GDP growth	−2.8	5.5	8.1	3.9	−3.4	−0.8	−4.4	−10.9	8.8	9.0	9.2	8.5
CPI-Inflation	3.38	0.16	0.53	0.93	−1.17	−0.95	−1.07	25.88	13.44	4.42	9.64	10.9
Budget Balance	−0.53	−2.03	−1.48	−1.36	−1.68	−2.39	−3.25	−1.46	0.48	2.6	1.77	1.78
Primary Balance	1.05	−0.33	0.5	0.87	1.22	1.01	0.54	0.72	2.31	3.88	3.7	3.54
Public Debt/GDP	33.75	35.68	34.52	37.58	42.99	45.04	53.76	145.85	138.27	126.45	72.83	63.55
Real Interest Rate	14.23	10.57	9.75	12.55	13.12	9.95	29.12	16.18	7.83	−2.24	−2.46	−4.23
Brazil												
GDP growth	4.4	2.1	3.4	0.0	0.3	4.3	1.3	2.7	1.1	5.7	3.2	4.0
CPI-Inflation	65.98	15.76	6.94	3.19	4.86	7.03	6.84	8.45	14.72	6.6	6.87	4.18
Budget Balance	−6.6	−5.42	−5.67	−7.4	−9.03	−3.38	−3.29	−4.17	−4.65	−2.43	−2.96	−3.00
Primary Balance	0.24	−0.09	−0.94	0.01	2.92	3.24	3.35	3.55	3.89	4.18	4.36	3.86
Public Debt/GDP	26.9	30.15	34.59	42.38	49.39	47.75	50.75	59.62	53.72	49.29	46.69	45.75
Real Interest Rate	n.n.	n.n.	65.5	78.8	66.3	47.7	44.6	47.3	46.9	43.3	44.9	42.1

Sources: WDI, IFS

constraints at the local level (hypothesis 3). Furthermore, I compare situations where such signaling of soft budget constraints and soft (or no) enforcement of rules indeed set the wrong incentives for local budget actors (in Argentina throughout, in Brazil in the earlier period). These are compared to a case in which specific fiscal rules, together with a credible sanctioning mechanism, contributed to a change in incentives for subnational budget actors (Brazil in the second period).

Both case studies follow the same structure, beginning with a summary of the evolution of fiscal (im)balances and institutional changes from 1990 to 2006. Afterwards, I explore in more detail how fiscal deficits (surpluses), government expenditure and revenue evolved over time, both on the national and on the subnational level. In addition to those fiscal outcomes, I discuss changes in public debt as an additional indicator of fiscal performance. Including an alternative measure seems warranted, given the potential for data on deficits to be biased by various means of creative accounting (Hallerberg et al. 2009b).

Looking at the subnational data for both countries allows me to show how a strengthening of central controls indeed leads to an adjustment in spending, revenue-raising and borrowing activities on the subnational level in Brazil. For Argentina, I show that such balancing of subnational accounts did not take place before the sovereign debt crisis in 2001. In the second part of each country study, I review the most relevant institutional reforms, fiscal laws and implementation strategies (or lack thereof) in the detail needed to understand how they relate to fiscal outcomes. Both chapters end with a summary of the observed interplay of national and subnational institutional changes, policy adjustments and (changed) fiscal outcomes. In Chapter 7, I then go on to draw comparisons between Brazil and Argentina during the 1990s and 2000s before I discuss my findings in light of selected competing and complementary explanations in the literature.

4.7 OUTLINE OF FURTHER MULTI-LEVEL EMPIRICAL ANALYSES

As stated before, my empirical approach to understanding the determinants of fiscal deficits in Latin America is bound to provide but a first overview. Further cross-country time-series data would be necessary to test my theoretical framework. Given data constraints, in particular with regard to subnational fiscal deficits and also information on existing subnational fiscal rules and budgetary institutions, rigorous empirical testing of my theoretical arguments drops out as an empirical strategy. Being constrained today, however, should not preempt investigations into

Table 4.4 The IADB Index of Budgetary Institutions

The IADB-Index of Budgetary Institutions (IBI)		
Sub-Indicators	No. of Index-Items	Max Score (Weight. Avg.)
(1) Fiscal Rules Subindex	10	40
Narrow Fiscal Rules Subindex	3	10
Medium Term Frameworks Subindex	2	10
Borrowing Constraints Subindex	3	10
Reserve Funds Subindex	2	10
(2) Hierarchy Subindex	9	30
Restrictions on Legislature Subindex	3	10
Restrictions on Ministers Subindex	3	10
Cash Management Subindex	3	10
(3) Transparency Subindex	3	30
Comprehensiveness of Budget Bill	1	10
Inclusion of Extra-Budgetary Items	1	10
Size of Extra-Budgetary Funds	1	10
Total	22	100

Source: Filc and Scartascini (2004, Annex 1)

the relationship between fiscal institutions and fiscal imbalances in the future. In imagining the ideal framework for testing hypotheses 2 and 3 on the added and potential conditional effects of horizontal budget process decentralization and vertical fiscal decentralization, a few ideas come to mind. A consistent analysis, allowing me to test my theoretical claims, should mainly serve two purposes: first, it should allow me to investigate whether horizontal decentralization is indeed correlated with subnational budget discipline, controlling, among other factors, for existing subnational fiscal rules and constraints; second, it should serve to show the conditional effect of vertical fiscal decentralization on general government fiscal outcomes, depending on the strength of national-level institutions. To achieve both goals, data analysis should be carried out in a multi-level framework. Multi-level models allow for improved empirical testing when the data of interest are grouped into more than one category (e.g. states within countries). As discussed in Chapter 3, my aim is to eventually test the claimed conditional effect of central-level budget institutions on individual sub-states' fiscal decisions. This means that I would be dealing with a phenomenon that extends over two levels of analysis – the macro

Table 4.5 Budgetary institutions: items

Question-Items for the Index of Budgetary Institutions	
(1) Fiscal Rules Subindex	
Fiscal Limits	In developing the budget, are there fiscal rules placing limits on executive fiscal policy discretion?
	If there are fiscal limits, can the executive branch propose waiving or amending the limits?
Medium Term Fiscal Frameworks (MTFF)	Is there consistent medium-term fiscal framework stating targets or ceilings for expenditures, deficits and revenues for the medium term?
	If the answer is yes, does it state targets or ceilings for each subsequent budget year within that term?
Reserve Funds	Does the annual budget include any central reserve funds to meet unforeseen expenditures?
	Are there laws, regulations or policies which define the permitted uses of the budget reserves?
(2) Hierarchy Subindex	
Hierarchy Within Executive	Are there fixed spending limits set for initial ministry spending plans?
	Who has the last word?
	How are disputes between ministries and the central budget authority resolved?
	What percentage of the initial executive's budget proposal is decided by the President/Prime minister/Principal Executive (i.e. not decided between the ministers)?
Executive-Legislative Relations	If the budget is not approved by the legislature before the start of the fiscal year, what are the consequences?
	Are there any restrictions on the right of the legislature to modify the detailed budget proposal of the executive?
	If applicable, what is the legal basis of these restrictions?
Cash Management	What instruments are used to monitor budget execution?
	Can the central budget authority withhold funds that are appropriated, but not available on a legal or entitlement basis?
	Can the central budget authority withhold funds for entitlement programs or other areas where legal obligations have been made on behalf of the state?
(3) Transparency Subindex	
	Is the budget document presented to the legislature comprehensive (does it include all government expenditures)?
	Do budget documents cover extra-budgetary funds and activities?
	What types of extra-budgetary funds are found (and how many)?

Source: Filc and Scartascini (2007)

(central/federal) level and the micro (state) level. In order to test my theoretical argument (hypothesis 3), a hierarchical model framework could take us a big step forward in understanding if and how national-level institutions and subnational fiscal strategies interact.

NOTES

1. The countries are Argentina, Bolivia, Brazil, Chile, Colombia, Costa Rica, Ecuador, El Salvador, Guatemala, Mexico, Nicaragua, Panama, Paraguay, Peru and Venezuela.
2. In IMF reports and in the EIU data, the term 'Public Sector Borrowing Requirement (PSBR)' sometimes replaces General Government Budget Balance, describing the same quantity.
3. Note that primary balance data are available only for a much smaller sample of countries, excluding Brazil, among others.
4. The top of the box represents the 75th percentile and the bottom line is the 25th percentile, while the line inside the box represents the distribution median. The lines extending beyond the box (whiskers) represent the minimum and maximum values of the distribution. However, by default the statistical analysis software package used here lets the whiskers exclude a value if it extends beyond 1.5 × the inter-quartile range in either direction. That value is shown separately as a point on the graph.
5. Data on the Dominican Republic is missing in the second survey. Also, the researchers used a 0–10 scale, while in the first study (Alesina et al. 1999) a 0–100 scale was used. In both cases, higher values indicate stronger centralization. Further changes to the original survey include the introduction of additional survey questions, for instance to provide more information on cash management in each country. The respective data for Latin American countries is available from a new Database on Budget Practices and Procedures, developed by the OECD and the World Bank in collaboration with the IADB. Further documentation is provided on the OECD homepage: www.oecd.org.
6. The construction of the three sub-indices draws largely on the earlier theoretical and empirical contributions of von Hagen (1992), von Hagen and Harden (1995) and Eichengreen and von Hagen (1996), among others, that used similar indices to measure budget process centralization in the context of European countries.
7. Recent empirical research has shown that transparency, i.e. the degree to which 'debt cannot be hidden from the public', is crucial for reducing public debt (Alt and Lassen 2006). Furthermore, transparency is necessary to prevent governments from engaging in different forms of 'creative accounting', allowing them to hide fiscal deficits (Milesi-Feretti 2003, von Hagen and Wolff 2008).
8. Note that I display here the inverse of the scaled Index of Budgetary Institutions used by Alesina et al. (1999) and Filc and Scartascini (2007). I am using the inverse scale, running from small to large decentralization, to make results more easily interpretable. Higher index scores now correspond to higher degrees of institutional decentralization.

5. Fiscal stabilization, subnational fiscal indiscipline and institutional reform in Brazil

This chapter discusses improvements in fiscal accounts and public debt-to-GDP ratios in Brazil at the national and state levels and takes a closer look at economic policies and the politics of institutional reforms from 1990 to 2006. In a nutshell, I argue that the general improvements in Brazil's fiscal stance and public indebtedness can be explained by the government's commitment to budgetary institutional reform, changing incentives for budget actors, both on the national and the subnational level. Under initially soft budget constraints, the high level of vertical fiscal decentralization in expenditure led to increasing fiscal problems and debt accumulation on the subnational level, creating liabilities for general government finances. After the government decided to implement stronger fiscal rules between 1997 and 1998, the subnational governments finally reached and maintained balanced budgets.

Below, I begin with a brief overview of macroeconomic policy in Brazil, accounting also for external influences (section 5.1). Afterwards, I describe the evolution of fiscal imbalance over the 1990s (5.2), before I turn to potential institutional explanations for the outcomes we observe (5.3 and 5.4). The aim is to get a better understanding of the effects of horizontal decentralization (5.3), as well as of the effects of vertical decentralization under the conditions of more and less decentralized national-level budgetary institutions (5.4). In section 5.4, I discuss the negative consequences that stem from a mismatch between subnational spending responsibilities and own-source revenue-raising rights, relying on additional data that are unavailable for the broader sample of countries in the region. In the last section (5.5), I summarize the evidence on institutional decentralization and fiscal imbalance and present some first conclusions.

5.1 BRAZIL, 1990–2006: AN OVERVIEW

Brazil's successful fiscal consolidation since the end of the 1990s makes it a crucial case for research on the effect of institutions on macroeconomic fundamentals. Introducing the Real Plan in 1994 – a new currency regime aimed at stabilizing the exchange rate and bringing down inflation from unsustainable levels – significantly changed the set of available policy options for the government. It made fiscal stabilization a necessary and, at the same time, an even harder task. The currency-related increase in government debt, combined with the inability to follow the previous practice of floating outstanding obligations, put severe fiscal pressure on federal and subnational governments alike. By the mid-1990s, Brazilian fiscal deficits relative to GDP, both on the national and subnational levels, were rising to alarming levels. Current expenditure was trending upwards and, after the Asian crisis in 1997, high and increasing debt-financing costs, coupled with declining GDP growth rates, put a heavy weight on government finances. In September 1998, after the government had increasingly come under pressure from financial markets that were betting against the fixed exchange rate regime, President Cardoso turned to the IMF and other bilateral and multilateral donors for financial assistance. Large-scale financial assistance was provided by the IMF and others on the basis of the government's fulfillment of fiscal targets.[1] For a moment, the government seemed to have gotten ahead of market turbulences and capital withdrawal from the country. But by December of that year, the government's failure to reach a simple congressional majority for a new pension law, increasing workforce contributions to the system in December 1998, led IMF staff and international private creditors to worry about the time consistency of fiscal adjustment promises. Fears that the opposition leader, Lula da Silva, whose popularity during the precedent presidential campaign had been rising, could gain more influence over the center-conservative Cardoso government, were fueling the fire further (Martínez and Santiso 2003). After the Brazilian currency, the real, had become the target of speculative attacks, having lost more than half of the country's reserves (almost $40 billion) in the second half of 1998, the government was finally forced to let the currency flow on January 15, 1999.[2]

In this situation, some of the Brazilian states tried to default on their debt to the nation, unwilling to undertake the fiscal adjustment needed to guarantee Brazil's debt servicing and hence continued access to financial markets. A public default declaration by the governor of the south-eastern state of Minas Gerais, former Brazilian president Itamar Franco, turned into a power game for the federal government. President Cardoso, devoted to continuing on the path of primary fiscal surplus accumulation, finally got the upper hand in the fight with revolting state governors. To understand how it was possible for Cardoso to succeed over subnational interests, we will take a deeper look at fiscal institutional reforms that started much earlier, after a banking crisis in 1995 and a large bailout for the states in 1997.

Arguably, Brazil's commitment to servicing its (external) debt and to reducing the rate of public debt to GDP was tested a second time during the financial crisis in 2002. The financial markets had substantial concerns that a newly elected left-wing president, Lula da Silva, would turn his back on fiscal and debt consolidation and 'declare war' on international creditors. In the six months before the election of October 2002, sovereign risk spreads therefore soared to unforeseen levels. Creditor fears lasted for another year after Lula was elected. But, despite all prior concerns, Lula followed largely on the path of fiscal consolidation set out by his predecessor. The new president successfully stabilized fiscal accounts and the public debt. Thanks to the by-then established strengthened budgetary institutions, including balanced budget and expenditure rules, Lula was able to control spending pressures from various budget actors, including line ministries, legislators and subnational governments. Brazil was thus able to avoid default during both crises, in 1998 and 2002. The country reduced its debt overhang despite the initially not so bright economic outlook and financial market 'punishment' (the risk premium on Brazilian government bonds). Domestic political opposition to adjustment could not stop the federal government from implementing fiscal targets that had been negotiated with the IMF. In return, the country received financial assistance from the fund until late in 2005 when it paid back its full outstanding debt ahead of schedule. Brazil finally returned to investment grade in 2008.

How did all this become possible in a country with a historical track record of sovereign defaults, having left a particularly negative and lasting impression with the declaration of a 'debt moratorium' in 1987? I argue that rather than by passing a single law, Brazil's often quoted Fiscal Responsibility Law (FRL) of 2000, stabilization became possible through a gradual evolution of budgetary institutions. In a series of institutional reforms, the government aimed to centralize decision-making processes on the national level and also to constrain budgetary powers from subnational budget actors. Once the new institutions were established, the federal government had at its disposal new 'tools', allowing the implementation of fiscal adjustment where it was most needed, i.e. when creditor fears regarding a 'return to old habits' (including the IMF's) were at their strongest.

5.2 FISCAL IMBALANCE IN BRAZIL

In the next few sections, I provide a brief overview of government balances (nominal and primary) over time, before I take a closer look at the evolution of expenditure and revenue, both on the national and subnational levels of government. Additionally, I show how the public debt changed over time, before I turn to potential institutional explanations for fiscal outcomes in the following sections (5.3 and 5.4).

5.2.1 Fiscal Results

5.2.1.1 General and central government

Figure 5.1 depicts the evolution of nominal budget balances for the general government together with primary budget balances.[3] The plotted line indicates the balance target the Cardoso government imposed upon itself and negotiated with the IMF as conditionality in return for financial assistance in the fall of 1998. The strong drop in the nominal surplus after 1994 was triggered by the introduction of a new currency, the real, together with an exchange rate peg. Setting an end to high inflation, the new currency regime at once dramatically increased the costs of government expenditure, driving the budget deficit to peak at 6.6 percent of GDP in 1995. After 1997 the fiscal situation improved significantly, at least judging by the primary result, i.e. the budget result before interest payments on existing debt. Looking at the development of the nominal general government balance in the period between 1995 and 2006 (for which data are available from the IMF and domestic sources), we see that the public sector balance in Brazil remains negative, although it stabilizes at 3 percent of GDP and less after the financial market crisis of 2001, a critical threshold for countries to reach if they want to bring down the public-debt-to-GDP ratio.[4] We observe in Figure 5.1 two drastic increases in the nominal deficits, one during the financial crisis in 1998 when the general government deficit rose to −9 percent of GDP, and one in 2002 when it reached 5 percent due mainly to skyrocketing interest rates on Brazilian government debt.[5] Judging by the primary fiscal result, the budget results before interest, we observe that a significant fiscal adjustment took place following the reforms in budgetary institutions beginning in 1997. Strengthened control over budget decisions allowed the central government to keep its promise to maintain balanced budgets and reach primary fiscal surpluses that would allow a gradual consolidation of the public debt. Hence, the Brazilian government managed to fulfill the ambitious targets negotiated with the IMF, despite financial turbulences caused by creditor fears of sovereign default in 2002.

It is often argued that successful fiscal consolidation in Brazil can

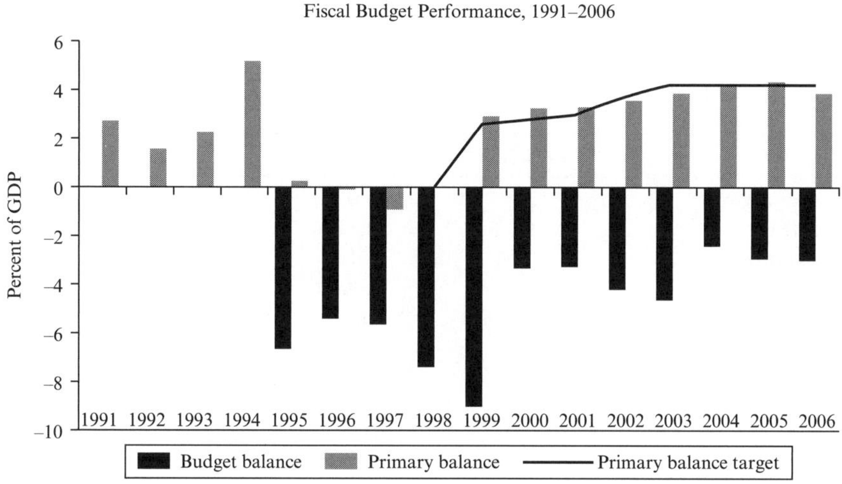

Figure 5.1 *Nominal and primary deficits and government fiscal targets, Brazil*

best be explained by a boom in exports and strong growth following the devaluation of the real in January 1999. To be sure, exports were still shrinking by 10 percent between 1997 and 1999 and did not pick up until 2000. Likewise, GDP growth dropped heavily at the end of the 1990s and a turnaround was not reached until 2000. Looking at the primary fiscal results, however, we observe that the budget was already balanced before the boom set in. Hence, while it may well be argued that the positive economic development in the 2000s created a supportive environment for the government's policies, it does not appear to be a causal factor explaining why the government engaged in reform as early as 1997.[6]

5.2.1.2 Subnational fiscal imbalance

In a large federal country like Brazil, in which significant fiscal authority in spending is delegated to 27 states (including the federal district) and around 5,500 municipalities, the fiscal performance of subnational governments arguably plays an important role in achieving an overall stability of government finances. Above, I assumed that under more decentralized spending schemes, subnational CPR problems would lead to increased spending and deficits, creating growing liabilities for the nation. Looking at Table 5.1, we may observe that subnational results are turning negative on average in the second half of the 1990s. In fact, the primary subnational deficit reached 0.67 percent of GDP in 1997, before a strong turnaround was achieved, starting in 1998.

Table 5.1 Primary fiscal results, Brazil

Primary Fiscal Results by Level of Government, 1991–2006 (in percent GDP)				
	1991–1995	1996–2000	2001–2005	2006
General Govt	2.4	1.03	3.86	3.88
Central	1.33	0.88	2.29	2.21
Subnational	0.54	−0.13	0.84	0.85
State	n.a.	n.a.	0.69	0.7
Municipality	n.a.	n.a.	0.15	0.15
Public Enterprises*	0.53	0.28	0.73	0.82
Federal	1.00**	0.35	0.53	0.58
State	−0.43	−0.06	0.20	0.24
Municipal	−0.01	−0.02	0.01	0

Note: *Results are rounded averages **Average for 1994–1995

Source: Giambiagi (2007)

These budget improvements follow a federal bailout for 22 out of the 26 (or 27 with the federal district) state governments and the introduction of fiscal targets and expenditure ceilings in the debt contracts, negotiated between the federal government and the states.[7] Under the Brazilian government's Program to Reduce State Involvement in Banking Activity (PROES), the first states began with debt restructuring in 1997 and the process was finalized with the last state signing an agreement at the end of 1998. Looking at disaggregated data (not shown here), subnational governments reached a primary surplus of 0.22 percent of GDP in 1999, which grew to almost 1 percent between 2004 and 2006.

The data indicate that the strong improvements in aggregate subnational government fiscal results were primarily driven by the state. Measured in percentage of total state-level revenue, 16 out of 26 states (without the federal district) noted a fiscal deficit in 1997. One year later, deficits had grown and exceeded 30 percent of total revenue in eight states. However, by 2001 state budgets were all balanced or in surplus, indicating a drastic improvement. After the federal bailout, the states were relieved of their debt burden. They did not, however, return to their 'old habits' of increasing expenditure and accumulating new deficits. Showing a similar development, deficits on the part of public enterprises were turned into persistent surpluses, following the restructuring and privatization of loss-making banks and firms under the PROES initiative.[8]

Overall, the data indicate that fiscal results on all levels of government and of publicly owned enterprises improved visibly after a series of central-level institutional reforms taking place between 1997 and 2000. However, to find out if this success can be traced back to the more fiscally responsible behavior of subnational governments, we need to take a look at spending and revenue.

5.2.2 Government Expenditure

5.2.2.1 General and central government

The literature often emphasizes the particularly high level of expenditure rigidity in the Brazilian budget, resulting from guarantees in the 1988 constitution. The earmarking and hardwiring of government revenue for payroll and social security expenditure for active and retired public personnel are seen as a serious obstacle to fiscal stability because they reduce the ability of the federal government to implement adjustment measures in hard times (e.g. Cline 1995, Bevilaqua 2002, Roubini and Setser 2004, Alston et al. 2009). The data indeed reveal a drastic increase in one of the largest categories of earmarked expenditure – personnel costs – in the early 1990s, growing by over 8 percent on average each year between 1991 and 1995.

In Table 5.2, showing data on the primary expenditure of the central government in percentage of GDP (1991–2006), we observe that the financial crises in 1998 and 2002 led to immediate cuts in total primary spending, but that spending had risen to pre-crisis levels within three years of each crisis. Both Federal Law 9646 and the Fiscal Responsibility Law of 2000 require that policy makers indicate a revenue source that provides resources in the equivalent amount of funds needed under a newly added spending scheme. Additionally, public wage bill expenditure is not allowed to increase beyond 50 percent of current revenue and incumbents are no longer allowed to increase public employment 180 days prior to an election. We observe that after the passing of the laws, wage bill expenditure remained relatively stable, even around elections. Expenditure in the other spending categories continued to grow after the first institutional reforms, however they increased gradually and within limits.

Table 5.3 compares the average growth rate for federal government primary expenditure during different periods. The data make it clear that in the four-year interval following the devaluation and introduction of a more flexible exchange rate regime, the total primary expenditure of central government fell on average compared to the period prior to the event. A significant increase takes place after President Lula takes office, however, given the extremely positive growth environment, these increases appear to remain within limits. We see that government expenditure

Table 5.2 Central government primary expenditure, Brazil

	Primary expenditures of the Central Government, 1991–2006 (in percent GDP)															
	1991	1992	1993	1994	1995	1996	1997	1998	1999	2000	2001	2002	2003	2004	2005	2006
Transfers to states + municip.	2.65	2.67	2.87	2.55	2.6	2.53	2.66	2.91	3.28	3.42	3.53	3.80	3.54	3.48	3.91	3.99
Public Wage Bill	3.80	3.93	4.52	5.14	5.13	4.84	4.27	4.56	4.47	4.57	4.8	4.81	4.46	4.31	4.29	4.52
Active	2.66	2.63	2.53	2.82	2.63	2.52	2.25	2.31	2.22	2.39	2.48	2.50	2.32	2.32	2.31	2.43
Passive	0.91	1.06	1.72	1.99	2.14	2.07	1.82	2.04	2.05	1.97	2.11	2.08	2.11	1.97	1.98	1.89
Transfers	0.23	0.24	0.27	0.33	0.36	0.25	0.20	0.21	0.20	0.21	0.21	0.23	0.03	0.02	0.00	0.20
Social Security (INSS)	3.36	4.25	4.94	4.85	4.62	4.89	5.01	5.45	5.50	5.58	5.78	5.96	6.30	6.48	6.80	7.13
Other expenditures	3.90	3.39	3.55	3.96	3.82	3.69	4.73	5.04	4.52	4.58	4.99	4.94	4.37	4.80	5.28	5.60
Total	13.71	14.24	15.88	16.50	16.17	15.95	16.67	17.96	17.77	18.15	19.10	19.51	18.67	19.07	20.28	21.24

Source/data: Giambiagi (2007)

Table 5.3 Growth rate of federal government expenditure, Brazil

Average Growth of Federal Government Primary Expenditures				
	1992–1994	1995–1998	1999–2002	2003–2006
Total primary expenditures	9.7	4.6	4.3	5.6
Transfers to states + municip.	1.8	5.9	9.1	4.7
Public wage bill expenditures	14.0	−0.6	3.5	1.8
Social security benefits (INSS)	16.5	5.5	4.4	8.1
Other expenditures	3.6	8.7	1.7	6.6
GDP	3.1	2.4	2.1	3.4

Source: Giambiagi (2007)

continued to grow at moderate rates after the shift to a more flexible exchange rate system. There is little evidence that policy makers fell back to their 'old habits' of trying to solve CPR problems with spending sprees that threaten overall stability.

5.2.2.2 Areas of adjustment

Table 5.2 provides information on the evolution of central government expenditure on active government personnel and on pensioners since 1991. The data show that, measured in percentage of GDP, expenditure on active and retired public employees and on pensioners remained relatively stable and that there are not many traits of spending cuts around the years of the financial and economic crisis. Nevertheless, reducing expenditure in a few areas was sufficient to bring down the overall level of expenditure. With these cuts, the government could send a signal to official and private creditors that it was willing to take unpopular measures to guarantee fiscal stability, keeping room in the budget for continuous debt servicing.

Expenditure on active military employees marks one area in which cuts were made. Between 1998 and 1999, expenditure on this group dropped from 0.52 percent to 0.37 percent of GDP, returning to the pre-crisis level in 2002 (0.55 percent). From 2003 to 2004, expenditure on military personnel was cut once more from 0.46 percent to 0.38 percent of GDP, remaining below 0.4 percent in the following years. Our picture of expenditure growth in the area of public personnel is further completed by data provided in an analytical study on Brazilian public sector employment by Gaetani and Heredia (2002). The authors show that from 1997 the rate of new civil servants at the federal level was gradually reduced. New entries into service fell from a high 9,055 in 1997 to only 2,927 in 1999 and to as little as 660 in 2001.[9] The overall number of civil servants in the direct administration was continuously brought down by more than 20 percent between 1995 and 2001. Looking at the total order of public employees, including those in state-owned enterprises, the number shrank by roughly 10 percent between 1995 and 2001.

Besides cuts in particular areas of the public wage bill, which spending areas were targeted by the Cardoso government to reduce growth in government expenditure? A look at the 'other expenditure' category of government expenditure shows a similar pattern of alternating phases of expenditure growth and cuts, as seen in the area of personnel expenditure. The lion's share in this expenditure category goes into executive expenditure on the health and administrative costs of different government branches, various social transfers including the support fund for workers (FAT), and a number of subsidies.[10] 'Other expenditure' fell by roughly 10 percent in 1999 and in 2003. However, looking at the four-year average before and after these expenditure cuts, we see that they had been growing before and they continued to grow after the years the fiscal cuts were implemented.

Next, exposing a familiar pattern of financially distressed governments, the Cardoso administration decided to make cuts in the area of public investment. Governments that are forced to implement a fiscal adjustment often target the public investment category of the budget for spending cuts (Table 5.4). Looking at the average per period expenditure of the different administrations, we see that investments indeed dropped by 0.9 under the Cardoso administration. Public investments fell significantly and to relatively equal amounts on the federal and subnational levels, compared with the earlier periods. Also, total government investments stabilized at 0.15 percent during the first term of President Lula da Silva (2003–2006 average).

Table 5.4 Growth rate of public investment by level of government, Brazil

Growth in Public Investment by Levels of Government, 1990–2006			
	Federal Government	States + Municipalities	Total
1969–1973	1.8	2.7	4.5
1974–1978	1.5	2.3	3.8
1979–1984	0.9	1.4	2.3
1985–1989	1.1	1.8	2.9
1990–1994	1.2	1.9	3.1
1995–2002	0.8	1.4	2.2
2003–2006	0.6	1.4	2

Source: Giambiagi (2007)

5.2.2.3 Subnational government expenditure

As the data show, subnational fiscal results improved significantly following the introduction of fiscal targets in the debt contracts following the 1997/98 bailout (Table 5.1). On the one hand, the states clearly benefitted from reduced debt servicing costs following the federal bailout. On the other hand, expenditure ceilings were effective in stabilizing costs. Public wage bill expenditure and subnational government investments, judged by the level of expenditure relative to total state-level revenue, were stabilized (reduced) (Figure 5.2). Evidence of cuts in investment projects is also given by the data in Table 5.4, indicating a slowdown in public investments made by subnational governments during both terms of President Cardoso and the first of Lula's terms. As Figure 5.2 shows, the expenditure ratios for social and health policies remained largely untouched by the austerity measures taken during the crisis. Following on from the 1988 constitution, increases in the spending responsibilities of subnational governments in the area of personnel and social policy expenditure have led to subnational expenditure growth since the beginning of the 1990s (e.g. Cline 1995,

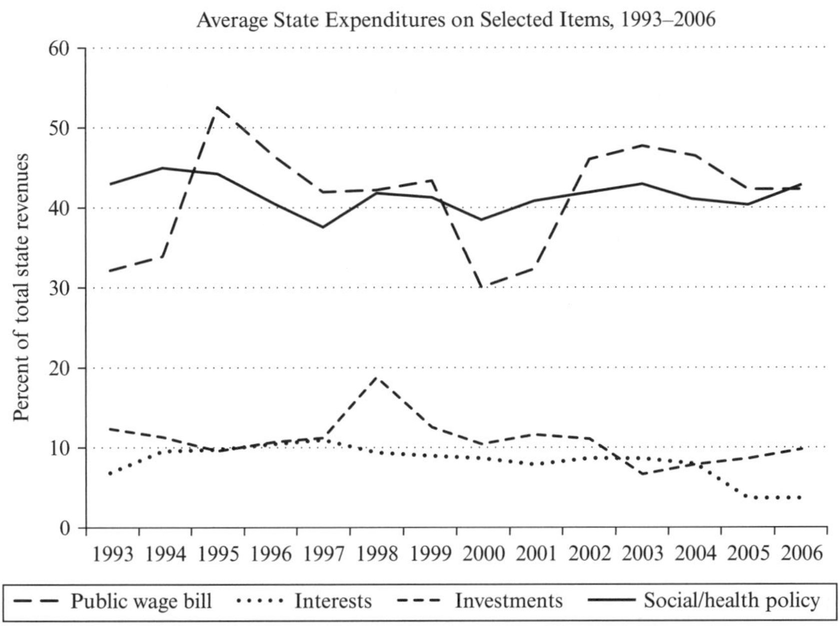

Source: Souza 2008

Figure 5.2 Evolution of average expenditure of the Brazilian states on four major items

Rodden 2006). Generally, changes in provisions on expenditure in those domains underlie particular safeguards by the constitution. Hence, social security expenditure, in particular expenditure on the beneficiaries of social security insurance (INSS), remained largely unaffected by the government's repeated attempts at primary balance adjustment. In summary, we observe that budget rigidities were reduced in the area of public wage bill expenditure but no significant adjustment in social policy expenditure took place.

5.2.3 Government Revenue

5.2.3.1 General and central government

To determine how the Brazilian government was able to reach increasing primary budget surpluses as an answer to the 1998 financial and economic crisis, a look at the evolution of revenue adds crucial information. Next to a stabilization of government expenditure, a significant increase in tax revenue, beginning in the year of the federal bailout for the states in 1997, allowed the government to turn around a primary budget deficit to continuous primary surpluses after 1999 (Figure 5.3). At almost 35.5 percent of GDP, today's tax burden in Brazil is high by international standards and also among emerging economies.[11] And, although Brazil started from an

Source: IPEA-Data, as cited in Alston et al. (2009, p. 61)

Figure 5.3 Evolution of tax burden, Brazil

already relatively high tax burden for an emerging market economy in the 1990s, we see a steady growth trend during the second term of President Cardoso, which is continued by his successor, Lula da Silva. Among political pundits in Brazil, it is popular to argue that Cardoso was able to stabilize the budget only by increasing tax rates and extending the tax base rather than by engaging in far-reaching expenditure adjustment (source: research interview with former Finance Secretary of Sao Paulo, Amir Khair, 2008). In general, taxes indeed increased in response to the additional financing pressure on the government after the federal bailout for the states in 1997 and the crisis in 1998/99. With some exceptions (import fees, the federal VAT, taxes on large-scale financial transactions, and 'other receipts'), tax revenue in percentage of GDP continued to increase gradually after the crisis. There is also evidence that the government extended the tax base by (re-)introducing certain taxes. Revenue from an import tax and the financial transaction taxes (provisional general tax, tax on large capital transfers, and after 2002 the newly introduced tax on outward financial transactions) went exclusively to the federal government's budget. Furthermore, as will be explained in more detail below, the federal government increased social security contributions after a congressional majority had been won to de-earmark revenue from the social security system to the benefit of discretionary funds at the president's disposal, beginning in 1994 (Alston et al. 2009, p. 61). Table 5.5 provides an overview of the evolution of revenue from taxes levied by the central government. Overall, beyond increasing government revenue, these steps effectively provided the president with more financial leverage over subnational governments.

5.2.3.2 Subnational revenue

The own-source revenue-raising activities of the Brazilian states have traditionally been relatively strong. Over the course of the 1990s until the bailout in 1997, however, the share of own-source revenue in total state revenue had been decreasing (see Figure 5.4). The year 1998 marked a turnaround and the share of own-source in total revenue increased again, moving up by close to 14 percent until 2004. The share of federal transfers in total state revenue has been increasing since the state debt crisis in 1997 for a while, although transfers dropped in the crisis year of 1999. After the crisis was controlled, the share of federal transfers rose once more by roughly 8 percent between 2000 and 2001, in response to extraordinary subnational financing needs after the recession and as compensation for the federal government's decision to re-distribute revenue from an export tax from the states to the central budget (Kandir Law).[12] After 2001, the state average share in transfers went down significantly again, while the share of own-source revenue kept increasing.

Table 5.5 Federal government tax revenue by type of tax, Brazil

Federal Government Revenues, Disaggregated by Type of Tax, 1991–2006 (in percent GDP)																
Composition	1991	1992	1993	1994	1995	1996	1997	1998	1999	2000	2001	2002	2003	2004	2005	2006
Import fees	0.42	0.39	0.45	0.47	0.7	0.50	0.55	0.67	0.74	0.72	0.7	0.54	0.48	0.47	0.42	0.43
Fed. VAT, industrial products	2.16	2.34	2.47	2.08	1.93	1.84	1.79	1.67	1.55	1.6	1.49	1.34	1.16	1.18	1.23	1.21
Income tax	3.39	3.8	3.94	3.76	4.11	3.99	3.89	4.68	4.84	4.78	4.98	5.81	5.47	5.3	5.8	5.91
Provisional *general* tax on financial activities (IPMF/CMPF)	0	0	0.07	0.99	0	0	0.74	0.83	0.75	1.23	1.32	1.38	1.36	1.36	1.36	1.38
Tax on *large* fin. transactions	0.59	0.62	0.81	0.73	0.46	0.34	0.4	0.36	0.46	0.27	0.28	0.27	0.26	0.27	0.28	0.29
Social contributions, large firms	1.31	1	1.38	2.14	2.16	2.12	2.04	1.91	3.02	3.38	3.56	3.54	3.5	4.08	4.08	3.98
Social security contributions	1.06	1.08	1.16	1.05	0.87	0.88	0.81	0.77	0.92	0.85	0.88	0.87	1.02	1.03	1.02	1.05
Tax on earnings	0.28	0.74	0.79	0.9	0.83	0.78	0.82	0.79	0.69	0.79	0.72	0.9	0.99	1.05	1.22	1.21
Tax on financial transfer abroad (CIDE)	0	0	0	0	0	0	0	0	0	0	0	0.49	0.44	0.4	0.36	0.34
Other receipts	0.86	2.08	1.18	0.91	0.84	0.82	0.96	1.92	1.26	1.37	1.18	1.3	1.4	1.47	1.02	1.1
Total	10.07	12.05	12.26	13.03	11.9	11.27	12	13.6	14.23	14.99	15.11	16.44	16.08	16.61	16.79	16.9

Source: Giambiagi (2007)

Figure 5.4 Average state tax revenue, Brazil

In contrast, we observe, over the course of the first Lula administration (2003–2006), that the average share of federal transfers in states' total revenue rose again, while the average share of own-source revenue more or less remained the same. This suggests that states became slightly more dependent on federal transfers, although they generally maintained a high degree of revenue autonomy compared to subnational units in other countries in the region. Being the most important source of revenue for the states, the state-level value-added tax (ICMS) provided growing revenue over the entire sample period (Table 5.6). At the same time, tax revenue from the federal-level value-added tax, the 'IPI', has been continuously decreasing.

5.2.4 Public Debt

5.2.4.1 General and central government

Brazil was a latecomer to the Brady Plan, which set an end to the 1980s debt crisis and left its economy with a manageable public debt ratio of around 27 percent of GDP, signing an agreement as late as April 1994. While the administration of President Itamar Franco (1992–1994)

Table 5.6 State-level value added tax, Brazil

Receipts from State-level Value-Added Tax (ICMS) (in percent GDP)							
1991	1992	1993	1994	1995	1996	1997	1998
6.73	6.44	6.08	7.3	6.69	6.6	6.34	6.22
1999	2000	2001	2002	2003	2004	2005	2006
6.37	6.98	7.24	7.1	7.02	7.12	7.22	7.39

Source: Giambiagi (2007)

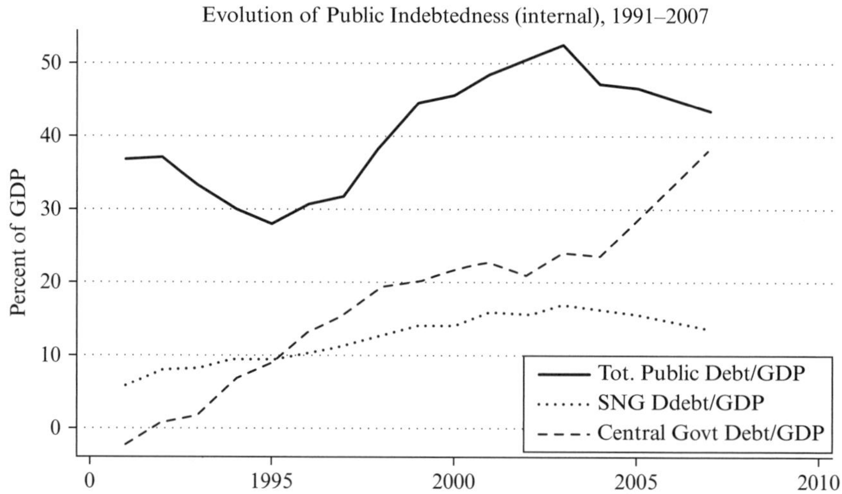

Source: BACEN, as cited in Giambiagi (2007, p. 31)

Figure 5.5 Public debt by level of government, Brazil

committed itself to macroeconomic stabilization, the most important step in reaching that goal – ending inflation through the introduction of a new currency system – led to a strong increase in government debt, in particular on the part of central government (Figure 5.5). Total public debt grew by almost 15 percent GDP between 1994 and 1999. Figure 5.5 compares the evolution of internal public debt in percentage of GDP between 1991 and 2006 by level of government, as reported by the government development agency IPEA (Giambiagi 2007). Additionally, the dashed line indicates how total (internal and external) general government debt grew relative to GDP for comparison.

After the Asian and the Russian crises in 1997/98, which led to a renewed and significant increase in borrowing costs for emerging market debtors, fiscal stabilization and debt stabilization became priorities for the government, which is reflected in a significant slowdown in the rate of change of both the total and the internal public-debt-to-GDP ratios after 1998 (Table 5.7).[13] The post-reform adjustment of the public debt growth rate is stronger on average for internal public debt than for external public debt.

5.2.4.2 Public debt creation on the subnational level

As shown in Figure 5.5, subnational government debt, continuously increasing in the first half of the 1990s, reached double digits in 1996. As the figure indicates, debt was stabilized for a while after 1998 although it continued to grow. Perhaps more importantly, as an indicator of fiscal and debt stabilization, the growth rate of subnationally issued debt dropped sharply after the new debt ceilings were introduced in the restructuring contracts with the states starting in 1997 (Table 5.7). While the subnational government internal public-debt-to-GDP ratio grew at 0.93 on average in the years 1992 to 1997, it fell to 0.36 percent on average in the post-reform period. This effect is particularly noteworthy given that after the currency peg had been abandoned, we might have expected to see subnational policy makers going back to 'business as usual' – with the bending of borrowing rules and continued over-borrowing – and expecting to be bailed out.

Clearly, the 1997 federal bailout provided the necessary short-term relief for the states. As shown in Figure 5.2, debt service as a share of states' revenue decreased after the bailout. However, the states were still left with a sizeable ratio of debt to GDP and their debt kept growing.[14] This is best understood by continuous capitalization of debt service in line with debt contracts between the federal government and the states. The restructuring contracts included the provision that any debt service in excess of a fixed percentage of total revenue was capitalized, i.e. it became part of the total debt stock to be repaid at a later point in time. As a consequence of these 'back-loaded' debt repayment schemes and under extremely high borrowing costs during the financial crisis in 2002, subnational government debts grew to worrisome levels in 2003 (roughly 17 percent of GDP). However, after the election the new government in 2003 successfully convinced the markets, through continued fiscal consolidation, that political risk concerns were unwarranted. Borrowing costs finally slowed down and the debt-financing problem of the states could be contained. No further bailouts by the federal government took place.

Table 5.7 Growth rate of public debt, Brazil

	Growth Rate of (Internal) Public Debt-to-GDP-Ratio, 1992–2006														
	1992	1993	1994	1995	1996	1997	1998	1999	2000	2001	2002	2003	2004	2005	2006
Total (external and internal) general government debt	0.3	−3.9	−3.2	−2	2.7	1.1	7.1	5.6	1.1	2.8	2.2	1.8	−5.4	−0.5	−1.6
Total (internal) general govt debt	4.9	0.4	2.7	1.5	4.1	0.7	5.3	2	1.5	2.2	−1.2	4.1	−1.5	3.9	3.5
General government debt	2.9	1.1	4.8	2.3	4.3	2.2	3.9	0.6	1.7	0.9	−1.7	3.1	−0.5	5	4.5
State and Municip. debt	2.2	0.2	1.3	−0.1	0.7	1.3	1.1	1.4	0.1	1.8	−0.3	1.4	−0.7	−0.7	−0.9

Source/Data: Giambiagi (2007)

To fully evaluate how the initially high debt accumulation and the increasing growth rate of public debt between 1991 and 1997 could be slowed down, it requires a closer look at the three consecutive state debt crises, ending with debt restructuring in 1989, 1993 and 1997/98, the last of which fundamentally changed the rules of subnational debt financing. I summarize in Appendix A: Part 1 the events that led to a turnaround in subnational indebtedness after 1998. Looking at the history of bailouts in Brazil, one can make a clear case that initial debt levels are decisive for creating the next crisis ('original sin'). Apparently, the combination of high remaining debt ratios and, perhaps, overly ambitious strategies for reducing debt may have left state governments with too little room to maneuver after the first two debt bailouts. Yet, acknowledging the impact of 'inherited' debt stocks does not spare us from explaining why debt accumulated to such high levels in the first place. One question remains: what forced an end to the vicious circle of subnational deficit financing and public debt accumulation? Changing incentives for policy makers by reforming fiscal institutions in 1997, as I argue, provided a solution to the underlying CPR problem. To exemplify how fiscal targets work to prohibit spending bias, I describe in the required detail in Appendix A: Part 2 how fiscal conditionality was woven into debt-restructuring contracts. What this exercise shows is that debt consolidation at the subnational level largely followed a process of institutional centralization. Changing the rules of the game gradually, shifting more responsibility in spending and debt policies to the federal level, worked well in the case of Brazil and may provide a good example for other countries in which such a fundamental change may have seemed impossible for a long time.

5.3 HORIZONTAL BUDGETARY INSTITUTIONS, VERTICAL DECENTRALIZATION AND FISCAL PERFORMANCE

Brazil was able to significantly improve its fiscal stance and debt position soon after a series of institutional reforms took place between 1997 and 2000, judging by the data on fiscal and debt outcomes presented above, both on the national and subnational level. The second part of this chapter takes a closer look at these institutional changes, scrutinizing how their implementation affected fiscal outcomes.

Based on the argument developed in Chapter 1, stating that CPR problems at different levels of government were responsible for fiscal imbalance and extensive debt creation, I analyze how changes in budgetary rules have altered the incentives for budget actors. First, I look at the national level, or what I call the horizontal dimension of budget making. Second, I focus on the fiscal behavior of subnational budget actors, i.e. those in the vertical dimension.

5.3.1 Centralizing Budgetary Institutions on the National Level

In the literature, there is broad agreement that Brazil's institutional development over the past 15 years stands out as a positive example for Latin America and beyond. In its latest report on the quality of budgetary institutions, the IADB (Filc and Scartascini 2004) ranks Brazil first place above the other 19 Latin American and Caribbean countries included in the survey. Brazil's budgetary institutions are not only significantly more centralized than other countries in the region but also compared to industrialized countries including Germany and the USA.[15]

However, the quality of Brazil's institutions has not always been that great. In the IADB's first survey on budgetary institutions, carried out by Roberto Alesina and colleagues (1999) in the late 1990s, Brazil ranks only 11th out of 20 Latin American and Caribbean countries. Not only did Brazil's budget process at the time look much less coordinated than in other countries in the region showing a comparable level of economic development – such as Mexico, Chile or Uruguay – but budget control was even lower than in traditionally much less developed countries in the region, including Paraguay and Ecuador, and below the average of Latin American and Caribbean countries.[16]

How was it possible to recentralize the budget process sufficiently, allowing for significantly improved fiscal and public debt outcomes? First of all, we need to differentiate between the short-term fiscal adjustment policies of the government of Fernando Henrique Cardoso (1995–2002), introduced in the fall of 1998, and longer-term-oriented fiscal institutional reforms. During the financial crisis in 1998, the government was under pressure from the financial markets and also from the IMF who made its assistance conditional on efforts to reach negotiated primary surplus targets that would allow the country to get back on a sustainable track with its public debt and to continue debt service. A fiscal adjustment plan presented by the government in September 1998 included the goal of turning the primary budget deficit of 1997 (−1 percent of GDP) into a balanced budget. Additionally, Cardoso proclaimed the goal of achieving growing primary surpluses (2.92 percent in 1999, 3.24 percent in 2000) in the following year. According to Cardoso (in a research interview), these targets were cautiously set to more ambitious levels than those requested by the IMF, in order to convince both the fund's fiscal policy experts and the financial markets that the government was serious about avoiding a default. The first target for cuts in expenditure was the public wage bill, leading to significant short-term reductions in central government personnel expenditure in 1999 and also in 2003, as demonstrated above. Another target area was public investment.

In addition to the above short-term measures, the Cardoso government engaged in a series of reforms of Brazil's budgetary institutions, the foundations for which were laid several years before the 1998 crisis. Generally, approaches that explain the country's fiscal improvement point to the Fiscal Responsibility Law introduced to Congress in April 1999 and sanctioned in May 2000, as the centerpiece of institutional development. Suggesting that a major turnaround was possible by passing a single law, however, would over-simplify the actual process of institutional improvement. Rather, fiscal consolidation in Brazil became possible through a series of institutional changes that took place during the second half of the 1990s. The reforms changed the incentives of budget actors in different sectors and on all levels of government. To control the budget, the Cardoso government chose a mostly statutory reform approach, relying on targets for expenditure and debt accumulation. Most importantly, to guarantee compliance with the new institutions, the government relied on a mix of 'carrots' and 'sticks'. This included a shift to ex ante regulation of budget decisions and ex post enforcement mechanisms.

The Fiscal Responsibility Law (FRL) of May 2000 defines expenditure ceilings, fiscal targets and debt ceilings, while the Fiscal Crimes Law (FCL), sanctioned in the same year, flanks the former, providing a new enforcement mechanism. For the first time in Brazilian history, the FCL holds individuals responsible for fiscal mismanagement through the penal law.[17] As a way of making transgressions of the FRL financially painful for subnational governments, the law allowed the president to withhold 'voluntary' transfers to a non-compliant agency or state government, to stop any legal guarantees and withhold new credit operations. In addition to these 'sticks', the president used 'carrots' to create political alliances, usually in the form of financial transfers. Another 'carrot' Cardoso offered, though this had only a one-time effect, was a change in the electoral law in 1998, allowing incumbents to run for a second term in office.

The FRL changed the incentives for national-level budget actors within the government and in the legislative and judicial branches by establishing budgeting based on a 'golden rule', requiring new borrowing to stay level with capital expenditure on investment. Debt limits can only be reviewed in periods of negative economic growth and low growth (i.e. lower than 1 percent in four consecutive quarters). The law sets limits on the size and structure of the budget, conditional on revenue. This means that permanent spending mandates have to be linked either to corresponding increases in permanent revenue or to a reduction in other permanent spending commitments. As established by the FRL, budget decisions are guided by a new Medium Term Fiscal Framework (MTFF), stating spending targets, expected revenue and deficits or surpluses for the medium term and for each specific year. From its medium-term fiscal planning, the government derives short-term expenditure targets by project and government branch.

A crucial part is played by expenditure limits, reducing government spending on the public wage bill to 50 percent of net revenue on the national level (and 60 percent on the subnational level). In the case of 95 percent of the maximum limit for personnel expenditure being exceeded, the granting of new benefits, the creation of offices, new admissions (except for replacements in some sectors) and overtime will be suspended. If the maximum limit is surpassed, through voluntary transfers, the president can suspend the contracting of credit operations (except for debt refinancing and a reduction in personnel expenditure), and guarantees. Furthermore, to reduce political business cycle-related spending sprees, the FRL prohibits increases in expenditure on public employees in the 180 days before the end of a political mandate.

Another key area defined in the FRL is the debt limits on subnational governments. The limits – set at 2 percent (1.2 percent) of net recurrent revenue for state (municipal) level governments – are defined by the Senate and can only be lifted during an economic crisis.[18] If debt limits are surpassed for 12 months, the government can withhold discretionary transfers, deny guarantees and prohibit the contracting out of new credit operations. Furthermore, the FRL contains strict provisions on indebtedness and issuance of public debt by the central bank, prohibiting debt-restructuring operations among the various levels of government.

Looking back at the fiscal stabilization process in Brazil at the end of the 1990s, it should not remain unmentioned that both short-term adjustment measures and more long-term-oriented institutional reforms took place in a political system that, by the constitution of 1988, shows in general a strong tendency to centralize budget decisions in the hands of the president. As Alston et al. (2009, p. 81) point out, when designing the constitution, legislators tried to ensure that the president held strong institutional powers, in particular during 'state-of-emergency' situations, allowing him or her to enforce 'rescue measures' against political veto players with a mixture of instruments, including provisional decrees, vetoes and urgency petitions. Beyond these, the president is also in a strong position during 'normal' times. According to the 1988 constitution, the president holds a twofold veto over budget amendments proposed by the Brazilian Congress, allowing the rejection of the entire proposal or specific items. Once the budget bill is passed, the president maintains authority over executing specific budget amendments. The executive hence is capable of controlling the budget during the formulation stage but also during the execution stage, given that the budget is not mandatory but serves only an authoritative function.

5.4 SUBNATIONAL FISCAL RESPONSIBILITY UNDER STRENGTHENED HORIZONTAL INSTITUTIONS

A series of legal changes, in the second half of the 1990s, finishing with the Fiscal Responsibility Law (FRL) in 2000, introduced stronger controls of the federal government over subnational borrowing, defining the criteria for borrowing eligibility. Institutional reforms also made binding debt (and fiscal) targets for subnational governments enforceable through financial and legal sanctioning by the federal government, reducing the unsustainable borrowing of subnational governments.

5.4.1 Expenditure Decentralization and Fiscal Imbalance

The National Constitutional Assembly, leading to the new democratic constitution of 1988, provided the Brazilian states with large expenditure autonomy compared with other federations. Overall, subnational governments are responsible for 41 percent of total government expenditure, according to the IMF's GFS data in 2002. Expenditure decentralization is thus the second largest in Latin America, behind Argentina (44 percent) and significantly higher than in Mexico (26 percent), the other large federal country in the region.

During the first half of the 1990s up to a banking crisis in 1995 and the following fiscal crisis in 1996/97, we find evidence in line with my argument that expenditure decentralization fostered CPR problems, leading to growing subnational fiscal imbalance. Under soft budget constraints, vertical decentralization set incentives for subnational budget actors to solve CPR problems by increasing expenditure. Deficit financing was commonplace, leading to growing debt ratios at the state level. Market discipline was essentially undermined after repeated federal bailouts for the states and for state banks, leading capital market participants to underestimate the real risks of investing in Brazilian state bonds. Up until the third consecutive bailout in 1997, which coincides with a period of belt tightening for the federal government, there is little evidence of a credible and sustainable hardening of budget constraints on subnational governments.

5.4.2 Subnational Debt Crises: Paving the Way to Fiscal Conditionality in Debt Contracts

The financial situation of the Brazilian states up to the late 1990s was to a great extent determined by the moral hazard problem of subnational governments' borrowing contracts. The financial markets read the government's previous two bailouts for the states as a guarantee that the nation would step in whenever subnational debtors were in trouble, setting the wrong incentives and leading to continued lending by private investors, substantially underestimating the true risk of such lending. Additionally, federal bailouts undermined the fiscal responsibility of the states because they signaled soft budget constraints. The first subnational bailout occurred in late 1989, extending into 1990. The Brazilian states came under financing pressure as a consequence of the international debt crisis of the 1980s. Subnational governments had previously been increasingly gaining access to international financing. On one hand, states had borrowed from the World Bank and the IADB, and on the other hand from international private actors.

Dillinger and Webb (1999) note that borrowing from official lenders demanded federal guarantees whereas private borrowing did not. By the end of the 1980s, when they came into enhanced financing difficulties, several states stopped servicing their foreign debt, forcing the federal government to take on their liabilities. This situation led to the first in a series of bailouts and the federal government agreed to incorporate all federally guaranteed debts of the states into the long-term debt of the federal treasury.

After the fiscal crisis in late 1989 and early 1990, the newly elected Collor de Mello administration implemented a stabilization program aimed at reducing inflation. The program showed only short-term success and inflation accelerated after a short time in mid-1991. Nevertheless, the initial success of the anti-inflation measures affected the policy game between the federal and subnational governments. Under high inflation, the states could continue to increase deficit spending, given that they were able to 'inflate away' outstanding liabilities. The reduction in inflation changed the incentives for subnational governments. When inflation decreased, the states' demand for debt renegotiation with the federal government suddenly increased. The federal government was willing to assume those debts, introducing conditions for the refinancing of debts from the 1980s and state bonds through a new law (Law 8388). However, when inflation accelerated again, after the collapse of the second Collor Plan in mid-1991, the pressure on states to refinance their debts was reduced and thus their demand for renegotiations decreased. Additionally, there were two measures that took pressure off states' finances. In February 1991, Central Bank Resolution 1789 allowed the exchange of Central Bank bonds for state bonds, which was effectively a rollover of state bonds in the domestic financial market. Also, the Central Bank fostered the demand for states' debt instruments by authorizing the operation of mutual funds with state and municipal bonds in their portfolios. Bevilaqua (2002, p. 14) notes that, as a result, bonds became the main source of financing for Brazilian states and the net debt of subnational governments increased from 7.5 percent of GDP in 1990 to 9.3 percent in 1991.[19] The fast growth rates of subnational government bonded debt, at a real rate of growth of 40 percent, brought the federal government into the plan, which focused on amending the 1988 constitution to constrain state-level bond issuance. Disaggregated data on bond issuance show that states in the more industrially developed south of Brazil – Sao Paulo, Minas Gerais, Rio de Janeiro and Rio Grande do Sul – held the largest shares in total state bond issuance (Bevilaqua 2000). Apparently, the borrowing activity in the richest states was highest. Given the level of their economic and financial development, they enjoyed better access to capital markets. Subnational debt accumulation turned into a severe problem again in 1992. At the time, the financing pressure on states' banks grew significantly because they were faced with increasing difficulties in placing their bonds with private institutions. To gain some degree of freedom in their finances, states started to request debt renegotiations of their non-bonded debts with the central government. They were met in November 1993 (through Law 8727 establishing the conditions for bonded debt renegotiations) and there was a bailout of banks holding state bonds by the Central Bank in June 1994 (through Central Bank Resolution 2081). The agreement with central government included a rescheduling of non-bonded debt for 20 years, extending to all debts of state governments and their enterprises. The Central Bank bailout led to an assumption of the majority of state bonds by the Central Bank which had, by the end of 1993, not been holding any such bonds. Additionally, the Central Bank intervened in the two largest state banks – BANESPA of Sao Paulo and BANERJ of Rio de Janeiro – on December 31, 1994, in order to take care of both banks' substantial liquidity problems (see the BANESPA case study in Appendix A: Part 2).

The 1993/94 bailout included up-front debt forgiveness and a reduction in interests on the state debts, which were restructured for 30 years in most cases. Constitutional Amendment No. 3 introduced a ban on the issuance of new state bonds until December 1999, with the exception of those bonds financing the payment of judicial claims existing in 1988. The rollover operations of existing bonds were not affected. Paradoxically, the 1993 bailout led to an increase in bond financing, despite the federal government's initiative to at least stabilize the issuance of subnational-level government bonds. Additionally, wage increases, initially designed to correct for inflation, led to a large expansion in real payroll expenditure after the successful implementation of the Real Plan in 1994 followed by sustainable prize stability. The state's fiscal problems were intensified by a combination of the inflation correction of wages, introduced and implemented during the last term of Itamar Franco, in September 1994, and the first term of the Cardoso administration, in May 1995, together with the problem of rigidities in government expenditure, mainly on public employees (Cline 1995).

Bevilaqua (2002, p. 21) argues that the bailout eliminated the fiscal discipline that the financial markets were starting to impose on the states by refusing to hold their bonds and concludes that it was an important driver of deficit spending and over-borrowing in 1994. Another crucial factor contributing largely to the next states' fiscal crisis coming up in 1997 was a very high level of the Central Bank's real overnight lending rate, the SELIC, which had reached roughly 38 percent by the end of 1995 – more than three times the average interest rate for the following two administrations.[20] The data impressively show that next to fiscal indiscipline of the states, the evolution of interests put a strong burden on subnational finances.[21] Both factors led to serious fiscal difficulties in 1995, putting pressure on central government to develop yet another debt restructuring plan.

5.4.3 Toward Stronger Central Government Regulation of State-level Finances

After 1995 the federal government, increasingly under pressure from (post-Mexican crisis) recession-related lower government revenue and an increasing US dollar – making it more expensive to keep up the currency peg – took several steps to control subnational government borrowing and expenditure. The growth in subnational debt had been fostered by two main factors that the federal government was now aiming to control: (1) the extensive use of revenue anticipation loans (AROs), thus short-term debt borrowed to re-finance long-term debt; (2) subnational governments had accrued large arrears, which were essentially hidden debts. For instance, state governments went into arrears on payments to suppliers and public employees and on loans to state-owned banks.

In November 1995, the federal government took steps to implement a comprehensive rescue operation through Vote 162/95 of the National Monetary Council, authorizing the Caixa Econômica Federal (CEF) to provide emergency credit lines to the states for three different purposes:

the payment of wages and other outstanding arrears, the financing of voluntary retirement programs, and the refinancing of outstanding AROs. In exchange, the states were required to reduce payroll expenditure to 60 percent of net revenue by 1998, to privatize state assets and to increase the efficiency of state-level tax administration. Nevertheless, the financial rescue plan for the states late in 1995 failed and was doomed to do so, as Bevilaqua (2002, p. 27) concludes, precisely because the envisaged spending cuts to 60 percent of net revenue had been too ambitious. It was not until September 1997 that the federal government successfully negotiated with the states a comprehensive restructuring (Law 9496), combined with a final bailout, putting emphasis on states' obligation to adjust in return for rescue financing.

With the introduction of Law 9496, sanctioned in 1997, the federal level aimed to exert stronger control on the expenditure of the states. The law provided a framework for debt renegotiations between the states and the federal government through the PROES initiative (see Appendix A: Part 2). To reduce debt ratios, Law 9496 set targets for declining deficit ratios. Additionally, it set lower ceilings for expenditure on public employees and investment than previously guaranteed under the provisions of the 1988 constitution.

Expenditure on public personnel had to be brought down to 60 percent of current revenue after 1997. Furthermore, in the debt contracts with the federal governments under PROES, the states agreed on a list of 35 to 45 specific rules on fiscal and debt management, accounting and transparency, among others. As an important feature, Law 9496 for the first time introduced credible sanctioning mechanisms. The federal government was entitled to deduce outstanding debt service directly out of transfers to the states if they refused to meet debt-servicing targets. Also, the law made it impossible for states to borrow even from private banks if state governments failed to meet the deficit and expenditure targets. This rule was enforced through the Central Bank, which is responsible for private sector banking regulation. Taken together, Law 9496 and additional resolutions of the Central Bank, the National Monetary Council, and Congress effectively made balanced budgets and longer-term fiscal consolidation a precondition for new borrowing of the states.

Congress sanctioned the Fiscal Responsibility Law (FRL) in 2000 at a point where the strict fiscal and debt rules inscribed in the 1997 debt contracts with the states were showing their first successes, including the improvement of subnational fiscal balances. While in 1997 the number of states with a primary deficit was 16, it fell to 6 in 2000 and finally reached zero in 2004. In a way, the FRL further institutionalized successfully implemented rules. It was designed to structure annual budgets, both on the national and subnational levels, so that they would be consistent with the new multiyear budget plan (MTFF), required by the FRL. Also, budgets at both levels of government had to fulfill crucial transparency standards, mainly the banning of off-budgeting procedures. The FRL further established the rules on the public wage bill, emphasizing the ceiling on subnational government expenditure on personnel expenditure (no more than 60 percent of current revenue). Additionally, the FRL reduced the opportunities for office holders to rely on the public wage bill for political support around elections, prohibiting increases in expenditure on employees in the 180 days before the end of the mandate and declaring all labor contracts in violation of the FRL as invalid.

Steps by the government and Congress to introduce ex post sanctions, both for government institutions and the individual politicians in violation of the FRL, increased its credibility. The sanctions include both economic and legal measures. Not only can the president withhold funds allocated to budget actors missing budget targets, but if they transgress the fiscal laws, incumbents can lose their position and the right to hold public office for five years after a court has established violation of the fiscal law.

5.4.4 Recentralization of Budget Power by Increasing Discretionality of the Federal Budget

To achieve subnational government fiscal adjustment and to win the necessary political majority for a new long-term regulation of fiscal decision making, President Cardoso – similar to President Menem in Argentina – depended to a large extent on a system of 'pork and perks' (Treisman 2004).[22] In his campaign for institutional reforms, Cardoso could rely on a powerful tool: discretionary funds that had been filled with revenue since 1994, following a decision of Cardoso's predecessor to de-earmark certain tax-sharing funds and delegate them to a new fund that was at the sole disposal of the president. Indeed, data on the degree of revenue allocation in the Brazilian budget between 1979 and 2004, from Alston et al. (2009, p. 53), show that in 1987 non-earmarked revenue amounted to 55 percent of GDP whereas in 1990 non-earmarked revenue had fallen to only about 20 percent of GDP. The second 'tool' crucial for increasing presidential leverage over (state-level) veto players turned out to be tax revenue from newly introduced taxes, levied to overcome the crisis in 1998 and kept exclusively by the federal government.

In 1993, the government of president Itamar Franco (1992–1994) created the so-called Social Emergency Fund (FSE), which was initially designed as a temporary fund aimed at de-earmarking 20 percent of all taxes and contributions (Alston et al. 2009, p. 83). The FSE was followed by the Fund for Fiscal Stability (FEF), another temporary fund, and in

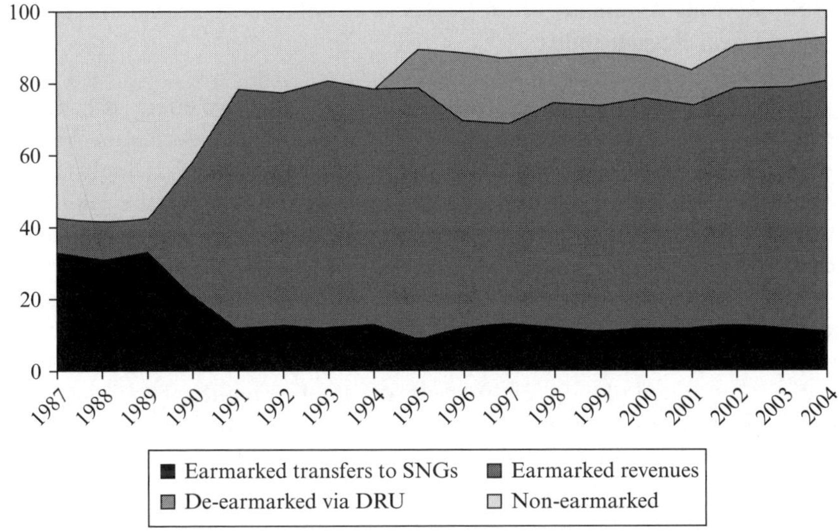

Source: Alston et al. (2009)

Figure 5.6 De-earmarking of government funds, Brazil

1999 by a permanent fund, the Delinked Budgetary Resource (DRU). These instruments were successful in keeping non-earmarked revenue at a level of around 20 percent and thus significantly higher than they would have been in the absence of the funds (compare Figure 5.6).[23] The funds provided the president with crucial additional financial leverage in the struggle for fiscal adjustment during the crisis in 1998 and afterwards.

Additionally, it was revenue from new taxes that allowed the president to reward political allies. Furthermore, federal revenue increased relative to subnational revenue due to the steady increase in social security contributions. The government was able to reach three consecutive constitutional amendments in 1994, 1995 and 2000 (lasting through 2003), allowing the re-channeling of social security revenue to other sectors, increasing its leeway in using tax funds. The central government steadily increased non-shared taxes, including export taxes and a financial transaction tax (finally repealed in 2010). While these steps attracted critique from tax experts for increasing the share-distorting taxes (see detailed discussions in Ter-Minassian 1997b and Mora and Varsano 2001), it provided the federal government with significantly increased revenue at its disposal, in particular during the economic boom after the 2002 financial crisis.

5.4.5 Revenue Autonomy of the States as an Alternative Explanation of Fiscal Responsibility

I highlighted above what I believe to be a mainly positive effect of central-level regulation and intervention in subnational fiscal decisions. Yet, a widely held view is that subnational fiscal discipline is linked strongly to the taxation autonomy of subnational government units. Does the relatively strong revenue-raising autonomy explain why Brazilian states were able to reduce their fiscal imbalances?

Compared with subnational governments in other Latin American countries, including Argentina, the Brazilian states enjoy significantly higher revenue-raising capacities. Based on the IMF's GFS data, own-source revenue made up 28 percent of total revenue of subnational governments in 2002, which is 10 percent more than Rodden's (2002) estimates for Argentina and also higher than in the third most decentralized country, Mexico (20 percent). The high revenue-raising capacities of Brazilian states and municipalities put them much more in a category with federations within the OECD world, including Austria, where own-source revenue covers 27 percent of total revenue, and Germany (33 percent), than with other middle-income countries. However, own-source revenue varies significantly among the Brazilian states, given the traditionally large economic disparities between different regions. Furthermore, revenue autonomy was reduced by several steps taken before and during the financial and debt crisis in 1998/99, including the Kandir Law in 1996. Rodden (2003, p. 17) notes that Brazilian states, along with Canadian provinces, are the only examples of subnational governments that fully administer their own value-added tax. As a result of tax competition between the states, income from the state-level VAT (ICMS) declines gradually. Revenue from the ICMS, which initially accounted for more than 90 percent of states' total revenue, was reduced to 85 percent in 2002. Additionally, federal legislation passed during the first Cardoso administration excluded the states from export tax revenue, handing over full control to the federal government. The Kandir Law, passed in 1996, exempted exports from the tax on the circulation of goods, effectively reducing state revenue. Although the federal government granted states some compensation for the loss in revenue, the revenue gap was – intentionally – never entirely filled.

The finding that diminishing subnational own-source revenue was followed by improved subnational fiscal outcomes contradicts, to some extent, the common view that by reducing revenue autonomy, subnational fiscal discipline is critically undermined. The reason was already discussed above: it seems that in the specific case of Brazil, those states that are able to collect the most own-source revenue

– the industrialized, more wealthy and hence fiscally more independent Brazilian states in the south and south-west – are those that accumulate the largest debts, putting the overall debt and fiscal sustainability of the country at risk.

5.5 SUMMARY: HORIZONTAL AND VERTICAL DECENTRALIZATION IN BRAZIL

Fiscal consolidation in Brazil during the second half of the 1990s became possible through reforms that (re-)centralized fiscal control on the national level and strengthened federal government control over subnational fiscal decisions. In the horizontal dimension, budget control was strengthened through the introduction of global fiscal deficit and debt targets in the Fiscal Responsibility Law (FRL), sanctioned in April 2000. Additionally, the introduction of ceilings for public wage bill expenditure forced politicians at all levels of government to tackle a key structural problem in government finances. The FRL set higher standards for public sector accounting and transparency.

In the years following the successful price stabilization with the introduction of the real in 1994, the government learned that the fixed exchange rate by itself could not prevent fiscal imbalances from re-appearing. More sustainable solutions to the underlying structural problems made it onto the list of political priorities. A deteriorating borrowing climate, falling foreign direct investment inflows after the Asian and Russian crises, and external pressure from the IMF and private creditor consortia all played their role in forcing the Cardoso administration to tackle fiscal problems by 1998. But the necessary condition for a successful fiscal adjustment was, in much likelihood, the government's own determination to harden budget constraints – if that was what was necessary to prevent a second default after the traumatic experience in 1987.

First steps in the direction of budgetary institutional centralization had in fact already been taken prior to the crisis, with the inclusion of fiscal conditionality in debt restructuring agreements with the states and the passing of Congressional Resolution 78 and Law 9646 in 1997. Following up on these legal acts, the federal government presented its new FRL to the Brazilian Congress in April 1999. For the FRL to become accepted by all sides as a credible instrument, it was crucial for the government to receive broad support, both from Congress and the state governors. To gain support from both, Cardoso made use of additional discretionary funds (DRU), released through legal changes by his predecessor in 1994, to provide side payments to political allies. Furthermore, Cardoso offered to extend the planned electoral reform, allowing the president to run for a second term, to incumbents on all levels of government. He thereby co-opted potential opponents of his fiscal consolidation plans, making them part of his inter-party 'coalition for fiscal stability'.

The first steps toward fiscal consolidation were hence taken even before the government decided to think aloud that the currency peg could be relaxed. The government agreed with Congress on a punishment mechanism for violations of fiscal rules that included both pecuniary sanctions and political as well as legal consequences for incumbents. It is noteworthy that the Fiscal Crimes Law in 2000 established, for the first time, the concept of individual responsibility for government malpractice. The fruits of these initiatives soon started to show, allowing Cardoso to balance the general government primary budget in 1998 and to build up surpluses – beyond what was agreed with the IMF – in the following years.

Recentralization of budgetary power vis-à-vis subnational governments had already started in 1994. The federal government had taken its first steps toward bringing subnational budgets under control by de-earmarking revenue from the revenue-sharing system. Paradoxical as it may sound, the subnational fiscal and debt crisis, beginning in 1995 with the near default of two of the largest state-owned banks, BANESPA of Sao Paulo and BANERJ of Rio de Janeiro, provided a window of opportunity for the federal government to rein in government expenditure by recentralizing budget and borrowing autonomy in exchange for financial assistance to the states.

In 1995, after the introduction of the Real Plan, subnational governments accounted for half of general government debts. Given the (estimated) systemic risk of letting two major debtor banks default, the federal government was forced to find a solution to the restructuring of subnational liabilities. Federal Law 9496, setting standards for debt reduction and fiscal consolidation on the subnational level, together with the government's PROES initiative which introduced conditionality into the bilateral debt-restructuring contracts with the states, provided important tools for the federal government to constrain subnational leaders. Two prior subnational debt crises in 1989 and 1993 were ended with a rescheduling of state debts, essentially shifting the immediate debt burden into the future without getting to the root of the problem. However, under PROES, the federal government made its debt relief for the states (in the range of 10 percent of their outstanding debt to the federal government) conditional on the restructuring and privatization of failed banks within two years. Furthermore, it set explicit fiscal targets for subnational governments. Law 9496 ended the use of short-term revenue anticipation loans (AROs) that had facilitated the fast expansion of subnational debt.

And the government limited states' ability to capitalize on interest payments that exceeded (undemanding) ceilings in previous debt contracts with the federal government, which too had led to a piling up of the debt stock.

In the power struggle between President Cardoso and the revolting governor of Minas Gerais, former president Itamar Franco, who declared a default of his state in January 1999, the central government's commitment to the new rules was challenged for the first time. Indeed, Cardoso remained unyielding and used his power to withhold cash flows to that state in the amount of debt that the governor had declared a default on. In the end, Cardoso won the battle and provided evidence that the new budgetary institutions had led to a fundamental change in the budgetary bargaining game between the federal government and the states. Over the next few years, state governors started to change their fiscal strategy, dropping earlier plans to default collectively on state debts. The next time the government came once more under financial market pressure, prior to the 2002 presidential election, leading to the electoral victory of left-wing candidate Lula da Silva, it took considerable persuasion by the Brazilian authorities and the IMF to calm the markets. Yet, the incumbent President Cardoso was able to convince both official and private creditors that his successor, left-wing or not, was bound by the existing laws to continue on the path of fiscal consolidation.

This was the likely outcome for two main reasons. First, the new government faced large incentives to reap the benefits of fiscal stabilization rather than to announce a radical change that would intensify capital flight with all of its negative consequence for the economy. Second, after the successful implementation of fiscal institutional reform at the end of the 1990s, the president and his economic team now had effective instruments at their disposal to control spending pressures and constrain public debt creation. Under these conditions, default seemed unlikely, which the markets finally acknowledged after the first few months of the first Lula da Silva administration.

NOTES

1. The IMF granted Brazil financial assistance amounting to US$41.5 billion; the first tranche – US$9 billion – was approved before December 1998 with the purpose of buttering up the Cardoso government's capacity to keep up the currency peg despite massive capital outflows.
2. Following the attack on the real, monthly outflows of foreign capital already exceeded the amount granted to the government in December. By January 1999, the government was forced to devalue its currency towards the US dollar, initially by 8 percent. By the

end of January 1999, depreciation of the real had reached 66 percent, standing at a real exchange rate of R$1.98/US$ on January 31, 1999.

3. The IMF and other international organizations often use the primary fiscal balance as a key indicator of a country's ability to adjust fiscally to financing pressures in the case of developing countries because it allows for a determination of structural household problems beyond debt-servicing needs.
4. At this point, Brazil would have fulfilled one of the main 'Maastricht convergence criteria', self-imposed by European Union members in 1992 with the aim of promoting prudent government finance. Besides the deficit ratio, the Maastricht treaty foresees a limit on the government-debt-to-GDP ratio of 60 percent. In Brazil, the public debt ratio always remained below 60 percent throughout the entire sample period for which data are available (1995–2006), reaching its highest value in 2002 (59.62 percent of GDP).
5. Brazilian government bond spreads over US Treasury Bills almost double between 1997 and 1998, peaking at 860 basis points (bp) in 1999. They fall for a couple of years but peak once more during the elections in 2002 at close to 1200 bp. In the following year, the bond spread drops to an average of 730 bp and continues to fall in the next few years, bottoming out at 240 in 2006.
6. A crucial factor in the IMF lending agreement prepared over the summer and approved on 2 December 1998 was the reduction in the government's primary fiscal balance. The primary balance data show that Brazil successfully decreased the deficit within the same year. At the end of 1998, the government was able to reduce the primary fiscal deficit, standing at nearly 1 percent of GDP in 1997, and reach a minimal surplus of 0.01 percent of GDP. Over the following years, it targeted a sophisticated primary fiscal surplus, extending the target suggested by the IMF. Indeed, the government arrived at its target and the general government primary surplus increased to 2.92 percent in 1999 and 3.24 percent in 2000. The exact calculated primary surplus goals of the government of President Cardoso were 2.6 percent in 1999, 2.8 percent in 2000 and 3 percent in 2001.
7. According to data presented in Bevilaqua (2002), the lion's share of the bailout went to the following states in descending order: Sao Paulo (57 percent), Minas Gerais (13.4), Rio Grande do Sul (10.7) and Rio de Janeiro (9.6).
8. Data from Giambiagi (2007) reveal that public enterprises owned by the states accumulated relatively high deficits in the equivalent of roughly 0.40 percent of GDP in 1994 and 1995. Beginning in 1996, these deficits are continuously reduced until they reach positive numbers in 1999. Since then, their surpluses have increased to roughly 0.2 percent of GDP between 2000 and 2004 and continue to reach relatively high surpluses. For public enterprises owned by municipal governments, the situation is similar. They were able to reach balanced results for the first time in 2000 and have avoided any deficit making since then.
9. It should be noted that the decision of the Cardoso government to reduce the number of new public sector employees was flanked by an initiative to increase the number of highly qualified employees holding university degrees. In an attempt to improve the quality of the bureaucracy, the Cardoso administration raised the percentage of university degree holders among new federal civil servants from merely 73 percent in 1997 to 94.1 percent in 2001. This compares with 39.2 percent in 1995.
10. Giambiagi (2007, p. 23, Table 11) provides a detailed overview of expenditure for specific categories.
11. According to a report by the UN Commission for Latin America and the Caribbean (ECLAC 2009), Brazil's tax burden amounts to 35.5 percent of GDP which is the highest in Latin America and very close to the OECD average of 36.8 percent. In the same year, the average for the LAC region was 18.4 percent of GDP and roughly 30 percent in Argentina.
12. According to the Kandir Law of 1996, exports are exempt from tax on the circulation of goods, effectively reducing state revenue. Promising the states that it would compensate them for the lost revenue, the federal government made additional transfers conditional

on states' continued debt service to the nation and on fiscal consolidation (including the 60 percent limit on state-level public wage bill expenditure relative to total state revenue).

13. Some caution in interpreting the subnational data in Table 5.7 is warranted, given that for subnational governments it includes information only on the internal public-debt-to-GDP ratio. However, it should be noted that since the beginning of the sample period until 1998, the share of external debt in the total public debt was continuously declining. After the currency crisis in 1998/99 until the end of the crisis in 2002, external debt increased once more, however it fell significantly after 2003. The average share of internal-to-total general government debt was 77 percent between 1991 and 2006.
14. Figure 5.2 shows the continuous decrease in states' average expenditure on public debt servicing over the total sample period (1993–2006). After an initial increase in 1995 following the introduction of the real, expenditure on interest continued to grow to high numbers, reaching almost 11 percent of total annual revenue in 1997. After the 2002 crisis was overcome, it finally fell to less than 4 percent in 2006.
15. Brazil received a score of 8.14 on the 10-point scale applied, where 10 indicates the highest degree of institutional centralization. This compares to a sample average of 5.84 for Latin American and Caribbean countries and implies that Brazil's fiscal institutions are more centralized on the national level than institutions in federations in the OECD, including Canada (4.68), the USA (5.08) and Germany (6.11).
16. The institutional score in the first IADB survey (Alesina et al. 1999) for Brazil is 54.49 on a 100-point scale, where 100 points indicates full centralization. To compare, the average degree of institutional centralization of Latin American and Caribbean countries was 57.09. Brazil also scored worse than other economically more advanced countries in the region, including Mexico (73.46), Chile (73.32) and Uruguay (63.48), and also worse than poorer countries like Paraguay (59.65) and Ecuador (55).
17. Individual politicians who do not comply with the fiscal rules face removal from office, prevention from occupying public office for five years and fines that in the past have ranged up to 30 percent of annual salary, and finally imprisonment.
18. During economic crises or monetary and foreign exchange shocks, which have to be acknowledged by the Senate, the president of the republic may forward a request to the Senate asking for the review of debt limits.
19. This compares to the high ratio of subnational debt to GDP in Argentina already in the years prior to the sovereign debt crisis. In 1996 provincial debt soared from zero to 5.1 percent of GDP. Although the subnational debt ratio slowed down for a couple of years afterwards, it started to grow again between 1998 and 2002 when the ratio reached more than 20 percent of GDP.
20. During the first government of President Cardoso (1995–1998), the real interest rate, SELIC, stood at 21.6 percent, which is equal to double the average real interest rate for the following two governments (10.2 percent in 1999–2002 and 11.3 percent in 2003–2006).
21. Commenting on their order of relevance, Bevilaqua (2002, p. 39) notes that although 'high real interest rates made debt service unbearable, the evolution of states' debt was probably not sustainable otherwise'.
22. This kind of 'pork and perks' politics under the two Cardoso administrations is also well captured in Alston et al. 2009, among others.
23. Alston et al. (2009, p. 84) report, based on government data, that non-earmarked revenue in 2003 was at 19.7 percent of GDP compared to only 12.7 percent without counting the DRU.

6. Fiscal federalism under decentralized budgetary institutions in Argentina

This chapter looks at fiscal imbalance, vertical fiscal decentralization and attempted reforms of budgetary institutions in Argentina since 1990. The evidence I find suggests that Argentina did not establish the kind of budgetary institutions at the central government level that were shown to be crucial for successful fiscal stabilization in Brazil. On the surface, Argentina appeared to be a case in point for a quick implementation of 'Washington consensus'-type reforms. For large parts of the administration of President Carlos Menem (1989–1995), his new economic policies, aiming for a radical transformation of the economy, seemed to pay off quickly. Looking back at that period, we are now able to say that reform successes were often overrated while large structural weaknesses remained. In this chapter, I focus on the remaining fiscal imbalances that began to resurface in the spring of 1999. Provincial-level fiscal and debt problems contributed not only to overall government financial instability but also to a loss of confidence in the debt-management capacity of the government on the part of financial investors. Below, I describe the process that later culminated in what at the time became known as the 'greatest default in history' – the Argentine government's public declaration of sovereign default in December 2001. Looking at the root causes of debt accumulation, I trace the process of fiscal policies and institutional reform (or lack thereof) from the beginning of the democratic transition in the early 1980s.

Through the democratic constitution of 1983, subnational governments in Argentina had been granted remarkable fiscal authority in the area of spending. Figure 4.5 (in Chapter 4) shows that Argentina keeps the top position in terms of spending decentralization among the group of Latin American and Caribbean countries, even above Brazil. I argue that the decentralization of expenditure increased the CPR problem and fostered fiscal indiscipline at the subnational level. In the absence of any hard budget constraints, provincial governors faced incentives to increase spending, exceeding by far what they were able (and allowed) to collect in own-source revenue and also what they could draw on in total revenue after receiving transfers from the federally orchestrated revenue-sharing mechanism (coparticipation funds) and from discretionary funds.

Although, at the beginning of the 1990s, President Carlos Menem (1989–1995) successfully stopped subnational fiscal expansion through two 'Fiscal Pacts', in 1992 and in 1993, negotiated with the provinces in return for federal assistance, these temporally limited agreements were not followed by lasting changes to the budgetary institutional set-up. Instead, the rules of the fiscal bargaining game between the federal government and the provinces remained more or less the same. I argue that the Argentine government would have been much better prepared to stabilize fiscally by the end of the 1990s had the fiscal decision-making process, including decisions on external borrowing, been less dispersed across different branches and levels of government. But the Argentine government abstained from adopting more centralized fiscal institutions when times were good, leaving it in a weaker position to implement adjustment when things were getting much worse after 1998. Instead of introducing more long-term-oriented budgetary institutional solutions to persistent CPR problems on the national and subnational levels of government, the latter continued to be answered by increasing overall public expenditure. Unresolved spending rigidities made it very difficult for the government to achieve primary fiscal surpluses in the amounts needed to stabilize the high and increasing ratio of public and publicly guaranteed debt to GDP after 1999. Surely, the government's decision to stick to US-dollar parity of the Argentine peso for so long increased pressure on the government to implement austerity. When it failed to deliver on crucial deficit and debt reduction targets, the market punishment was severe. As a consequence, debt reduction turned into an ever more difficult task.

Below, I present data on subnational and central government expenditure, fiscal results and debt, showing that structural fiscal vulnerabilities preceded the external shocks to the Argentine economy. One-time revenue from the privatization of state companies helped to conceal the deteriorating fiscal stance for a while. However, towards the end of the 1990s, imprudent fiscal behavior on the national level and fiscal strategies on the subnational level were interacting, creating fiscal imbalances that were hard to resolve, particularly in the quickly deteriorating external economic environment. Indeed, subnational expenditure (as a share of GDP) rose after 1993 and again, more drastically, in 1996. Only a couple of years later, given soaring debt-financing costs and continued economic depression, the federal government was trapped in a situation of insolvency. It managed to postpone sovereign default for a while but, as observers of the mounting debt problems generally agree, it could hardly be averted in the end.

At the peak of the crisis in 2001, Argentina's government lacked the institutional 'tools' to implement the kind of fiscal adjustment strategy that might have convinced the markets and international agencies of its willingness to repay the outstanding debt. Instead, the government's inability to resolve growing subnational fiscal imbalances and debt problems fueled the already heated debate. Both the IMF and private creditors increasingly voiced their concerns about the country's willingness to stay current on its (external) liabilities. Financial assistance was made conditional on the government's commitment to tackle structural fiscal problems, including the provincial financing crisis, but the president's position vis-à-vis the governors was too weak to strike a deal on fiscal adjustment. The failure to reach an internal compromise with provincial governments also put a question mark over the federal government's ability to implement fiscal adjustment at the national level.[1]

In the next few sections, I provide a brief overview of macroeconomic policy and external influences in Argentina (6.1) before I describe the evolution of fiscal imbalance in the 1990s (section 6.2). Next, I turn to potential institutional explanations for the outcomes we observe. The aim is to get a better understanding of the effects of horizontal decentralization (6.3) as well as the effects of vertical decentralization under the conditions of more and less decentralized national-level budgetary institutions (section 6.4). Here, as in the chapter on Brazil, I also discuss the negative consequences that stem from a mismatch between subnational spending responsibilities and own-source revenue-raising rights. In the last section, I summarize the evidence on institutional decentralization and fiscal imbalance, as well as market reactions in Argentina and present first conclusions. The chapter closes with a view on how to improve further cross-country analysis, based on my insights from the case studies.

6.1 ARGENTINA, 1990–2006: AN OVERVIEW

For almost a decade after successful monetary stabilization following the introduction of Argentina's 'convertibility' system of fixed exchange rates, fiscal imbalance in Argentina appeared to be a minor concern. When President Carlos Menem (1989–1999) came to office, following a solid electoral win (with 47.5 percent of the vote, followed by the conservative candidate with 33 percent) and blessed with a stable congressional majority (45 percent for the three-party coalition of his Justicialist Party, before the conservatives with 29 percent), he was able to sanction a series of economic policy reforms that were well received by the financial markets and international institutions, facing remarkably little resistance. The first major change was the aforementioned introduction of the fixed exchange rate system – widely known as the Convertibility Plan[2] – under the auspices of a currency board in April 1991, that showed itself to be extremely successful at bringing down inflation from historically high numbers within a year.[3]

Second, the government signed an agreement in principle under the Brady deal in April 1992 under then Economy Minister Domingo Cavallo and international private creditors, settling the debt problem that had weighed on the shoulders of governments since the default in 1982.[4] After Argentina signed the international debt agreement, it was left with a manageable public-debt-to-GDP ratio, particularly given the high growth rates of the early and mid 1990s (see Table 4.3 in Chapter 4).

Third, Menem sought to tackle the issue of pension reform in 1993, when the nation took on financial responsibility for the restructuring of the (loss-making) provincial pension plans with the goal of privatizing the system a little later. Further pro-market policy choices during the first Menem administration, establishing the country as a 'poster child' of macroeconomic reform spirit and modernization (Mussa 2002), included several tax reductions and tax harmonization (e.g. the elimination of taxes that were simultaneously levied by the provinces and the nation). As many observers have noted, privatization of the pension system turned into a major financial liability for the government as soon as debt-financing costs started to rise and economic recession broke out after the Mexican Tequila crisis in 1995. After having privatized the pension system, which required substantial financial involvement by the government, pension contributions were now missing in the budget (Brooks 2007). At the same time, federal revenue was falling due to an economic downturn. Pressure from provincial governors to compensate for their losses during the 1995 crisis through increased federal transfers and a loosening of recently agreed borrowing limits, created further liabilities for overall government finances in the years to come. Given high post-crisis growth rates, picking up in 1996, the government's finances seemed to recover for a while. Also, under favorable borrowing conditions, growing government expenditure and increasing indebtedness seemed unproblematic. This situation, however, turned around after Brazil's currency crisis in the second half of 1998 and led to the forced devaluation of the real in January 1999. First, this monetary policy decision created competitive pressure on Argentina's exports, leading to a significant drop in revenue. Second, turmoil in emerging markets (crises in Asia, Russia, Brazil and Ecuador) led to a tightening of credit, making it increasingly difficult for Argentina to finance the existing structural fiscal problems and to simultaneously keep up its currency peg, which remained in place until 2002. Provincial fiscal indiscipline and debt accumulation by then posed a threat to overall fiscal stability.

Over the 1990s, Argentine governments may indeed have established a picture of Argentina as a 'poster child' of macroeconomic reforms and modernization. Its successful stabilization efforts leading to the convertibility system particularly contributed to its positive image (Dornbusch 1995, Mussa 2002). However, as I show below, the same political leaders that successfully stabilized the currency and reduced inflation failed to eliminate structural inconsistencies with regard to the country's fiscal management, which remain a latent source of macroeconomic instability. In particular, governments failed to implement credible budgetary institutions. Although the Argentine Congress had accepted the establishment of fiscal laws, including fiscal targets and debt ceilings, in 1996 and 1999, budget actors were not adhering to new rules on several important occasions. The implementation of fiscal laws was prevented by follow-up budget bills that put a halt on agreed targets, postponing compliance to an uncertain future and, hence, undermining the whole concept of fiscal responsibility. When Argentina came under pressure after a series of external shocks to its economy, the government lacked the 'institutional tools' that might have allowed a faster adjustment to changing external conditions. Instead, as with 'Murphy's law', almost everything that could possibly go wrong went wrong. At the point where the government had effectively lost access to international markets and where it was denied any further financial assistance from international institutions, the default on external private debt became unavoidable.

6.2 FISCAL IMBALANCE IN ARGENTINA

Below, I provide a brief overview of government balances over time, before I describe how expenditure and revenue evolved, both on the national and subnational levels of government. After that, I take a closer look at changes in the public debt, before I turn to potential institutional explanations for fiscal outcomes, in sections 6.3 and 6.4.

6.2.1 Fiscal Results

6.2.1.1 General and central government

At the beginning of the 1990s, government revenue benefitted from economic growth and improved tax collection, allowing the government to secure budget surpluses until a turning point was reached in 1995 when the balance declined sharply as a consequence of the Mexican Tequila crisis. In 1996, the nominal central government budget deficit stood at 2 percent of GDP, and although the deficit dropped for 2 years, it continuously increased after 1998. The drop in the deficit in 2002 can be understood as a consequence of the first large-scale restructuring of Argentina's (external) debt, leading to a significant reduction in debt-financing expenditure. In that same year, the newly inaugurated government of interim President Ernesto Duhalde (2002–2003) also decided to drop the convertibility system and move towards a managed float, making it easier for the government to fill its financing gap. In the following years, the beginning economic boom – GDP growth picks up again, reaching 8.8 percent in 2003 – facilitated a return to budget surpluses.

Looking at the budget situation (Figure 6.1), net of debt-financing costs, which is indicated in the primary result, we see that primary surpluses decreased continuously from the beginning of the 1990s until they turned into a small deficit of 0.33 percent of GDP in 1996. Afterwards, Argentine primary budget results improved significantly over a period of three years, reaching a surplus of over 1.2 percent of GDP in 1999. However, the economic recession beginning in 1999 caused both GDP and government revenue to fall severely, leading the primary balance to drop to 0.54 percent of GDP in 2001. In September 1999, the government reacted by proposing a new 'Fiscal Solvency Law' (Law 25.152),[5] trying to commit itself to return to a balanced budget by 2003 in order

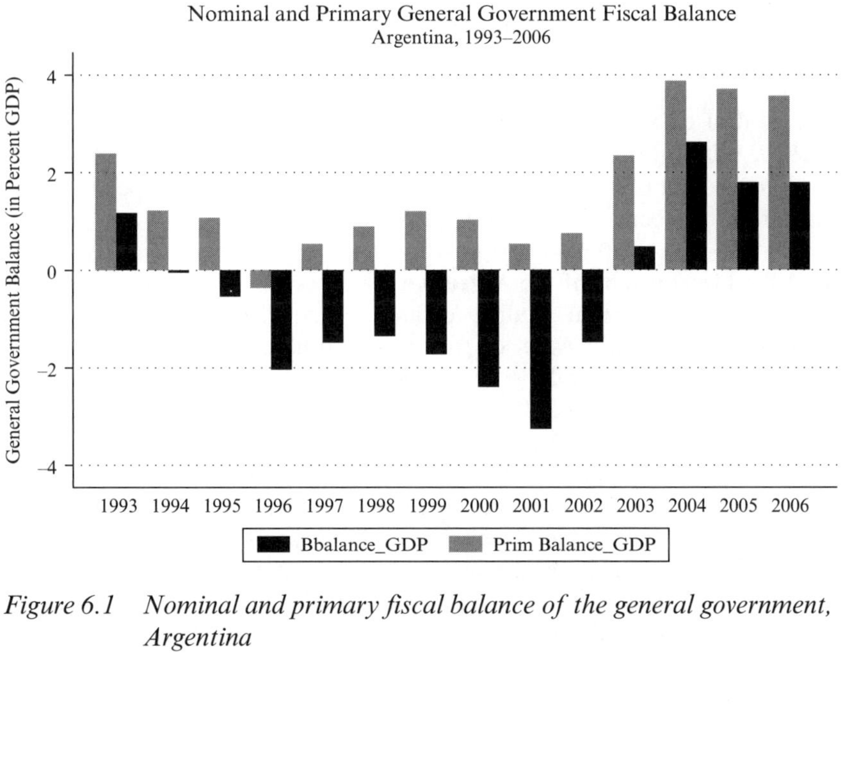

Figure 6.1 Nominal and primary fiscal balance of the general government, Argentina

to reduce the public-debt-to-GDP ratio. Specifically, the FRL includes a rule that primary public expenses may not be increased beyond the GDP's increase rate. Expenditure is generally not allowed to increase until the budget is balanced.[6] With the aim of guaranteeing that the government could react to those fiscal imbalances resulting from external shocks, the Fiscal Solvency Law initiated an 'anti-cyclical fiscal fund', to be filled with a portion of current resources (2 percent) and of capital resources (50 percent) annually until it reached 3 percent of GDP. Finally, public debt is prohibited from increasing beyond the fiscal deficit and other causes expressly set forth. As we know today, the government in the end remained unable to reach such ambitious targets in 1999. What followed instead were a large-scale sovereign debt default, currency devaluation and a massive restructuring of outstanding debt in the years that followed. Throughout the year 2000, the government fell short of the negotiated primary fiscal targets in every quarter. The actual establishment of an anti-cyclical fund was halted by annual decrees beginning in 2000 and has not been picked up again by any government despite strong economic growth and increasing government revenue since 2003. Although there can be little doubt that the devaluation and financial crisis in Brazil led to soaring debt-financing costs for Argentina, contributing significantly to the rise in public debt, it should also be noted that structural imbalances preceded the soaring interest rates on Argentine and other emerging market debt after the Brazilian devaluation.[7] This becomes even more apparent when we take a look at primary fiscal budget data, net of privatization gains (Table 6.1). We observe that the total government budget deficit came close to 3 percent of GDP already in 1998, increasing to almost 5 percent of GDP in 1999. Without the large one-time revenue from privatization, the average total government fiscal deficit would have been more than 5 percent over the period between 1992 and 2001 (Table 6.1).

6.2.1.2 Fiscal results of the Argentine provinces

According to nominal budget estimates provided by the Economic Commission for Latin America (not reported here), deficits for the provinces gradually deteriorated in the early 1990s, from a deficit of −0.1 of GDP in 1992, the first year for which data are available, to −1.26 percent in 1995, the year after the Mexican crisis. Following two 'fiscal pacts', negotiated between the government of Carlos Menem and the provinces in 1992 and 1993, in which the provinces agreed to stabilize their budgets in return for a fixed amount of federal transfers and the nationalization and restructuring of the loss-making provincial pension system, provincial accounts improved significantly for two years after 1995.

However, this trend turned around again in 1998 and provincial deficits

Table 6.1 Primary fiscal outcomes excluding privatization gains, Argentina

	Fiscal Results of the Central Govt and Provinces in Percent GDP		
Year	Central Govt	Provinces	Total
1992	−0.11	−0.29	−0.40
1993	0.14	−0.88	−0.74
1994	−1.14	−0.92	−2.06
1995	−2.34	−1.37	−3.71
1996	−2.98	−0.68	−3.66
1997	−1.54	−0.47	−2.01
1998	−1.79	−0.83	−2.62
1999	−3.00	−1.63	−4.63
2000	−2.18	−1.16	−3.34
2001	−3.87	−2.42	−6.29
Average	−1.88	−1.07	−5.36

Source: Economy Ministry of Argentina

increased significantly to almost 1.5 percent of GDP (−1.63 percent of GDP without privatization gains; see Table 6.1) in 1999, peaking at more than 2.3 percent of GDP (2.4 percent) in 2001. Also, when looking at the average provincial deficit of 1 percent of GDP in the period between 1992 and the crisis year of 2001, the Argentine provinces fared relatively worse than the Brazilian states, which were able to secure a slight surplus over roughly the same period.[8] Although the central government agreed with the IMF in September 2000 to restructure the provincial accounts to stop their fast deterioration and growing debt accumulation, provincial fiscal outcomes continued to deteriorate. Figure 6.2, showing the nominal and primary provincial fiscal deficit (before and after capital gains) clearly indicates the deterioration in provincial fiscal results, beginning in 1998. If we look at the line indicating the primary deficit, it turns out that the temporal financial recovery of the provinces and the primary surplus in 1997 was mainly due to capital gains during that time.

It was not until after the sovereign default declaration and the forced devaluation of the peso in 2002 that the federal government was able to reach a renewed agreement with the provinces about their adherence to a new Fiscal Responsibility Law, passed in 2004. With the introduction of the FRL, which foresees balanced budgets and expenditure limits that also apply to the provinces, provincial primary fiscal surpluses started to

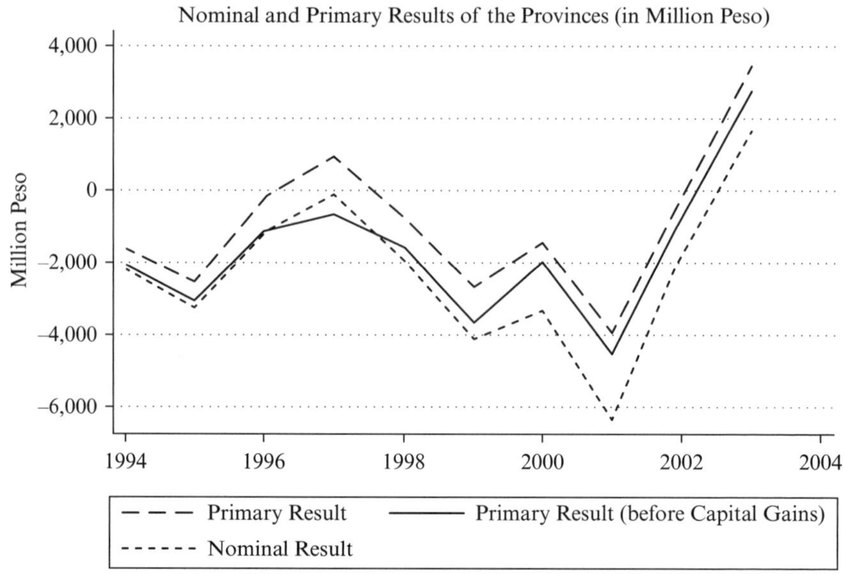

Source: Data from the Economy Ministry, Argentina

Figure 6.2 Fiscal results of the Argentine provinces, 1993–2004

increase from 2003. Surpluses then increased over the following years of economic recovery. However, a recession-related decline in government revenue led to a renewed provincial primary fiscal deficit of 0.72 percent of GDP in 2009, according to data reported in Artana et al. (2012, p. 7, based on data from the Economic Ministry and the authors' own calculations).

6.2.2 Government Expenditure

6.2.2.1 General and central government

From the beginning of the 1990s, general government nominal expenditure continuously expanded until 1995 when it leveled out at around 19–20 percent of GDP for a couple of years. From 1997 onwards, expenditure relative to GDP grew again until the height of the macroeconomic crisis in 2001, peaking at more than 22 percent of GDP, up from roughly 18 percent in 1993. (See Figure 6.3.)

At the peak of the default crisis, we observe that government expenditure fell sharply by roughly 3 percent of GDP between 2001 and 2002. Since then, we see a continuous growth trend and the Argentine government's outlays, measured in percentage of GDP, reached pre-crisis levels

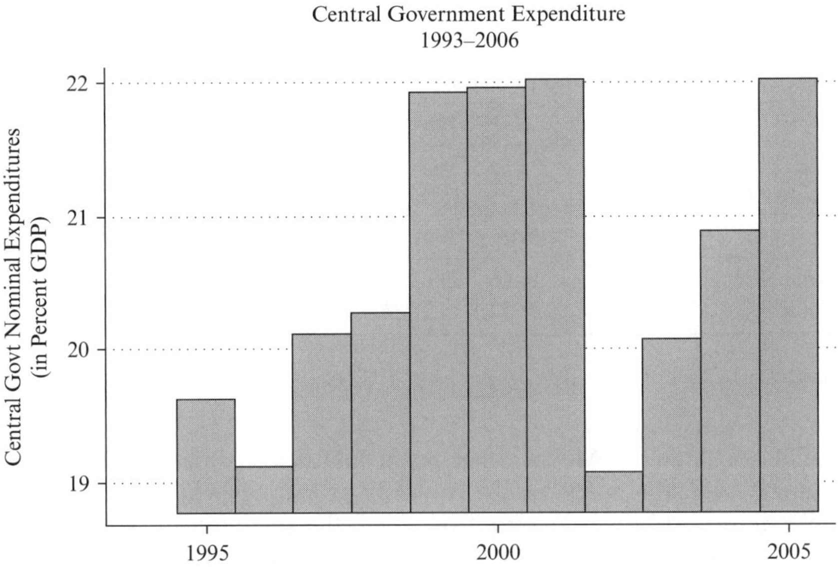

Figure 6.3 *Nominal central government outlays (including loans), Argentina*

Table 6.2 *Primary expenditure, Argentina*

General Government Primary Expenditures (in Percent GDP)											
1993	1994	1995	1996	1997	1998	1999	2000	2001	2002	2003	2004
24.12	24.58	24.33	23.46	22.64	23.11	25.06	24.20	25.58	21.95	22.80	23.50

Source: Economy Ministry, Treasury Secretary, Republic of Argentina

in 2005 and increased further in the following years. To see whether the high level of expenditure is mainly related to high interest rates beginning in 1999, a look at the primary expenditure data, net of debt service expenditure, seems warranted. Table 6.2 presents data for total government primary expenditure, between 1993 and 2004, available from the Argentine Economy Ministry. According to the data, primary expenditure increased from 1998, after it fell between 1996 and 1997, following the first Fiscal Solvency Law. Primary expenditure soared in the election year 1999 and remained high until the default in 2001. Afterwards, for the two years in which Argentina was effectively excluded from the financial markets and

Table 6.3 General and central government budget revenue, Argentina

Government Revenues, 1993–2006							
	1993	1994	1995	1996	1997	1998	1999
Total Govt Revenue*	25.54	24.41	23.4	22.2	23.44	23.33	23.95
Central Govt Revenue**	19.21	18.75	19.1	17.09	18.64	18.9	20.25
	2000	2001	2002	2003	2004	2005	2006
Total Govt Revenue	24.96	23.62	23.79	26.75	28.69	nn	nn
Central Govt Revenue	19.57	18.78	17.62	20.54	23.48	23.78	24.22

Sources: * Economy Ministry of Argentina **EIU data

could not draw on IMF or other bi- or multilateral financial assistance, primary expenditure fell visibly. However, primary expenditure picked up once more and kept increasing from 2003, the year after the government finally decided to abandon the convertibility system. In 2003, Argentine growth also returned to high levels, rising above 8 percent for the next half-decade. Government revenue also rose after 2003 (Table 6.3). Taken together, this suggests that spending in Argentina remains pro-cyclical.

6.2.2.2 Subnational government expenditure

Expenditure data for the Argentine provinces between 1990 and 2001 show a significant increase at the beginning of the decade (Figure 6.4). Under the first Menem administration (1989–1995), the provinces were burdened with increased spending responsibilities in health and education. Remmer (2007, pp. 366–7) argues that the crux of extensive provincial expenditure was increased personnel expenditure, as a consequence of a 40 percent increase in public employment in the course of the 1980s. According to her study, that trend persisted into the 1990s, 'with spending on provincial administration more than doubling between 1990 and 1995 alone'. A visible improvement in provincial finances was made after the federal government struck a deal with the provinces – the 'Fiscal Pact' of August 1992. This first fiscal pact cut through the rules on fiscal transfers established in the Coparticipation Law of 1988 that defined the quotas from a shared tax pool to the provinces. Given their weak fiscal position, the provinces signed an agreement that allowed central government to divert 15 percent of revenue from the shared tax fund back to the social security system. At the same time, central government guaranteed to provide the provinces with pre-fixed minimal monthly transfers equivalent to their respective expenditure in 1992 (US$725 million). In the following year, a second fiscal

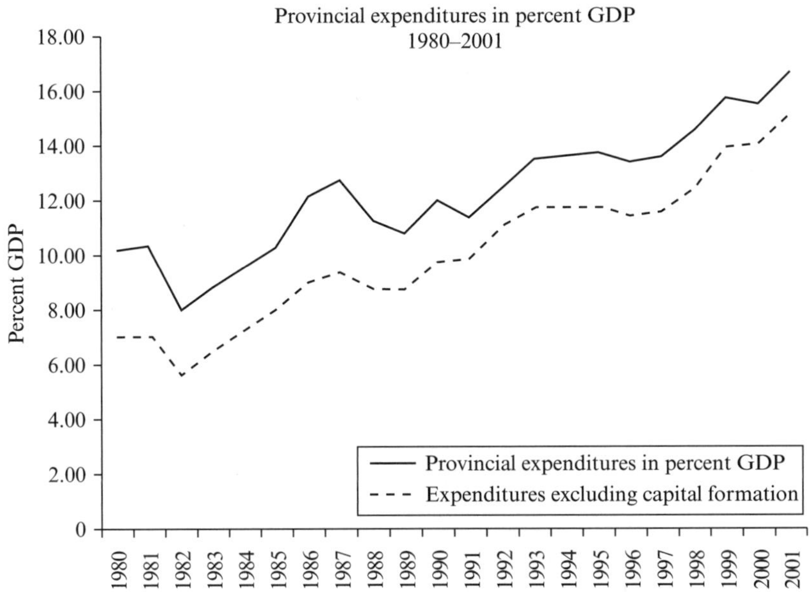

Source: Data from Universidad Torquato di Tella, as cited in Remmer (2007)

Figure 6.4 Nominal provincial expenditure, Argentina

pact was signed that led to the integration of the (loss-making) provincial pension funds into the federal pension system. The provinces were once more granted a pre-fixed amount of monthly transfers, raised by roughly 2 percent compared to the previous year.

As a consequence of the two fiscal pacts, the increase in provincial expenditure slowed down between 1993 and 1995, stabilizing at around 10 percent of GDP. However, beginning in 1997, the outlays of the provinces increased once more. During the recession starting in 1999, we observe rapidly growing primary expenditure (i.e. before capital expenditure), arriving at roughly 14 percent of GDP in the crisis year of 2001. Looking at Figure 6.5, displaying primary provincial expenditure in absolute peso values (after transfers to the municipalities), we observe a steady increase, slowing down only gradually in the second recession year in 2000 and once more in 2002 after an agreement with the federal government over 'transitory provincial financing' (i.e. an increase in federal transfers), starting in the following year, in return for provincial adherence to the Fiscal Responsibility Law sanctioned in 2004. Between 2001 and 2004, primary provincial expenditure increased by almost 43 percent.

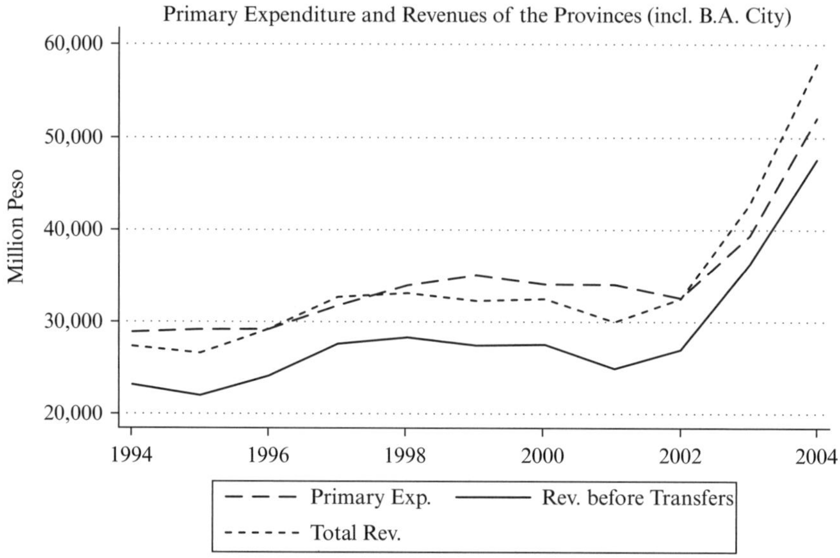

Source: Data from the Argentine Economy Ministry

Figure 6.5 Provincial primary expenditure and revenue, Argentina

Given the economic boom, which means growing own-source revenue, and facilitated by a big increase in federal transfers after the 2002 agreement with the federal government, the high and increasing levels of expenditure do not weigh too heavily on budget outcomes. However, as Artana et al. (2012, p. 7) observe, the high level of provincial expenditure turns out to be problematic once more, given rapidly falling revenue during the 2009 recession, provoking a return to a primary subnational deficit of close to 1 percent of GDP.

6.2.3 Government Revenue

6.2.3.1 General and central government

The revenue of the central government visibly suffered during the economic recession following the external macroeconomic shocks in 1994 and 1999, although the decline was deeper and longer after the second crisis in which Argentina lost badly, competitively, compared to Brazil. It was not until after the devaluation early in 2002 that central government revenue started growing again, at an average annual rate of 1.67 percent of GDP between 2004 and 2006. A driving factor of the recent increase in central government revenue is the introduction of new taxes and tariffs during the debt crisis in 2001. These include the re-introduced export tariffs and a financial transaction tax that had been abolished in the early 1990s, improving, above all, the revenue base of the central government. Bonvecchi (2010) notes that in addition to increasing revenue from the income and value-added taxes, during the economic recovery, starting in 2003, revenue from export duties and the reintroduction of the Bank Debits Tax contributed fundamentally to growing central government fiscal surpluses after 2002.[9] These particular revenue sources strengthened the financial leverage of the federal government, given that they remained almost exclusively with the latter.[10]

Hence, while the general tax burden increased by 5.80 points of GDP between 1998 and 2005, the lion's share is collected and kept by central government and the provinces only receive a share equivalent to 0.2 percent of GDP (Artana 2007). Additionally, post-devaluation inflation helped the government to stabilize its fiscal stance because, in spite of growing inflation rates, income tax (both for individuals and corporations) was not indexed, benefitting government revenue.

In sum, looking at Table 6.4, it can be said that post-crisis taxation in Argentina was significantly higher than during the Menem administration, which was characterized by tax reductions and declining revenue for the central and the general government.[11] Cross-country data on the overall tax burden in Latin American countries from the UN Economic Commission for Latin America and the Caribbean (CEPAL) show that in 2007, taxation in Argentina reached levels higher than in the previous decade and also much higher than in the rest of Latin America (except Brazil), coming close to levels seen in industrialized countries.[12]

Table 6.4 Vertical fiscal decentralization: revenue and expenditure, Argentina

Vertical Fiscal Decentralization in Argentina, 2004			
Area of Decentralization	Central Govt.	Provinces	Municipalities
Total Expenditures	57.3	35.2	7.5
Primary Expenditures	50.6	40.6	8.8
Total Revenues	54.8	37.8	7.4
Taxes and Soc. Security Contributions	66.4	33.4	0.2

Source: IMF-GFS

6.2.3.2 Provincial revenue

Total provincial revenue dropped due to the crisis in 1995, picking up once more in the following year until it exceeded expenditure for the first time in 1997. In the years that followed, until the new agreement on increased federal transfers in 2002, total provincial revenue remained below the level of expenditure, explaining the rapid growth in provincial (external) debt. Figure 6.5 indicates the gap between provincial own-source revenue (before federal transfers) and total revenue, revealing a substantial transfer dependence. In the literature, the high degree of transfer dependence of (Argentine) subnational governments is often taken as an indication of soft budget constraints. Looking at Figure 6.5, it becomes obvious that until the mid-2000s a relatively high level of transfers has prevailed, despite the fact that provincial revenue grew after 2002 to levels that would demand significantly lower transfers. At the same time, there are no known initiatives to 'save' the extra revenue in any kind of 'bad weather fund' arrangement. Hence, it seems that what we observe are more of the same 'old habits'. Own-source revenue declines relative to federal transfers. For a number of post-crisis years, given the increasing revenue, this factor did not translate into growing provincial deficits. However, during the recent recession in 2009 the provinces accumulated a primary deficit of almost 1 percent of GDP.

6.2.4 Public Debt

6.2.4.1 General and central government

At the conclusion of its Brady deal in 1992, putting an end to the 1980s debt crisis, Argentina was left with a manageable public debt burden of less than 30 percent of GDP (see Figure 6.6). However, in the following years, reflecting the gradual increase in total government expenditure and declining revenue, public debt relative to GDP grew continuously. In the five years before the Brazilian crisis (1993–1997), public debt relative to GDP grew significantly by more than 17 percent (43 percent between 1993 and 1999).[13] Given the high real interest rates, soaring to two-digit numbers in 1998 (see Table 4.3 in Chapter 4), there is little doubt that a large share of the growth in public debt ratios must be attributed to unfavorable financing conditions.

Additionally, a significant increase in overall government debt in 1998, attributed to the government's official recognition of previously unrecorded debt in the previous year, put the government in a difficult position (Sturzenegger and Zettelmeyer 2006, p. 169). As Figure 6.6 shows, public debt ratios, both at the central and subnational government level, began to increase prior to the rise in debt-financing costs in 1998. And

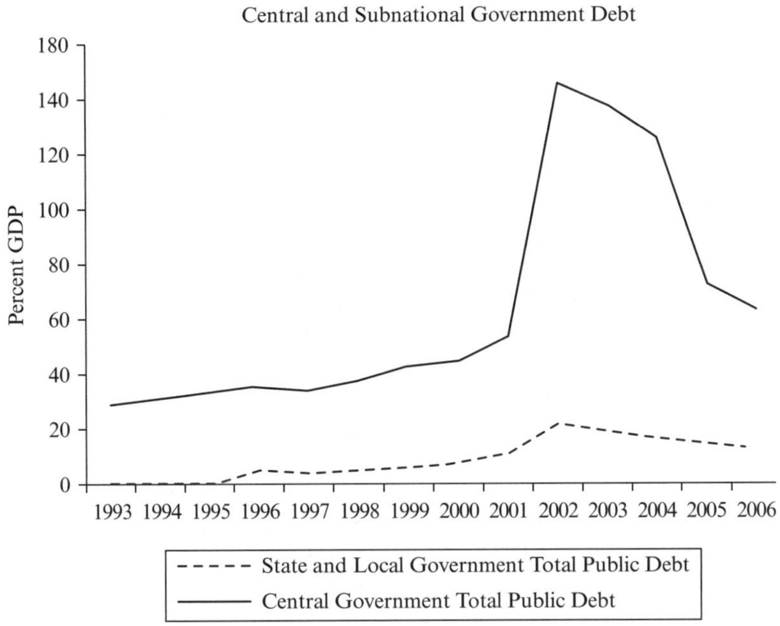

Source: Data from ECLAC 2009

Figure 6.6 Central and subnational government debt, Argentina

although real interest dropped significantly below the 10 percent mark in 2000, public debt in that year grew by more than 2 percent of GDP. Given rising creditor concern about the risk of sovereign default over the course of the recession, culminating in skyrocketing bond spreads in 2001 – with over 1355 basis points on average in that year, compared to an average annual bond spread of 570 in 1999 (and 292 bp in 1997) – and the forced currency devaluation and appreciation of the peso at the beginning of 2002, public debt had risen sharply to 146 percent of GDP by the end of that year.[14]

After three major restructurings of Argentina's public debt over the following years, involving major haircuts for private investors, the public debt ratio dropped significantly to roughly 64 percent of GDP in 2006. Although, without doubt, the debt restructuring meant a remarkable reduction in Argentina's debt in 2006, the country was left with a public-debt-to-GDP ratio that was more than twice as large as the one after the signing of the Brady deal in 1992 that put an end to the 1980s debt crisis.

6.2.4.2 Provincial debt creation

Figure 6.6, based on ECLAC data, also shows the evolution of subnational government debt relative to GDP. Between 1993 and 1995, the provinces did not accumulate any noticeable debt, however the situation changed in the years after the Mexican crisis and provincial debt stood at 5.1 percent of GDP in 1996. After a year of declining provincial debt in 1997, the debt ratio picked up once more and increased significantly until the debt restructuring and federal bailout for provincial debt in 2002. The hike in provincial debt was followed by a federal government bailout, assuming $11 billion of provincial debt, equivalent to 10.8 percent of GDP (Sturzenegger and Zettelmeyer 2006).[15] The average annual growth rate of provincial debt during that period corresponds to about 4 percent of GDP. After the debt restructuring, the public debt ratio falls at an average annual rate of more than 2 percent of GDP. Again, we observe a significant increase in the debt ratio prior to the deterioration of debt-financing conditions. In 2002, the subnational debt ratio peaked at 22 percent of GDP. Although it declined after the default, the public debt ratio of the provinces still remained above pre-crisis levels at the end of the 2000s.

In 1999, Argentina's creditors began to worry about the government's ability to stay current on its debt service not 'only' because the public-debt-to-GDP ratio was increasing. Other factors played important roles, putting a question mark over the government's ability to tackle the debt problem in due time. These included the fact that the growth in external debt in the second half of the 1990s had increasingly been financed with short-term debt. According to data presented by Roubini and Setser (2004), short-term debt grew from roughly 30 percent of exports to close to 90 percent between 1994 and 1999. In addition, Argentina's decreasing exports after Brazil's devaluation in January 1999 led to a soaring total-debt-to-exports ratio, another crucial indicator for investors. Between 1997 and 1999, the ratio of total public debt (i.e. public and publicly guaranteed debt) to exports had jumped from 38 to 52 percent. That ratio remained at around 50 percent until it jumped to more than 160 percent in the default year of 2001, falling below 100 percent only after the final restructuring deals were signed in 2005.

Taken together, decreasing economic growth in 1999, an increasingly unfavorable borrowing climate, the acknowledgement of previously hidden debts and, additionally, a large amount of debt coming due in the spring of 2001, all increased the pressure on Argentina's fiscal position. Yet, the government did not come up with a fiscal adjustment strategy comparable to that put forth by President Cardoso in Brazil when the real had come under pressure and debt ratios were soaring. Instead, the government of President de la Rua relaxed fiscal targets and failed to strike a deal with the provinces over a reduction in subnational deficits and debt reduction. The conflict with the provinces was not settled until after the debt default.

Looking at the pre-crisis data, there is evidence that government finances had already been suffering from structural problems before the external shocks. As the evidence presented above suggests, subnational fiscal problems were a relevant structural weakness. They were obviously related to spending pressure given the (flawed) institutional incentives inherent in the country's (fiscally) federal system. After Argentina's default and subsequent large-scale debt reductions, the remaining ratio of central government debt to GDP, the relatively slow progress in reducing public debt at the lower levels of government, and the rising trend in inflation, all certainly point to a remaining risk of fiscal crisis and debt instability in the future.

6.3 FISCAL DECENTRALIZATION, BUDGETARY INSTITUTIONS AND FISCAL PERFORMANCE

Argentina is often characterized as a country with highly centralized political institutions, notwithstanding its strong federal tradition. One reason is that according to the constitution of 1983, the president holds relatively strong veto powers over Congress. Additionally, the president can rely on constitutionally granted, far-reaching decree powers. Often, the perception of Argentina's political system as a centralized institutional model is based on a considerable 'Menem bias'. By this I mean a tendency to over-estimate presidential control, in particular in the budget-making sphere, based on the impression that was left by President Carlos Menem (1989–1999) during his first term, when his party held a majority in both houses of the Argentine Congress and controlled the majority of governorships in the 24 provinces (including Buenos Aires City). However, partisan-based dominance of the political space, which may be interpreted as 'centralization' of the political process, is not the same as a centralization of the budget process in the way that I described above (in Chapter 3). In contrast, given Argentina's budgetary institutional characteristics, it appears that presidents sometimes have a very hard time implementing fiscally responsible policies. Part of this weakness is related to the high reliance on discretionary solutions. The high dependence of various budget actors on discretionary funds makes the president very powerful during the good times. However, during economic downturns (and periods of decreasing government revenue), presidents lose their ability to rely on a system of 'pork and perks' to build political coalitions (Braun 2006, p. 39).

In the following sections, I focus on the institutions that shape fiscal policies in Argentina, in an attempt to correct the common 'Menem bias' persistent in many descriptions. As before, I start by describing how budgetary institutions (horizontal decentralization) evolved over the time period covered (1990–2006) before I discuss vertical decentralization and its effects on overall fiscal performance. Fiscal policy making in the past and present in Argentina tends to be affected by considerable CPR problems. Since the beginning of the 1990s, CPR problems appear to have been solved, with few exceptions, by increasing spending and borrowing, both on the national and subnational levels of government. Although the federal government took several initiatives to reform fiscal rules, governments to date have either failed to respect the new rules whenever the economic situation worsened or have willingly abandoned the rules in an attempt to win political support from those groups that would have lost under a strict application. In response to macroeconomic crises, including the Mexican crisis in 1994 and the economic crisis in 1999, political pressure on the federal government has increased. Various budget actors have requested compensation for their losses through increased transfers. With regard to the potentially destabilizing role of subnational fiscal behavior, it seems that the remaining soft budget constraints on subnational budget actors continue to be a threat to overall fiscal stability, at least when economic growth and government revenue should drop again.

6.3.1 Horizontal Fiscal Institutions

Relying on the Index of the Inter-American Development Bank as a measure of decentralization in national-level budgetary institutions, Argentina's budget process during the 1990s appeared more decentralized than that of the average Latin American and Caribbean country. Not only do the country's budgetary institutions appear to be more decentralized than in any other economically advanced countries in the region including Chile and Ecuador, but Argentina's budget process in the early period seems less coordinated than in neighboring Brazil, a country that shares many similarities, including a long tradition of fiscal federalism. Unlike in Brazil, the degree of budget process decentralization in Argentina does not change significantly over time, although, according to the second, most recent IADB survey on budgetary institutions (Filc and Scartascini 2004), Brazil has undergone a remarkable reform process. In contrast, Argentina made less effort here, and the distance between the two countries has widened significantly.[16] Given the shift towards more centralized budget processes and increased transparency in Brazil, the question naturally arises as to why Argentina fell behind so much in comparison.

6.3.1.1 Reform initiatives

To begin with, it was not obvious during the first half of the 1990s that Argentina would fall behind Brazil in terms of institutional improvement. With Argentina taking a lead in exchange-rate-based price stabilization and other pro-market reforms during the first term of President Menem, many observers might have expected a different result. Indeed, over the 1990s and 2000s, Argentine governments have at different points made efforts to improve budgetary decision making, attempting to allow for more stable government fiscal outcomes, in line with other macroeconomic stabilization policies.

First, in September 1992 the Menem administration introduced a new Financial Administration Law (No. 24.156), which set out new rules and procedures defining the budget process on the national level. The law introduced, for the first time, a single account and quantitative fiscal targets into the public administration at the budget formulation stage, included numerical restrictions on budgetary amendments by Congress, and aimed more generally at providing the executive with more control over the allocation of funds and a centralization of the budget process in the Economic (and Financial) Ministry (Bonvecchi 2010). It also led to the creation of two monitoring agencies – one overseeing Congress and the other the executive – which, however, remain politically dependent to date.

Over the course of the early 1990s, the government discussed several steps to improve subnational fiscal discipline. First, the federal government focused on implicit and explicit bailout guarantees given to subnational governments. A ministerial resolution was introduced to prohibit any federal agency from using its resources to pay a creditor on behalf of a province, thus banning explicit or implicit debt bailouts granted to certain provinces in earlier years. Additionally, the central government had hoped to prevent future bailouts by changing the Central Bank Charter in September 1992, reducing the role of the bank as a 'lender of last resort'. Second, by banning the use of coparticipation transfers as collateral in debt contracts with private (external) creditors, the federal government tried to constrain subnational debt expansion, inhibiting a crucial financing instrument. Until then, the provinces had often relied on the expected revenue from automatic coparticipation transfers as collateral in debt contracts with public and commercial banks. Third, starting in 1991 with the introduction of the convertibility plan, the government had already stopped the provincial governments from rediscounting their debt at the Central Bank. Since the late 1980s, when inflation reached its highest levels, provincial governments have been used to financing a large share of their expenditure by borrowing from provincial banks, which, in turn, rediscounts the credits at the Central Bank. This practice allowed the provincial banks to 'export' their credit risk to the nation, meanwhile reaping the benefits from the inflationary policies of central government. By 1990, provincial banks were providing more than 60 percent of the credit needs of provincial governments, at very low or zero interest rates (Webb 2003, p. 194). In the 1990s, provincial debt grew rapidly and the Central Bank lent large amounts through rediscounts in an attempt to prevent provincial bank collapse, given the poor recovery of loans and extensive personnel expenditure.[17] Finally, to ensure that the provincial debt was paid, Bancode la Nacion, which was responsible for distributing the coparticipation transfers, was given the authority to hold back funds in the amount of debt service to be paid by the provinces before transfers were distributed.

In addition to these policy measures, the federal government aimed to take control of growing subnational spending through the so-called 'Fiscal Pacts' in 1992 and 1993. Under the first pact reached in August 1992, the federal government agreed to increase inputs into the subnational social insurance system but reduced transfers to the provinces in equal amounts. To ensure continued provincial solvency, the federal governments decided to fill up the provincial accounts through transfers needed to keep the overall budget at the same level as in 1992. However, it soon became evident that a reshuffling of central funds was not sufficient to back up the provincial finances. Large financial holes in the provincial pension systems led central government to finally take control of pension funds and absorb provincial debts in the second Fiscal Pact in 1993. Furthermore, the federal government agreed to an increase in minimum fixed transfers to the provinces.

With the beginning economic downturn that was triggered by the Mexican crisis in 1994/95, however, central government soon came under pressure from the provinces to allow the continued use of transfers as collateral and to turn a blind eye to provincial bank rediscounting at the Central Bank.[18] This return to 'bad old habits' under the economic downturn seems likely to have encouraged the provinces to overspend, further fueling their borrowing, especially after the central government had decided to shift more spending responsibilities to the provinces. It is often argued that new fiscal and borrowing rules designed to harden budget constraints on the provinces during the first Menem administration never reached a point where they were regarded as credible, given the long history of bailouts and transgression of fiscal rules. Webb (2003, p. 199) notes that even after finance minister Cavallo's reach for more centralized borrowing control, the 'provinces were behaving as though they had a soft budget constraint'. In the aftermath of the mid-decade economic downturn, provincial debts increased greatly.

Nevertheless, given successful stabilization through increased central control over subnational government in the early and mid-1990s, it is somewhat puzzling to see the government incapable of striking a comparable deal in the years that followed. One plausible explanation is that Menem missed the right moment to follow up on the fiscal pacts, with more fundamental reforms of budgetary institutions. It appears that from the mid-1990s onwards, Menem was increasingly losing the political and financial resources to win the needed political majorities for such a project. Another explanation could be that Menem simply had other policy priorities. Some historical facts speak to that point. For example, any attempts at signing another fiscal pact between the provinces and the federal government were abandoned in 1994, the year Menem struck a deal with the opposition leader, former President Raul Alfonsin, to win a political majority for a constitutional change that would allow a second presidential term. Clearly, the constitutional reform designed by the Constitutional Assembly of 1994 would increase Menem's power base. However, by definition it also increased the leverage of the opposition.[19] Asking for increased provincial fiscal adjustment – through another fiscal pact or fiscal responsibility legislation – was for that reason politically difficult. Instead, the federal government was requested by the 1994 Constitutional Assembly to come up with a new law that would re-organize (and ideally fill) the tax-sharing system by 1997.

Soon after the electoral victory in 1995, however, several economic and political events kept Menem from fulfilling his mandate to reform the tax-sharing system. The Mexican crisis in 1994/95 and electoral defeat in the mid-term elections in 1997, among other things, significantly reduced the government's room for maneuver, minimizing chances that the president could now take on the task of re-organizing subnational financing with the aim of making the existing system more efficient. Internal quarrels in his own coalition and growing despair among the governors of his own ruling coalition made a re-organization of federal-fiscal relations more and more unlikely. Clearly, for President Menem who had often relied on a system of 'pork and perks' to build political alliances, the air was becoming thinner during those years.

Being aware of the deterioration of the fiscal stance in general, the Menem administration started a second reform initiative in February 1996 with the passing of a new Fiscal Law (No. 24.629), which introduced multi-annual fiscal planning, specified fiscal targets for the following years and led to an increase in power of the executive with regard to changing the budget past the drafting stage. In line with the new law, the Argentine Congress tied its hands in fiscal matters, delegating its rights to make budgetary amendment (cuts) in areas where government branches were unable to identify sufficient revenue, matching expenditure, to the president. While this meant, *de jure*, a significant increase in central control of budget decisions, the law nevertheless fell short of specifying sanctions in the likely case of government agencies or individuals acting against the fulfillment of fiscal targets. Although, initially, the law included individual liabilities and penalties for budgetary actors that were not complying, these provisions were watered down in the approval process (Abuelafia et al. 2009).

Yet another reform initiative was taken in March 1998 when Congress started to debate a new budget law (No. 25.152), which became known in the process as the first 'Fiscal Solvency Act'. It included numerical rules and deficit ceilings for each of the following years, as well as a schedule for a reduction in the deficit, aiming at a balanced budget by 2003. Additional cornerstones of the law included, at least initially, the establishment of a 'Countercyclical Fiscal Fund' and the introduction of new budget transparency and information dissemination standards.

It should be noted, however, that despite these legislative acts, budget constraints had effectively become weaker by the late 1990s. This political reality at central government level, together with a total lack of regulation on the source or scope of provincial debt, added in no small amount to the erosion of the budget and borrowing control of the federal government. The lack of central control finally became very obvious during the 2001 economic and sovereign debt crisis. Provincial governments at the time took far-reaching fiscal decisions without the approval of the federal government. Several of the provinces began issuing their own bonds (bonos) as payment to suppliers or public employees in the absence of any federal government approval. As Wibbels (2004, p. 214) points out:

> (h)aving all of the characteristics of money, these bonos effectively appropriated the right of seignorage historically vested solely with the central government. In a troubled economic environment, each of these mechanisms contributed to extensive quasi-fiscal deficits, expansive monetary policy, and increased public indebtedness.

Provinces issuing their own script during the 2001 crisis included Buenos Aires, Salta, Jujuy, Catamarca, Tucumán and La Rioja.

Under economic pressure after Brazil's devaluation, earlier initiatives to reform fiscal institutions were soon abandoned. The first 'victim' in that sense was the earlier declared goal to reach a balanced budget in 2003. At the onset of the economic crisis, a congressional majority opted for a hold on the planned countercyclical fund and a drop in annual fiscal targets included in the 1999 Fiscal Solvency Act, shifting the deadline for a balanced budget several times into the (uncertain) future. Renewed initiatives of the federal government to force Congress into accepting fiscal austerity at the peak of the sovereign debt crisis in 2001 were equally doomed to fail. A radical austerity plan, presented by the newly inaugurated Minister of the Economy, Ricardo Lopez-Murphy, which foresaw among other things, a cut in educational spending, was dropped after three weeks of mass protest, forcing the minister to resign. Afterwards, a final, desperate attempt to reach a radical cut-down in the government's deficit, the so-called 'Zero Deficit Law', presented to Congress in July 2001 by Economic Minister, Domingo Cavallo, equally failed. Although the law was passed by Congress, the government never had a chance to implement any of its fiscal targets in the turmoil breaking out after the IMF decided to stop its payments to Argentina on December 5, 2001.[20] From the data presented above, one can easily see the government's inability to control debt expansion once the economic crisis was under way in 1999. Given the evolution of real interest rates between 1999 and 2001, it is questionable whether those fiscal policy reform initiatives, taken at the peak of the crisis, would have sufficed to achieve a stabilization of government finances without significant financial assistance and/or debt relief (e.g. Mussa 2002). However, even if a reform of budgetary institutions might have done little to prevent Argentina's insolvency in 2001, we might have expected to stake hurtful reform measures in the aftermath of the default. Although the government, pre-occupied with the immediate necessity to negotiate its debt with its creditors after the default declaration, did not make a fast move toward such fiscal institutional reform, a new Fiscal Responsibility Law was indeed sanctioned in 2004.

The new Fiscal Responsibility Law (No. 25917), which was introduced into Congress in June and passed soon after in August 2004, included for the most part the same measures that made up the 1999 Fiscal Solvency Act, such as fiscal balance targets, transparency standards and multi-annual budget planning. As per the previous version, the law set numerical limits on the growth of expenditure. However, as in previous cases of attempted institutional reform in Argentina, it remained questionable whether the new law led to a credible strengthening of budget constraints. Doubt remains, in particular with regard to control over provincial borrowing and the achievement of fiscal targets. The first reason to remain doubtful is the insufficient regulation of provincial borrowing. Although all external borrowing now has to be approved by subnational legislatures and Congress and the ratio between debt service and total revenue is limited to 15 percent of current revenue, net of transfers to municipalities, the government has put no constraint on the use of expected future tax-sharing transfers as collateral, a practice that has been identified to have severely weakened budget constraints in earlier periods. This practice clearly contributed to a large overhang of subnational debt on several occasions in the past, in particular during the half-decade before the collapse of the provincial finances in 2001 (Webb 2003).[21] A second reason for concern is that since 2004 the provinces have been exempt, through the passing of successive annual budget laws, from fulfilling spending limits and budget transparency requirements, defined by the FRL and sanctioned in that same year (Bonvecchi 2010).

The 2004 FRL ties the expansion of primary expenditure to GDP growth and the achievement of fiscal balance, both on the national and subnational levels. However, it grants exclusion of certain types of expenditure to the provinces. Finally, in an attempt to improve auditing and adherence to the new FRL, the law foresees the establishment of a new institution, the 'Federal Council of Fiscal Responsibility', charged with monitoring the FRL and reporting transgressions of the law. By way of the law, the new fiscal council includes Financial Ministry representatives from each province and the federal government, and has the power to enforce sanctions for deviations from the law (Braun 2006, p. 25). However, these sanctions appear relatively vague, varying from the publication of deviations to limits on federal government budgetary transfers to the provinces. Financial sanctioning could indeed, as in Brazil, provide the government with an effective tool to coordinate subnational fiscal behavior (more). However, it remains to be seen how effective this way of sanctioning fiscal indiscipline will turn out to be, given that transfers from the revenue-sharing system (i.e. the lion's share in transfers) are excluded and cannot be withheld in the case of non-compliance.[22]

6.3.1.2 Reflections on the rule by decree

While it remains a challenging task to present direct evidence that we observe fiscal deficits (mainly) because certain budgetary institutions were absent, there may still be indirect evidence supporting the general argument made above that the Argentine government was lacking control over the budget process. One such, admittedly rather imperfect, indirect measure of the government's control over the budget process could be the extent to which the president relied – and continues to do so – on 'emergency decrees' (Decreto de Necesidad y Urgencia or DNU) as a policy tool. It seems plausible that in the absence of regular budgetary institutional 'tools', allowing the president to submit and implement the necessary fiscal policies to improve budget outcomes, he was dependent on an alternative instrument – emergency decrees. Data presented in Kim (2012) show that, indeed, the use of DNUs increased significantly, for the first time after the return to democracy under the first Menem administration.[23] Over the full length of his time in office, between 1989 and 1999,

President Menem passed a total of 545 DNUs. Emergency decrees soared for a second time during the 1998 economic downturn until the peak of the economic and fiscal crisis in 2002. After the sovereign default and the inauguration of the new Justicialist government in 2002, the use of DNUs dropped significantly, however remaining above pre-crisis levels. The high number of DNUs issued under the administration of President Nestor Kirchner (2003–2007) – in total 270 Necessity and Urgency Decrees – stands out in particular, compared to the number of such decrees during the preceding administrations of President de la Rúa (73 decrees between 1999 and 2001). That means that even though Kirchner came to office in 2003, backed by a Justicialist party that won the congressional elections with a comfortable lead over all other parties (36 percent of the vote for the Justicialists, followed by 14.2 percent for the conservative UCR and 8 percent for the left-of-center ARI Party), the government relied on DNUs as a 'normal' policy tool. This continued reliance on DNUs seems even more remarkable after the electoral backing for the 'Kirchner system' in the 2007 presidential race. The newly elected President Christina Fernández de Kirchner (wife of Nestor Kirchner) now rules with an enlarged congressional majority, backed also by a majority of provincial governorships, including the powerful governor of the province and the mayor of the City of Buenos Aires.[24] Although Congress passed a law in 2006 that constrains the use of DNUs, allowing Congress to take back policy decisions implemented through a presidential decree, President Kirchner continues to rely on them as a policy tool in the areas of monetary and debt policy.[25] Structural inefficiencies in the budget process, as well as in the political decision-making process more generally, are hard to defy. While this evidence is far from providing direct proof of an ineffective budget process, it does suggest that presidents continue to prefer the decree option to having to go through the regular political decision-making process in different areas including fiscal and debt-related issues.

6.3.1.3 Increasing the share of discretional transfers to recentralize fiscal authority

When looking at Brazil, I discussed how a recentralization of revenue and an increase in the share of discretionary funds – so-called ATNs (*Aportes del Tresoro National*) – after 1994 provided the president with crucial additional resources he could later use as 'pork' to win subnational support for his fiscal stabilization agenda. Although we observe in Argentina during the second half of the first Menem administration a similar tendency to recentralize revenue, this did not lead to a similar outcome.[26] After the taxing authority of the president was increased and when tax revenue was readily available, President Menem could indeed rely on a larger amount of discretionary funds to win political support for two fiscal pacts with the provinces that successfully reduced provincial deficits in 1992 and in 1993 (Eaton and Dickovick 2004, p. 101).[27] However, Menem at that point missed an opportunity to introduce a more permanent institutional solution. As revenue was drying up, following on from a combination of the government's decision to reduce social security contributions in 1993 and a general decline in income tax and VAT revenue after the Mexican crisis in 1994 and, a second time after 1998, the president saw his financial leverage over the subnational provinces decline (Braun 2006). Reforms of the budgetary institutions with the objective to stabilize government finances, reducing the budget-making and borrowing autonomy of subnational governments, were increasingly hard to achieve. Indeed, rather than fiscal discipline we observe more of the opposite behavior. The federal government came increasingly under pressure from the provinces to augment transfers during the economic downturns in 1995 and 1998. Under the remaining soft budget and borrowing constraints, the provinces had strong incentives to either engage in intensified political bargaining with the president over discretionary funds, or resort to external borrowing (which remained largely unrestricted), or try a combination of both. As the data on revenue before and after federal transfers, presented above (Figure 6.5), indicate, they did succeed in securing transfers until the federal government was practically insolvent and incapable of transferring any more funds in 2001. Also, subnational borrowing increased after the federal government turned a blind eye to provincial borrowing activities (Figure 6.6).

6.4 SUBNATIONAL FISCAL DISCIPLINE UNDER HORIZONTAL DECENTRALIZATION

Argentina is a federal country both in political and in fiscal terms. Its fiscal federalism is characterized by a relatively centralized revenue system and, at the same time, by decentralized spending responsibilities. While the federal government currently collects roughly 76 percent of total tax revenue, this accounts only for about half of the total public expenditure.[28] Provincial own-source revenue is small compared to the Brazilian states and subnational governments in other federal countries. Also, own tax revenues vary significantly among the different provinces, based on their degree of industrialization (Remmer and Wibbels 2000).

To guarantee that subnational governments would be guaranteed sufficient revenue and to balance regional inequalities, the Coparticipation Law (Coparticipación Federal de Impuestos (CFI)) of 1988 spelled out the total share of transfers to the provinces in total (sharable) government revenue, defining specific quotas for each province.[29] Tax-sharing transfers, which are automatically distributed to the provinces according to fixed quotas – last modified by a constitutional reform in 1994 – constitute about 95 percent of total federal transfers to subnational governments. The constitutional changes of 1994 hence further 'lock in' the coparticipation system, making the specific rules and quotas very difficult to change in the political process. Beyond the potential to create policy inertia, these institutional choices allowed the Argentine provinces to remain highly dependent on transfers from the tax-sharing system. Federal transfers cover roughly 60 percent of their revenue. At the same time, subnational governments retain a relatively high degree of borrowing autonomy, although the center has at several times in the past decade tried to extend its control in that area. Taken together, the mix of expenditure autonomy, high transfer dependence and borrowing autonomy, certainly provide a fruitful ground for subnational imbalances (Rodden 2006).

In this section, I analyze the evolution of federal-fiscal relations under a decentralized spending scheme since the return to democracy. My aim is to show how central-level institutions affect the behavior of subnational budget actors. Furthermore, I highlight those areas in which institutional reform either did not take place at all or they failed to show sustainable improvements because laws were not respected, and subsequently, transgressions of the laws were not punished. Following the same pattern as in the previous chapter on Brazil, I proceed in two steps. First, I discuss how expenditure decentralization drives CPR problems at the subnational level. The goal is to show how – given the high degree of spending decentralization – subnational fiscal decisions depended on central-level institutional constraints. Second, I look at the revenue side and investigate why it is that under a pronounced and highly path-dependent revenue-sharing and transfer system, fiscal indiscipline becomes even more likely.

6.4.1 Expenditure Decentralization and Fiscal Imbalance

Judged by the share of subnational government expenditure in total government outlays, Argentina is a highly decentralized country, in comparison to other Latin American and Caribbean and also other federally organized countries (Figure 4.3).[30] Around 48 percent of total government expenditure is made by provincial and local governments, according to the IADB. However, several observers find that expenditure decentralization could be even greater than IADB estimates suggest.[31]

As a general trend, we observe that subnational spending responsibilities for crucial public goods increased significantly after the return to democracy (tables 6.4 and 6.5). The spending responsibilities of the

Table 6.5 Expenditure by sector and level of government, Argentina

Expenditures by Sector and Level of Government						
Sector	Central govt.		Provinces		Municipalities	
	1986	1994	1986	1994	1986	1994
Basic Education	33.7	0.4	63.7	96.5	2.6	3.2
Higher Education	83.9	78	16.1	22		
Health Care	14.8	12.7	75.3	73.7	10	13.6
Sanitation	32.4	7.9	67.6	92.1		
Housing	13.5	6.5	75.4	69.6	11.1	23.9
Social Welfare	65.9	16.2	34.2	83.8		
Urban Services			3.6	6.7	96.4	93.3
Total	70.8	54.2	25	38.5	4.3	7.3

Source: Sanguinetti (1995), as cited in IMF (1996 Vol 1: 11)

provinces (education, sanitation and social welfare) and of the municipalities (housing, health care, basic education) increased remarkably during the first Menem administration, as shown in Table 6.5 (see also Remmer and Wibbels 2000, Wibbels 2004).[32] Wibbels (2004, p. 220) suggests that Menem singled out spending areas that included high fixed costs like health, primary education and social welfare expenditure (see also Eaton and Dickovick 2004, p. 101). It is possible that the federal government hoped to improve subnational fiscal discipline by forcing provincial governors to prioritize better with regard to their spending. Increasing provincial obligations to provide services in the mentioned high fixed-cost areas might have led them to cut down on expenditure in other, more flexible areas. However, as was shown above, there is little evidence that the increasing delegation of expenditure responsibilities improves subnational fiscal discipline. Instead, it appears that expenditure increased after the central government decentralized spending authority to a larger number of budgetary veto players. We may observe the increase in subnational spending after the successful price stabilization with the introduction of the convertibility system in 1991. With increasing expenditure responsibilities, subnational budget actors soon started to put pressure on the federal government to grant them higher fiscal transfers. To counter the increasing demands made by the provinces, Menem engaged in two fiscal pacts, in 1992 and 1993. As discussed above, this effort to rein in subnational finances turned out to be only partly successful. Clearly, the pacts fell short of providing a sustainable solution to structural problems.

6.4.2 Subnational Revenue Autonomy

Compared with the high degree of decentralization in expenditure, fiscal authority in the area of revenue remains much more centralized. Based on data for the 1990s provided by Rodden (2002), subnational governments in Argentina had much less control over revenue than over expenditure. According to IMF GFS data, provincial and municipal revenue together equal only 18 percent of total government revenue during the 1990s, although domestic estimates by Daniel Artana (2007), based on data from the Argentine National Budget Office, suggest that own-source revenue of the provinces and municipalities increased significantly, making up 24.4 percent of total revenue in 2004.[33] Compared with other, federally organized emerging market nations – such as Brazil or India – or with OECD countries, including the USA and Switzerland, the subnational own-source revenue-raising capacity of Argentine subnational governments looks relatively less well developed.[34] It was mentioned earlier that during the first Menem administration the federal government engaged in reform with the aim of recentralizing tax revenue. By the 1983 constitution, the central government already had control over the majority of taxes.

The provinces were granted the exclusive right to levy taxes and define tax bases only in the area of property, motor vehicles and stamp taxes. The bulk of provincial revenue stems from the gross receipts tax (see Table 7.1 in Chapter 7), which is collected by the provinces as a piggy-back tax, in addition to a federal value-added tax (see Table 6.6). The share of revenue stemming from tax in which the provinces hold exclusive taxing authority, from property, stamp and vehicle taxes, is comparably small. One way that the Menem government tried to recentralize control over revenue was to reduce the proportion of tax that was shared by the nation and the provinces. Wibbels (2004, p. 219), based on other sources,

Table 6.6 Major provincial taxes, Argentina

Sources of Provincial Tax Revenue in 1994		
Type	Percent of Total	Exclusive Taxing Authority
Gross Receipts	56.2	no
Stamp	10.1	yes
Property	17.4	yes
Automobiles	9.9	yes
Other	6.4	depends

Source: Interior Ministry of Argentina, as cited in IMF (1996b, Vol2: p. 11)

finds that 'seven out of the eight major tax reforms initiated between 1989 and 1993 benefitted the nation by shrinking the provincial proportion of shared taxes'. Additionally, the government tried to gain more control by recentralizing tax bases that – by the constitution of 1983 – had been delegated to the subnational level (Remmer and Wibbels 2000, Wibbels 2004). Wibbels (2004) estimates that shared revenue for the provinces decreases by about 28 percent as a consequence of recentralizing policies. As indicated in the discussion on expenditure decentralization above, the reduction in provincial taxing authority is parallel to an increase in spending responsibilities.

The Argentine provinces vary significantly in their ability to collect own-source tax revenue. Based on data from the United Nations Economic Commission on Latin America (ECLAC) for 2002, the four most developed provinces (the Province of Buenos Aires, City of Buenos Aires, Cordoba and Santa Fe) together account for about 78 percent of all provincial revenue collected. In contrast, the eight least developed provinces (Corrientes, Chaco, Formosa, Jujuy, La Rioja, Misiones, San Juan and Santiago del Estero) collected little more than 5 percent of own-source provincial tax revenue. If we look only at the important gross receipts tax, the inequalities become even more obvious. Roughly 60 percent of the gross receipts tax is collected in the province and municipality of Buenos Aires, with another 20 percent of the total coming from the other three wealthy provinces – Mendoza, Cordoba and Santa Fe.

6.4.3 Mismatch between Expenditure and Revenue under Soft Central-level Constraints

Subnational own-source revenue has never matched subnational expenditure and, based on data from the Argentine Ministry of Economy (Figure 6.5), it is obvious that the gap between provincial revenue and expenditure increased between 1997 and 2001, narrowing only after the debt default in 2002 and the subsequent economic upswing. In a pre-crisis report, the IMF (1996b, p. 10) warned of an increasing decoupling of revenue from expenditure, giving rise to a growing subnational fiscal gap, noting that 'the present provincial (and local) revenue structure in Argentina is, and seems likely to remain, inadequate for even the richest provinces to become essentially self-financing'. Without doubt, after the historical decision in 1934 to give up taxing authority in return for federal transfers through a tax-sharing system, subnational governments have always been at risk of becoming too transfer-dependent. A crucial political question for Argentina therefore has to be how much transfer dependence is too much for the federal government to balance. As the quote from the pre-crisis IMF report suggests, government policies under the first Menem administration (1989–1991) tended to reduce the fiscal capacity of subnational governments to the extent that overall fiscal stability was put at risk. On the one hand, the provinces were given more spending responsibility in cost-intensive areas (most notably health). On the other hand, the federal government reduced provincial revenue authority, leaving them in a situation where they were structurally underfinanced. Wibbels (2004) argues that this decision was deliberately taken by Menem to force subnational governments to (better) prioritize their spending decisions. In order for subnational budget actors to cut spending in areas other than those delegated to them, budget constraints needed to be hard. In reality, however, they remained effectively soft. Subnational governments could still borrow and, in fact, were driven to increase their external borrowing under worsening economic conditions in 1994/95, using expected revenue transfers as collateral without federal government interference.

Alarmed by a big increase in subnational deficits during the first years of the Menem administration (1989–1991), which could no longer 'easily' be financed after the introduction of the convertibility system, the government sought an agreement with the provinces over enhanced budget discipline. Under the political constellation, the president's Justicialist (Peronist) Party, controlling the majority of the 24 governors, was able to strike a deal with the provinces in a relatively short time. These agreements, the fiscal pacts of 1992 and 1993, both aimed at reducing subnational fiscal imbalance in return for financial assistance and the integration of the loss-making provincial into the national pension system. However, they did not tackle the underlying mismatch between subnational revenue and expenditure. Rather than improving the subnational own-source revenue-raising capacity, they increased the subnational dependence on transfers. But, at the same time, the government refrained from making transfers conditional on the achievement of certain – long-term – fiscal consolidation. That is, the federal government never made a serious attempt to enforce fiscal conditionality. Increasing the transfer dependence of Argentine subnational governments, together with unconstrained borrowing opportunities, all under an increasingly uncoordinated and transparent budget process at the national level, contributed to growing fiscal imbalance and debt accumulation. For the purpose of future empirical analysis, it would be useful to model the effect of such subnational fiscal mismatch – by design of the fiscal-federal structure – under the conditions of more or less centralized budgetary institutions at the national level.

6.5 SUMMARY: HORIZONTAL AND VERTICAL DECENTRALIZATION IN ARGENTINA

Argentina may have been the poster child of pro-market reforms to international institutions and the financial world, but its weak budgetary institutions meant that the government had very little room for maneuver after the country was hit by a series of external shocks. Argentina, unlike Brazil, did not engage in any groundbreaking institutional reforms during good economic times. A recentralization of taxing rights, guaranteeing an increase in non-earmarked funds at the president's disposal, allowed Cardoso to use his financial leverage over the states. Financial aid was made conditional on states' fiscal discipline and debt reduction. In Argentina, the president did not have comparable discretionary funds at his disposal. Although President Menem successfully recentralized taxes during his first term, his political agenda was defined by a strong commitment to reducing the overall tax burden. As a consequence, the federal government was, by the end of the 1990s, in a weaker position vis-à-vis subnational governments. In the period following the fiscal pacts, when the federal government was relatively strong, it did not use this leverage over the provinces to reform fiscal institutions nor did it hold on to hard borrowing constraints on the provinces. The political window of opportunity soon closed and at the beginning of the economic crisis in 1998, the federal government's position, both financially and politically, was severely weakened. Menem's general emphasis on small government, reflected in declining government revenue until 1996 (Table 6.3), made it even harder for his successor to strike a deal with important budgetary veto players over fiscal austerity measures. The brief stint in office of Economy Minister Ricardo Lopez-Murphy, who was ousted only three weeks after his entering office, after mass protests against his fiscal adjustment plan presented to the Argentine public in March 2001, illustrates very well the government's reduced room for maneuvering. By the time sovereign risk premia had begun to soar to unforeseen levels, in mid-2001, expressing creditor fears about a nearing debt restructuring, the government – as most economic experts agree – had practically no space to implement a fiscal adjustment in the amount needed to even stabilize the debt ratio and achieve a reduction over the next few years.

NOTES

1. Andrew Powell (2002) is one of the prominent voices, having pointed out that the Argentine government's failure to re-arrange fiscal relations with the provinces was a main determinant of the crisis in 2001. Powell (2002, pp. 1–2) explicitly notes that,

'until the end of 2000 – and arguably even until the second quarter of 2001 – the fiscal adjustment that Argentina most certainly required to resolve its crisis was feasible. Instead, Argentina did virtually nothing. The real roots of the crisis had more to do with Argentina and the difficulties in effecting a fiscal adjustment than with the particular exchange rate regime. Argentina's crisis was avoidable. If some combinations of key events and decisions at particular moments had turned out differently, the crisis could have been averted . . . Had any one of these occurred, then the risk of default would have decreased'.

2. The Convertibility Law, which was enacted on March 27, 1991, and became effective on April 1, 1991, established a currency board with an explicitly legislated, fixed exchange rate of 10,000 Australes per US dollar. Future changes in the exchange rate were only possible through a renewed legislative act. The currency board was required to provide full backing in US dollars for any issue of Australes, and subsequently for the new peso that was introduced a little later. During the convertibility system, which was revoked by the Argentine Congress on January 6, 2002, through an Emergency Act, the US dollar was allowed as parallel legal tender.
3. Under the Convertibility Plan, inflation fell from a monthly rate of roughly 11 percent in March 1991 by 1.5 percent from 1991 onwards. What was even more remarkable than the short-term success was the fact that inflation stabilized at relatively low levels. Previous reform initiatives had failed to maintain whatever successful stabilization was achieved in the short run. By 1993 the yearly inflation rate had fallen to 8 percent.
4. An agreement in principle between Economy Minister, Domingo Cavallo, and international private creditors was reached on April 7, 1992.
5. The Fiscal Solvency Law (25.152) was preceded by a series of complementary laws passed in 1998, including the Law of Financial Administration and of the Systems of Control of the National Public Sector (24.156), the Investments National System law (24.354), the Complementary Rules law for the Budget Implementation and the Administrative Reorganization (24.629) and the Note of the Multiyear Budget implementation of the National Budget Office.
6. As was explained above, the growth in public debt is tied to the government's ability to reach certain primary budget targets. For a government to keep the public-debt-to-GDP ratio at least constant, it needs to reach a certain primary surplus, which depends on the difference between real interest rates and GDP growth.
7. In 1999, restructured debt that had been issued on low-interest terms in the early 1990s was coming due and had to be replaced by market debt at much higher interest rates.
8. Brazilian states reached a slight surplus of 0.2 percent of GDP on average during a comparable period, 1991–2000.
9. In a detailed account of fiscal reforms including taxation in Argentina since 1988, Bonvecchio (2010, p. 7) reports that the Bank Debits Tax and revenue from export duties jointly contributed revenue of around 4.5 percent of GDP, suggesting that 'if policy had otherwise remained the same, the entire public sector surplus is explained by extraordinary taxes introduced by way of emergency economic legislation'.
10. Revenue from export taxes remains exclusively with the federal government, and only one fifth of total revenue from the tax on financial transactions is distributed to the provinces, thus this is a very small share compared with their usual portion of shared taxes which is more than half on average.
11. The average revenue-to-GDP ratio between 1993 and 1999 for the central government is 23.75 percent, increasing to an average ratio of 25.56 percent of GDP in the period after 2000. For the central government, the increase in the average tax ratio is higher. Central government revenue increases from an average of 18.85 percent during the Menem years (1993–1999) to 21.14 percent of GDP in the post-Menem period (2000–2006).
12. In 2007, Argentina had an overall tax burden of 29.2 percent of GDP. Among Latin American countries, only Brazil has a higher tax burden (34.2 percent of GDP), coming close to levels in some of the industrialized countries, including New Zealand (33.7), Canada (34.6) and Spain (36.5) (ECLAC 2009).

13. The increase of the government-debt-to-GDP ratio by 17 percent over a period of five years in Argentina at the end of the 1990s compares well to current crisis cases in the European Union. In Greece, we observe an increase in the debt ratio by about 17 percent between the beginning of the 2000s and the crisis year of 2009, based on OECD public debt data for the central government. Yet, it needs to be taken into account that Greece's initial public debt ratio was much higher (108 percent of GDP) than Argentina's. Compared with Spain, where the public debt ratio increased by 53 percent in four years, starting at a level more comparable to Argentina (30 percent of GDP), Argentina's increase in the public debt ratio over the 1990s seems less disastrous.
14. Interestingly, although Argentina suffered from a significant increase in interest payments relative to GDP in response to the worsening debt situation, the country never experienced real interest rates comparable to those paid by other defaulting countries in Latin America, in particular those in Brazil, both in the 1990s and in the years between 2000 and 2006 studied here. We also observe a remarkable difference between Argentina and other debtors in the ratio of debt interest payments to GDP. In 2000 to 2006, average debt interest payments stood at only 2.31 percent of GDP in Argentina, compared to 7.18 percent in Brazil and 3.47 percent in Ecuador.
15. Artana (2007, p. 20) notes that on the terms of the federal bailout, the government was offering the provinces the 'pesofication' of loans, an extension on their maturity and a relatively low real interest rate on the new indexed bonds of 2 percent per annum.
16. On the (rescaled) budgetary institutional decentralization variable (0–100 scale, 100 indicating the highest degree of decentralization), Argentina scores 50 during the 1990s. That means that during the 1990s the IADB researchers (Alesina et al. 1999) perceived budget institutions to be less centralized than the Latin American average (43.14). Not only were Argentina's fiscal institutions found to be significantly more decentralized than those in unitary countries in Latin America, including Chile (27) and Ecuador (45), but clearly also more decentralized than Brazil's (42). In their most recent report on the quality of budgetary institutions, IADB researchers (Filc and Scartascini 2004, 2007) classify Argentina's institutions as more centralized than in the earlier period (42), which is equivalent to the sample average. Yet, the distance between Argentina (42) and Brazil (19) has widened. Based on these two waves of surveys, Argentina appears to have made very little progress in strengthening its fiscal institutions.
17. Webb (2003, p. 194) reports that by 1989 Central Bank subsidies to subnational governments and others were estimated at about US$8 billion, equal to more than 5 percent of GDP and close to half of the overall public sector deficit.
18. The provinces once more began requesting credits from the Banco de la Nación, without the interference of central government. Webb (2003, p. 201) notes that such credits 'required painful adjustments on the part of the provinces', as the bank was entitled to deduct the debt service from federal tax receipts. The fiscal pain created by bending to rules supposedly made them sustainable. Alternatively, the bending of rules and a return to old borrowing habits may be interpreted as indicating an erosion of hard budget constraints.
19. The deal, which became known as the 'Olivos Pact', allowed Menem, on the one hand, to achieve the needed majority for a constitutional change that allowed him to be re-elected for a second term. On the other hand, the president gave up his authority to name the mayor of Buenos Aires City, a crucial (fiscal) veto player, and to change the heads of the Central Bank and the National Tax Agency without the approval of Congress.
20. Alienation by the Argentine government's unilateral decision to announce a 'bank holiday' on December 3, 2001, without prior consultation with the IMF management, finally leads the fund on December 5 to halt the disbursement of $1.3 billion scheduled for that month.
21. Since the beginning of the 1990s, central government has tried to constrain the borrowing autonomy of subnational governments on several occasions, but the provinces and municipalities still retain relatively large borrowing autonomy. Before the 2001 debt

crisis, Argentina rated among the most decentralized countries in terms of borrowing decentralization, according to Rodden's (2002) study of subnational borrowing autonomy in 32 OECD and non-OECD countries between 1986 and 1996. Rodden's index measures the borrowing autonomy of subnational governments and other government agencies and public enterprises on a 5-point scale, with higher values indicating more decentralized borrowing control. Argentine state governments score 4 out of 5 points on borrowing autonomy, the second highest score in the entire data set. Argentina is only outscored by Brazil, which between 1986 and 1994 reached the highest possible score (5). In the period covered in Rodden's data set, the degree of subnational borrowing autonomy, both in Argentina and Brazil, stands out when compared with such federal countries as the USA (with a score of 3 on the borrowing autonomy index), Canada (3.25) and Switzerland (3), which generally allow for a large degree of fiscal autonomy on the subnational level. It should be noted, however, that Brazil made large efforts to constrain the borrowing autonomy of the states and, by restructuring the banking system, was able to significantly reduce the level of borrowing through state-owned local banks after 1994. In Argentina, in 2002 central government assumed control of all external and all foreign-currency-denominated borrowing of subnational governments. Provincial debt needs to be approved by provincial legislatures, and municipal debt by municipal legislatures, respectively. Also, provinces are required to keep their total debt service expenditure below 25 percent of current revenue. However, it is not clear to what extent and how provincial governments are sanctioned if they transgress these rules.

22. Based on World Bank data on the volumes of federal transfers in Argentina for 2004, discretionary transfers make up 5 percent of all transfers to subnational levels of government, equivalent to less than a quarter of a percent of real GDP.
23. According to Kim (2012, p. 16) the data is collected from three sources: the Official Gazette of the Argentine government, the Annals of the Official Gazette, and the Directorate of the Argentine System of Juridical Information (SAIJ) within the Ministry of Justice and Human Rights.
24. In the 2007 presidential race, the Justicialist candidate, Christina Fernández de Kirchner, won in the first round with 45 percent of the vote. She entered office ruling over an enlarged majority for the ruling party coalition 'Front for Victory', led by the Justicialist Party, both in the House and the Senate.
25. Between her election to office in 2007 and 2012, President Cristina Fernández de Kirchner signed a total of 13 DNUs, including a recent decree that led to the removal of the Central Bank president and a decree allowing the use of Central Bank reserves for foreign debt repayment.
26. In the Ley de Convenios (Tax Sharing Law) in 1988, the federal government accepted that the share of discretionary transfers – ATNs – in total transfer should be reduced to 1 percent. This decision was taken to make the provinces less dependent on central government transfers. Although during the first and second Menem administrations, the central government took steps aimed at recentralizing revenue, and was successful to some extent, discretionary funds at the president's disposal still remained lower than in Brazil (Eaton and Dickovick 2004).
27. Under the first fiscal pact, the provinces agreed to the diversion of 15 percent of their total (automatic) coparticipation funds to the loss-making, now re-nationalized, pension system. This decision led to a relative increase in discretionary funds at the disposal of the president, allowing Menem to commend his political allies for voting in favor of and implementing his political projects, and to punish provincial leaders of the opposition party (UCR). With the relative reduction in automatic transfers, Menem apparently hoped to force provincial governments to prioritize their expenditure (more so). However, the government's deliberative distribution of funds to particular provinces, conditional on their political support rather than on their fiscal performance, meant an ex post softening of budget constraints (Eaton and Dickovick 2004, Wibbels 2004).

28. Artana (2007) estimates that the provinces spend more than suggested by Government Finance Statistics (GFS) data *and* that they are to a much lower degree responsible for collecting their own revenue. The latter can be explained by the fact that a large portion of what GFS counts as own-source revenue actually comes from transfers from the nation. The problem of the overestimation of own-source revenue in the GFS data sets has been addressed in depth, among others, in Rodden (2004).
29. The coparticipation system goes back to 1934 when federal government struck a deal with the provinces that led to a significant recentralization of taxing rights – most notably export taxes – in return for the federal government's compensation for Great Depression losses. Today, all the major taxes, other than social security contributions, are subject to sharing with the provinces. Some taxes, such as levies on financial transactions and on small tax payers, are partially shared, while a few taxes – most notably export taxes – are entirely appropriated by the federal government. The pool of shared taxes is distributed in two rounds: first, the so-called 'primary' distribution, dividing the Coparticipación Federal de Impuestos (CFI) funds between the federal government and the provinces; next, the 'secondary' distribution, dividing the provincial share among the subnational units according to redistributive coefficients set by tax-sharing legislation. Historically, the CFI accounted for the bulk of intergovernmental transfers in the country, averaging nearly 70 percent of the total between 1988 and 2008. With the two fiscal pacts, the federal government agreed to guarantee a base of 34 percent of all federal revenue to the provinces, which turned out to become more and more problematic under the economic downturn between 1999 and 2002 (Bonvecchi and Lodola 2010).
30. Data from the Argentine government, analyzed by Rodden and Wibbels (2002), show that expenditure decentralization in Argentina reached 38 percent on average between 1978 and 1996. This is not only clearly higher than the Latin American average but outscores even the average value for Brazil (24 percent) and other, developed, federal countries including the USA (29 percent) and Germany (30 percent). The only country with a higher degree of fiscal decentralization based on expenditure during that period is India, where 41 percent of total government expenditure was made by subnational governments.
31. Artana (2007), based on data by the Argentine Ministry of Economy, indicates even higher numbers for expenditure decentralization, with total subnational expenditure totaling 49.6 percent.
32. Argentina's federal constitution assigns exclusive responsibilities to the nation for external relations, money issue, exchange rates, regulation of international and interprovincial trade, border security and legislation on civil, commercial and criminal matters, labor and social security. Responsibility for the remaining public service provision is shared between central government and the provinces or municipalities, albeit with subnational governments having significant duties compared with other (federal) countries. How can we explain the above-described increase in expenditure decentralization over time? As Sanguinetti (1995, quoted in IMF 1996a, p. 11) points out, legal changes in 1991and 1993 increased the expenditure responsibilities of subnational governments.
33. Although the GFS data for 2004 tell us that more than 45 percent of total revenue is allocated by subnational governments, making it seem to be in the same category as decentralized federations like Canada or the USA, this estimate is significantly biased. The reason is that the GFS data set counts transfers from the federal government among the revenue of states (Rodden 2004, Artana 2007). Although in recent research, authors have collected data on own-source revenue, before transfers from revenue-sharing systems these data are not available for a larger sample of countries.
34. Subnational revenue autonomy, measured as the share of own-source revenue in percentage of total government revenue, remains much smaller in Argentina, compared with other federal countries around the world, e.g. Brazil (27 percent), India (34 percent), the USA (39 percent) and Switzerland (45 percent).

7. Comparing institutional reform success in Argentina and Brazil

Subnational fiscal indiscipline, which often comes as a negative consequence of decentralizing fiscal authority, can indeed become a source of fiscal instability, affecting an entire country. However, under the condition that national-level budget decisions are centralized and based on rules that aim at maintaining long-term stability, allowing a larger degree of vertical fiscal decentralization need not be a recipe for disaster. Brazil's successful fiscal stabilization over the second half of the 1990s makes this point very clear. Today, Brazil combines strong central-level budgetary institutions and a more transparent budget process with the granting of a high degree of fiscal autonomy to subnational governments. In contrast, the evidence on Argentina suggests that the country never succeeded in reforming its budgetary institutions to a similar degree. Subnational common pool resource problems in Argentina persist, leaving the government in a weaker position to balance potential economic shocks.

To be sure, the extreme fiscal and macroeconomic imbalances in both countries at the end of the 1990s cannot and should not be described as purely endogenous.[1] Nevertheless, the governments in Argentina and Brazil before and even during the crisis were given choices. Based on the evidence presented above, much speaks for the view that policy makers in Brazil successfully changed the country's economic destiny by reducing institutional problems that inhibited fiscal stability and effective crisis management. Argentina went down a different road, jeopardizing the trust of financial investors and throwing the country far back in its economic development.

In the first part of each case study, I showed where fiscal imbalances, including spending increases, deficits and public debt accumulation, started and for how long they persisted (and continue to do so). Next, I pointed to what I believe to be the crucial decisions on institutional changes (or lack thereof) that allowed for (prohibited) fiscal consolidation. In the following sections, I draw some first preliminary conclusions on the institutional approaches that worked to reduce the CPR problems and on the initiatives that failed, based on the in-depth case analyses of Argentina and Brazil in the above chapters.

7.1 CENTRAL-LEVEL BUDGETARY INSTITUTIONS

With regard to the first hypothesis about the supportive role of national-level budgetary institutions, the evidence for Brazil suggests that the country effectively reformed those institutions towards the end of the 1990s, which was then followed by a period of fiscal improvement. It is important to note that fiscal stability, defined here as a balanced primary budget, had already been achieved in the year of the financial crisis in 1998. Over the following years, the government was able to secure a drastic increase in its primary surplus. Although the improved export competitiveness, after the devaluation of the real in January 1999 and with a high demand for Brazilian exports in world markets at the beginning of the 2000s, clearly contributed to growing government revenue and facilitated debt reduction, much speaks for the view that the causes of Brazil's success pre-date the export-led economic upswing. Among proponents of the view that institutional reform was a game-changer in Brazil, most credit is usually given to the role of the country's Fiscal Responsibility Law (FRL) in 2000. There is wide agreement that the FRL strengthened the position of the president vis-à-vis the legislature. In general, the FRL described a successful piece of legislation because it fulfills three crucial requirements: (1) it sets detailed ex ante fiscal rules, extending to specific targets on expenditure; (2) it includes mechanisms that define how the central government has to react when targets are missed; and (3) it defines explicit sanctions that extend to government agencies as well as to individual budget actors. While these observations on the characteristics of the FRL seem reasonable, my analysis of Brazil's fiscal turnaround suggests that looking only at the FRL may be an approach too narrow to describe the full range of necessary institutional changes that allowed for the improvements. It seems more appropriate to say that fiscal consolidation resembled a gradual process, in which one institutional step was taken at a time to achieve, over time, a fundamental – and sustainable – change in the rules of the fiscal bargaining game.

In the case of Argentina, a stagnation of reforms best characterizes the second term of President Menem and the subsequent government of President de la Rua. At the beginning of the 1990s, during the first administration of President Menem, Argentine policies resembled those in Brazil. Budgetary stabilization after the introduction of the fixed exchange rate regime in 1991 seems to have been a policy priority of the first Menem administration. However, early reforms were soon abandoned under increasing economic pressures – first after the Mexican crisis in 1994/95 and, for a second time, in 1999. Although the government had passed in 1996 and, subsequently in 1999, fiscal solvency and responsibility laws that looked similar to those of Brazil and other countries, it failed to safeguard transparent and responsible budget making. The different fiscal laws and initiatives in Argentina never fulfilled the criteria that made Brazil's legislation a success. And it did not take long until – by congressional votes – the agreed fiscal targets initially set out were 'paused' through amending legislation, passed during the economic recession.

After Argentina's sovereign default in 2001, the situation has not improved. Although another Fiscal Responsibility Law was passed in Congress in 2004, subsequent annual budget bills have once more halted the introduction of stabilizing initiatives, including the introduction of a fiscal stabilization fund that would have allowed savings on the earnings of a period of successful export expansion after the default of more dire times. Furthermore, there is ample evidence that fundamental flaws in fiscal-federal relations that have aggravated the fiscal situation in previous crises, continue to exist. One example is a deal between the provinces and the federal government, granting the former a 'pause' in the implementation of budget transparency standards and the fulfillment of specific budget targets included in the 2004 FRL. Another example of structural flaws in the country's political decision-making process, including but not limited to fiscal policy, is the excessive use of emergency decrees (DRUs) as a way of making any legal changes possible. The extensive use of decrees clearly points to an inefficient budget decision-making process. In other words, despite generally positive economic conditions and a sharp increase in government revenue for a decade after the sovereign default, no steps have been taken by the Argentine government to resolve latent problems in the budgetary institutional set-up.

7.2 VERTICAL DECENTRALIZATION UNDER STRONG AND WEAK BUDGETARY INSTITUTIONS

Regarding the initial working hypotheses, stating that vertical fiscal decentralization is increasing overall fiscal stability (hypothesis 2), and that the risk of overall fiscal imbalance depends to a large extent on strong central-level institutions (hypothesis 3), my two cases provide valuable information. Table 7.1 compares the reform steps in the area of budgetary institutions that had an effect on subnational government fiscal decisions in both countries. All of these measures have been discussed in detail in the case studies above. On first look, both countries seem to have engaged in similar reform measures. Yet, once we zoom in on the reforms, it becomes clear that the institutional changes in Argentina were often watered down or

Table 7.1 Reform of budgetary institutions: Argentina vs Brazil

Institutional Reforms with Effect on Subnational Fiscal Decision-Making				
	Argentina		Brazil	
Federal Bailouts		1993, 2002		1989, 1993, 1997
Short-Term Stabilization Agreements				
Fiscal conditionality for bailouts	✓	Fiscal Pacts in 1992, 1993	✓	1997: Law 9496
	–	But: softened in 1995, abandoned in 1999		Senate Resolution 78
Subnational Primary Balance Targets	✓	1992 and 1993	✓	1997, re-enforced in 2000 FRL
	–	1996, 1999, abandoned by budget laws		
	–	2004, paused by budget law		
Subnational Expenditure rules	✓	in 1996	✓	1997, re-enforced in 2000 FRL
	–	1999, 2004, paused by budget laws		
Subnational Borrowing rules	(✓)	1996, 1999 (abandoned), 2004	✓	1997, re-enforced in 2000 FRL Debt ceiling
Prohibited:				
Anticipated Tax Revenue as Collateral	–	in 1993, but abandoned in 1995	✓	1997
CB Re-Discounting of SNG Debt	✓	in 1993	✓	1997
Budgetary Institutions (Long-Term)				
Fiscal Responsibility Law (FRL)	–	1996 and 1999 (failed)		2000 FRL
	✓	2004 FRL		
SNG Transparency Rules	–	1999, 2004 But: abandoned in 1999 and since 2004 by annual budget laws	✓	Yes, in 2000 FRL
Sanctioning Mechanism				
– Financial	✓	President can withhold discretionary transfers to SNGs (about 5 percent of total)	✓	President can withhold discretionary transfers to SNGs (about 10 percent of total)
– Individual-level	–	No	✓	Fiscal Crimes Law, 2000 Incumbent on all levels of govt. face threat of loosing office and prohibition to run again

abandoned only a few years after they had passed the Argentine Congress. In contrast, institutional reform in Brazil started later and seems to have progressed more slowly, at least until the late 1990s. However, successive administrations were able to achieve a fundamental change in the rules of the budget process and fiscal bargaining in Brazil. At the beginning of the 1990s, both governments, in Argentina and Brazil, were facing subnational fiscal crises that threatened overall fiscal stability. Subnational debt accumulation posed a new threat, given that – after the introduction of fixed exchange rate regimes – it was no longer possible to launch subnational bailouts and 'inflate away', increasing federal government expenditure as was previously done. Both governments therefore took steps to reduce the fiscal imbalance at the subnational level by forcing the latter to accept primary deficit targets, limits on expenditure and borrowing in federal financial assistance programs, with the aim of overcoming the ongoing crises.

The two fiscal pacts in Argentina in 1992 and 1993 under President Menem and the state financial assistance programs (PROES) in Brazil under President Cardoso in 1997/98 serve as examples that fiscal conditionality can indeed reduce fiscal imbalance – for a time. Yet, the example of policy reversal in Argentina around 1995 provides a warning message that fiscal targets that were introduced in debt contracts need to be re-enforced in subsequently binding legislation. Otherwise, they can and are most likely to be overthrown when economic pressures grow stronger. In Brazil, the subnational debt restructuring-cum-fiscal conditionality represented a first step on the path towards more sustainable fiscal stabilization through a series of reforms of the country's budgetary institutions. Argentina quickly changed its course, with President Menem foregoing the chance to sustain achieved macroeconomic stabilization success by passing follow-up fiscal responsibility legislation in due time.

Fiscal conditionality in the debt contracts with Brazilian state governments were not easily achieved by Cardoso, even though his party held the majority of state governorships. One achievement of the Cardoso administration was to use the president's relatively strong financial leverage over the states at a time when even the industrial power houses in the south and south-west of Brazil were deeply hurt by increasing debt-financing costs. Federal financial aid in this situation was tied to the fulfillment of tough ex ante fiscal and debt targets. It meant that the federal government prescribed how much could be spent by subnational governments on the public wage bill, a crucial political tool for state-level incumbents, cutting deeply into the fiscal autonomy of states that – historically – tend to be powerful political players with strong leverage over national-level political decisions. But unlike other political leaders that had failed to achieve fiscal and macroeconomic consolidation through narrow economic orthodoxy,

Cardoso wisely relied on a mix of 'carrots' and 'sticks'. His government relied on 'sticks' when no other alternative was available. An example is the political showdown involving President Cardoso and the governor of the state of Minas Gerais, Itamar Franco, a former president and party ally. In January 1999, Franco tried to force the federal government into abandoning fiscal conditionality, hurting the states by threatening to default on debt service payments to the government. President Cardoso countered Franco's move by threatening to withhold tax-sharing transfers to the state of Minas Gerais in equal amounts to due debt-servicing fees. In the end, Cardoso won over Franco, who – faced with insolvency – simply depended on the federal transfers to remain in office. Another piece of evidence on the willingness and ability of the federal government to enforce newly established fiscal responsibility laws is the fact that those incumbents who could be charged for severe fiscal mismanagement did, as a consequence of the Fiscal Crimes Law, end up in prison. Other ways of winning consensus for institutional reforms included an elaborate system of political 'pork and perks' (Samuels 2002, Treisman 2007). Here, Cardoso was the lucky beneficiary of earlier steps taken by his predecessor that led to an increase in discretionary funds at the disposal of the president. Furthermore, the president's capacity to provide pork to his political allies improved with the increasing revenue from re-invoked and newly introduced taxes on financial transactions, imports and capital earnings going directly to the federal government, without the requirement for it to be shared with the states.

A crucial point to take away from this specific case is that the relatively comfortable financial position of the Brazilian government in those years is not simply a consequence of increased revenue under an increasingly favorable economic environment beginning in 2002. During both of Brazil's financial crises, in 1998 and 2002, the government had fiscal room for maneuver because it decided to either keep tax rates at a certain level or even increase them against resistance from various groups. This factor also seems noteworthy when compared with the macroeconomic policy decisions of Argentina in the 1990s, which were focused – often to the applause of international organizations and private investors – on a radical reduction in the tax burden. President Menem's decision to first recentralize provincial pension plans and to privatize them afterwards effectively deprived the federal government of growing revenue during economic upswings after laying down the considerable burden of re-capitalizing the loss-making system. As a consequence, Menem lacked the comparable discretionary tax funds to win acceptance from crucial veto players for budgetary institutional reforms. In the case of Brazil, financial support for the states was one of several 'carrots' that were offered to them. Another supportive element was Cardoso's offer to subnational leaders to change the electoral law in 1998, which made it possible for the president to run for a second time, to office holders at state and municipal levels.[2] Further supportive measures, offered early on with the launch of the PROES initiative in 1996/97, included technical support for the states in designing a debt restructuring strategy and improving fiscal planning.

7.3 ALTERNATIVE WAYS OF REACHING SUBNATIONAL FISCAL DISCIPLINE

7.3.1 Party Discipline

In the academic literature on the determinants of macroeconomic stability, theories based on party discipline and party alignment of subnational leaders within the national government, remain very popular. However, in explaining why fiscal consolidation became possible for Brazil and not for Argentina, they do not help so much. Both presidents, Cardoso in 1997 and Menem in 1993, held similarly strong majorities in Congress as they took steps towards increasing central-level control of subnational fiscal activities. Furthermore, for most of their terms, both presidents knew the majority of subnational governments to be aligned with their own party.[3] Despite the fact that Menem could draw on the political resources of a strong, well-organized party apparatus, he did not succeed in reforming the budget process and passing legislature allowing for a fundamental change in the rules of the fiscal bargaining game between the provinces and central government.

One factor that arguably contributed to the success of reforms in Brazil that does not appear in any hard data but that has been reconfirmed literally by all interview partners for this book and in narrative accounts of Brazilian crisis management under the Cardoso administrations, is the close institutional cooperation between the Central Bank, the Finance Ministry and the presidency. This may be interpreted as evidence that there were generally fewer internal veto players within the ruling coalition during Cardoso's presidential terms. However, the close coordination had little to do with party discipline. In fact, it was members of Cardoso's own coalition that revolted publicly against the fiscal adjustment measures proposed by the president. One example of the lack of party discipline is the government's failure in December 1998 to win a majority in the House vote on pension reform that entailed, among other things, an increase in pension contributions by employees. In Cardoso's own words, the 'party leadership was not very alert' at that moment. Failing to gain a majority was even more embarrassing, given that, according to Cardoso, gaining it 'would not have been very costly' (source: research interview with Cardoso, February 2008). Another prominent example of missing 'party discipline' is the threat of former President Itamar Franco, in his position as governor of the state of Minas Gerais, to default on his state's outstanding debt. Among other examples, these may be interpreted as evidence that fiscal consolidation was reached despite a lack of party discipline.

In Argentina, it seems that the opportunity to implement far-reaching changes in budgetary institutions was missed, even though party discipline was traditionally high and subnational governments had been 'aligned' with the president's party for the first and for half of the second administration of President Menem. Neither President Menem, nor his successor, President de la Rua, were able to capitalize on a long tradition of party discipline in order to implement fiscal consolidation strategies. Even under the regained unity of the Justicialist Party, during the first and second Kirchner administrations, attempts at achieving fiscal consolidation failed and a fundamental change in the rules of the federal bargain was never made. This was despite the fact that members of the Justicialist Party and close allies held a majority of provincial governorships. The fact that both Kirchners, during their respective terms as presidents, continued to rely on emergency decrees to implement policies suggests that the national-level (fiscal) policy process was largely inefficient.

7.3.1.1 Could 'market discipline' have done the trick?

In both case studies, we find evidence suggesting that the transfer dependence of subnational governments remains a major concern for stability. Both governments, in Argentina and in Brazil, still need to come to terms with a fundamental structural weakness in fiscal-federal relations, the mismatch between the highly decentralized spending authority of subnational government and the subnational government capacity to raise the equivalent own revenue, particularly in poor states/provinces. Above, I referred to President Menem's potential miscalculation, namely that by increasing the expenditure responsibilities of the provinces while keeping their revenue autonomy at a low level, he could force them into prioritizing on their spending. Under the remaining soft budget constraints, i.e. a high reliance on federal transfers for covering local spending and the simultaneously high borrowing autonomy of the provinces, the opposite happened. Subnational expenditure continued to grow and around 1995, in response to economic pressures after the Mexican crisis, subnational debt increased sharply. Although the risks of letting the provinces borrow freely and allowing them to use the expected revenue from tax-sharing funds as collateral in debt contracts with (foreign) borrowers must have been known – in fact, this practice had been banned in the Fiscal Pact of 1993 and in the Fiscal

Solvency Law of 1996 – the federal government tolerated the subnational debt expansion. Among other sources, this toleration strategy is discussed in IMF reports, as well as in the financial press coverage between 1999 and the default in 2001, strongly criticizing the growing subnational deficit and debt build-up. Once we consider the vanishing political decision-making space of President Carlos Menem in the second half of his second term and the unstable majorities of the successor government, it seems less surprising that the government was unable to tackle the subnational fiscal problem in the run-up to or during the sovereign debt crisis in 2001.

However, whether increasing the revenue autonomy of subnational governments would have been the right recipe remains an open question in the context of emerging market countries. On the one hand, there is merit in the public choice view that by increasing the revenue independence of subcentral governments, the efficiency of public expenditure can be improved. Competition might prevent governments from over-spending (and over-taxing) and, assuming there is such a thing as a credible no-bailout commitment by the central level, subcentral governments may be forced to act as 'quasi sovereigns', making fiscal decisions under the critical eye of the market. If they failed to maintain fiscal stability and lose the trust of investors, subnational governments would be voted out of office by their respective constituencies in local elections. On the other hand, the idea of truly independent 'quasi sovereigns' seems incommensurable with the political and economic reality in the countries of concern. Given the high degree of inequality in living conditions among the regions and subnational governments in those countries, it is hardly conceivable that a central government would decide to leave its subnational governments to their own fiscal fate without extending a hand to them in times of crisis. Given the sheer lack of a sufficient tax base to cover even minimal local expenses, a withdrawal of the central government from subnational financing cannot be counted as a viable solution. Finally, there is another factor that has largely escaped previous research on subnational revenue autonomy.[4] As the case of Brazil during the 1990s shows, providing the states with large revenue-raising autonomy and, simultaneously, large borrowing autonomy can be a recipe for disaster, yet for other than expected reasons. Over-borrowing took place mostly in the richer industrialized states, including Sao Paulo, Minas Gerais, Rio Grande do Sul and Rio de Janeiro. Given their strong industrial productivity and hence high taxing capacity, those states were able to accumulate huge debts without intervention by the federal government, compromising the overall fiscal stability of the nation. Striking a balance between government solicitude and subnational independence is no easy task. Along the lines of Rodden and Eskeland (2003), one could therefore argue that a combination of hierarchical budget control and market discipline is likely to work best for vertically decentralized emerging market economies.[5] In this context, it surely helps to think of fiscal stabilization as a dynamic bargain with different fiscal actors on different levels of government. While increasing subnational fiscal independence and aiming for more market discipline in the long run, strong fiscal constraints and a certain degree of hierarchical control over subcentral budget and borrowing policies seem in order to (re-)stabilize subcentral budgets and to set incentives for fiscally responsible policies.

NOTES

1. Changes in the international economic environment, in investor appetite or risk perception of emerging market debt after the Asian and the Russian crises, and a slowdown in exports have all been identified to be playing a crucial role. Likewise, there is a growing consensus among macro economists and political economists that the rigid peg of domestic currencies to the US dollar and the refusal to shift to a more flexible regime earlier on, both in Brazil and Argentina, contributed to the crises in both countries.
2. In Argentina, term limits for provincial governors continue to vary from one province to another. President Menem's successful lobby for a constitutional change in 1994, allowing him to run for a second time, led to an increase in the number of provincial senators from two to three per province. Furthermore, constitutional reform changed the status of and nomination procedure for the government of the City of Buenos Aires. The capital received the status of a province and its mayor (now governor) was chosen for the first time through open elections and no longer nominated by the federal government.
3. In 1993, when Menem successfully negotiated fiscal deficit targets and spending ceilings with the provinces, his government coalition held strong majorities in both houses of parliament. From 1995 to 1997, he even had an absolute parliamentary majority. Furthermore, until 1995, the majority of Argentina's 24 provinces were led by his Justicialist party members.
4. An exception is the World Bank's World Development Report (2000, Ch. 5) for 1999–2000, which mentions the problem that macroeconomic instability can be threatened by high revenue-raising autonomy of subnational governments, although the authors conclude that this is most likely to be the case in 'large federations or very decentralized wealthy countries'. They assume this relationship to hold when revenue is decentralized before expenditure responsibilities, forcing central governments to maintain spending levels with a smaller resource base, leading to larger central government deficits.
5. A similar point of view is presented in Ter-Minassian and Craig (1997), who argue that a number of pre-conditions must be fulfilled for a government to successfully apply a 'laissez faire' approach, i.e. for 'market discipline' to work as an efficient constraint.

8. Conclusion: balancing subnational fiscal autonomy and overall fiscal stability

In the present study, my research was led by the question of how governments can forge their country's macroeconomic destiny and what institutional conditions will allow them to do so. More specifically, my aim was to investigate the role of budgetary institutions in fiscal stabilization in emerging market nations. In the theoretical parts of the book, I developed an argument about interactions between national-level budgetary institutions and subnational fiscal discipline in countries allowing their subnational governments different degrees of spending autonomy. Budgetary institutions include the rules, laws and hierarchical procedures that determine how well the government and the legislature on the national level can coordinate to pass fiscally responsible government budgets. My point is that more centralized budgetary institutions on the central or horizontal level of government are likely to improve fiscal outcomes on all levels of government for more than one reason. The first is that finance ministers and/or leaders of a country find it easier to constrain those budget players – within government and in the legislature – who have the strongest incentives to 'over-fish' the common pool resource, the national tax pool. Second, I argue that centralizing budget processes on the horizontal level also affects subnational fiscal discipline. While the ability to constrain subnational budget actors through central-level institutions in fiscal-federal frameworks has to some extent been recognized in previous contributions, the potential for a *signaling* effect of central-level efforts to restructure the budget process has largely been overlooked. Going beyond the existing literature, I submit that in order to change existing patterns of subnational fiscal behavior it may be crucial to start by scrutinizing the potential flaws in national-level budget processes.

Based on the findings in the institutional literature, we might suspect that greater decentralization of spending decisions along the vertical axis carries two main risks for fiscal stability. One is a structural issue and the other is a problem related to crisis management. In other words, by increasing the number of unconstrained veto players with spending authority policy makers might increase the CPR problem, adding another layer of budgetary actors with incentives to free-ride on the common tax pool. Subnational fiscal indiscipline can, over time, contribute significantly to overall fiscal instability. But vertical decentralization can also pose a more immediate threat to stability during an economic crisis, raising the costs for national governments to implement a fiscal adjustment against a large number of veto players.

How can horizontal centralization contribute to mitigate such problems? First, we may find that by increasing the degree of centralization and transparency at the horizontal level, governments signal their commitment to fiscal consolidation to lower-level budgetary actors. Institutional reform aimed at (re-)centralizing the budget process, thus affecting national-level budget actors, may indirectly affect the spending and borrowing behavior of subnational budget actors. This is because a tightening of budgetary institutions at the national level sends a strong policy message to subnational politicians, providing them with new information about central government policy priorities and a willingness to follow through, even on unpopular austerity measures. Hence, for budgetary institutions to work effectively, reform plans should ideally spell out the principles that are going to guide fiscal policy, forcing budget actors at all levels of government to consider what is good for the whole nation in the medium and even the longer term, rather than considering only their own narrow political gains.

Second, budgetary institutions, including fiscal responsibility laws, provide 'tools' for central governments to enforce fiscal rules through specific sanctioning mechanisms. These rules and enforcement mechanisms can be extended to constrain subnational governments. For example, when the Brazilian government decided that it was necessary to harden budget constraints at all levels of government, it simultaneously introduced similar fiscal rules applied at all levels of government, enforceable by the federal government. These went as far as introducing limits on certain types of expenditure (e.g. on the public wage bill) and on borrowing by government agencies. To be credible constraints, fiscal laws generally need to include minimum transparency standards (e.g. a ban on off-budgeting practices) and to identify a credible sanctioning mechanism, in order for them to be enforceable. The Brazilian case illustrates how central governments can enforce fiscal discipline, extending to subnational levels of government, for example by including provisions to hold back fiscal transfers in the case of non-compliance with transparency standards.

8.1 AN INTEGRATED APPROACH TO FISCAL INSTABILITY: VERTICAL FISCAL DECENTRALIZATION AND CENTRAL-LEVEL INSTITUTIONS

My theoretical argument about the interaction of horizontal and vertical fiscal decentralization combines two branches of institutional literature that have dealt with the negative effects of CPR problems for fiscal stability but which have evolved largely independent of one another. My approach provides a new perspective, pointing to potential ways in which central-level institutions may condition the effects of fiscal federalism.

Both branches of literature – the budgetary institutions and the fiscal federalism literature – start from the same theoretical premise that decentralization of fiscal decision making creates large numbers of veto players with incentives to over-use the common pool resource, i.e. the national tax pool. Showing the importance of fiscal rules and delegation approaches for reducing spending bias and stabilizing fiscal budgets and public debt levels, the budgetary institutions literature contributes greatly to our understanding of sustainable budget making. Furthermore, much has been gained by contributions showing how important it is for policy makers to implement the 'right type' of budgetary institutions, depending on the underlying political system characteristics (Hallerberg and von Hagen 1999, Hallerberg 2004, Hallerberg et al. 2009b). However, what remains overlooked in the budgetary institutions literature, with few exceptions, is the relevance of destabilizing effects rooted in insufficient control over subnational budget actors. Subnational-level fiscal behavior is often treated as a second-order problem and little attention is given to the consequences of delegating fiscal rights to lower levels of government. In the study at hand, my goal is to reach a better understanding of fiscal instability in the case of emerging market nations, in particular in Latin America and the Caribbean. To this end, considering the potential for budgetary institutions to change subnational fiscal behavior provides an important opportunity.[1]

In both the fiscal federalism and the public choice literature, focusing primarily on the effects of providing subnational governments with greater fiscal decision-making powers, the role of the central level in reaching subnational fiscal decisions remains under-theorized (Oates 2005, Rodden 2006). Depending on the school of thought, vertical fiscal decentralization is seen as an impediment to or a pre-condition for general government stability. However, little attention is paid to the institutional context or to the general degree of budget process control by a central government.

My analysis in previous chapters aimed to provide a first step forward in the direction of a more nuanced approach that considers a broader institutional context. In my perspective, fiscal decentralization – defined as delegating spending authority to subnational governments – can play out differently, depending on how transparent and structured the national level turns out to be. My approach builds on the assumption that central government institutions change the incentives for subnational budget actors, affecting their budgetary choices. And for the emerging market cases at hand, I hold that central rules constrain subnational budget actors much more effectively than self-imposed rules.

Earlier approaches by Jonathan Rodden and colleagues and the emerging work of the IMF researchers offered some guidance at the beginning of my analysis (Rodden 2002, Rodden and Wibbels 2002, Plekhanov and Singh 2007). These approaches relax the theoretical assumption that vertical decentralization generally leads to either more or less fiscal discipline of subnational budget actors. For Rodden (2002), decentralized spending control only poses a threat to fiscal stability on the condition that subnational governments remain both highly dependent on central transfers and also unconstrained in their borrowing decisions. That finding highlights the role of the institutionalized control of subnational fiscal activities in achieving and maintaining fiscal stability. But, at the same time, the approach remains narrowly focused on the regulation of borrowing activities. Plekhanov and Singh (2007) refine Rodden's argument on borrowing constraints, suggesting that the effectiveness of the type of borrowing controls that Rodden (2006) describes, depends on a broader set of fiscal management standards. My approach builds on these and other contributions, arguing that the effects of vertical fiscal decentralization are indeed likely to depend on a broader budgetary institutional context in which fiscal authority is delegated from the central government to subcentral government units. Much in line with Oates' (2005) suggestion quoted at the beginning of the first chapter of this book, I argue that the negative effects of vertical decentralization can be reduced under strong central-level budgetary institutions, and – no less importantly – this would allow us to still reap the benefits of fiscal and further political decentralization without jeopardizing overall fiscal stability.

8.2 EMPIRICAL EVIDENCE

To allow for a systematic empirical evaluation in the second part of the book, Chapter 3 develops my above stated argument on the potential interdependence of institutional effects in fiscally decentralized systems. It presents three main hypotheses, which I discuss later in light of the quantitative data and qualitative evidence on a set of emerging market economies in the Latin American and Caribbean region. In Chapter 4, the available institutional and macroeconomic data allowed me to assess the relevance of my first hypothesis – on the role of central-level budget institutions in achieving overall fiscal stability – relying on a graphical analysis, comparing data for 15 Latin American countries over time. Figure 4.4 in Chapter 4 indicates the negative relationship between the degree of horizontal institutional decentralization and nominal budget balances for the countries in my sample in the mid-1990s and, again, at the beginning of the 2000s. For both cross-sections of data, a strong and significant correlation between decentralized budgetary institutions and fiscal outcomes was found. Specifically, for the countries in my sample it appears that higher values on the aggregate horizontal decentralization variable correspond to significantly lower nominal budget outcomes. Looking at the broader Latin American picture, the empirical evidence thus suggests that a more (or less) transparent and stringent budget process at the central government level corresponds to improved (or worse) fiscal outcomes.

For my two country case studies, Argentina and Brazil, I detect a significant reduction in the size of nominal budget deficits in the latter and a significant – albeit still relatively small – deterioration in the former. Adding further evidence from the in-depth case analyses of the two countries over longer time frames in chapters 5 and 6, the following picture evolves: in the case of Brazil, reforms of the country's national-level budget institutions allowed for an impressive improvement in the fiscal stance at a time when the country needed it most, during a period of severe financial distress. Institutional recentralization prior to and during the financial crisis in 1998 helped the Brazilian government to convince its external creditors of its compliance with international contracts and its resolve to do what was necessary to stabilize financially. Looking only at nominal fiscal balance data, the Argentine government seemed to perform, for a long time, much better than expected given severe underlying fiscal institutional problems. However, as the in-depth case study of Argentina (Chapter 6) reveals, inconsistencies in the budget decision-making process and a lack of transparency continue to place a heavy toll on the country's fiscal performance to date. The high level of inflation that has plagued the Argentines ever since the sovereign debt default in 2001 is but one indication of the government's incapacity to find a sustainable solution to its structural fiscal problems.

In the second part of my theoretical approach, I established that adding the vertical fiscal axis to the picture of fiscal imbalance and debt accumulation provides crucial additional information on the sources of macroeconomic instability. Countries that decide to decentralize fiscal control along the vertical axis of government (fiscal federalism) are often found to carry a higher risk of overall fiscal imbalance. To reach a deeper understanding of this problem, I juxtaposed two potential explanations for it. Hypothesis 2 states that the negative budgetary effects of vertical decentralization may be expected to add to the negative effects of a decentralized budget process on the central government level, leaving a country with a higher overall risk of incurring general government deficits. Going beyond the additive effect, hypothesis 3 suggests that an interaction takes place between the strength of budget institutions on the national level and the behavior of subnational budget actors in a vertically decentralized system. As shown in the case studies on Brazil and Argentina (chapters 5 and 6), expenditure decentralization indeed turned out to be particularly problematic for fiscal stability, both in Brazil in the earlier period and for Argentina throughout the full time period under scrutiny. Both countries were struggling with subnational government insolvency, forcing central governments to provide bailouts for subnational governments and state-owned banks and public enterprises, creating a number of follow-up problems including creditor moral hazard. Both also lend support to the view that subnational fiscal behavior indeed depends on central-level institutions. Put differently, it depends on a strengthening of national-level budgetary institutions as to whether subnational governments change their fiscal behavior. Institutional reforms at the national level promise to have a signaling effect on subnational budget actors who would otherwise face strong incentives to exploit the national tax base.

8.2.1 Lessons from Reforming Budget Institutions in Argentina and Brazil

During the first half of the 1990s, both Argentina and Brazil matched the type of countries that display a high degree of horizontal and vertical decentralization (see Table 8.1), exposing them to a high risk of fiscal imbalance. Under loose horizontal control, subnational fiscal indiscipline seems likely to turn into a severe problem for general government fiscal stability. Indeed, in line with my predictions, we observe in Argentina and Brazil during the second half of the 1990s a deterioration of overall fiscal results (and an increase in public debt ratios). The two governments could no longer lean against an economic downturn – for example, after the Mexican crisis in 1994 – by 'floating' outstanding liabilities, after both countries decided to peg their exchange rates to the US dollar. That meant that new policy options had to be identified. For both countries, there is evidence of a relatively high degree of budget process decentralization in the initial phase. However, their institutional paths separate at the end in 1997. Before that point, the presidents and finance ministers of both

Table 8.1 Matching Latin American countries

Vertical Decentralization		1996 Horizontal Decentralization: low	1996 Horizontal Decentralization: high	2004 Horizontal Decentralization: low	2004 Horizontal Decentralization: high
	low	*Type 1*	*Type 3*	*Type 1*	*Type 3*
		Chile	Bolivia	Chile	Costa Rica
		Costa Rica	Ecuador	Ecuador ↓	Guatemala
		Panama	Guatemala	Panama	Nicaragua
		Paraguay	Nicaragua	Peru	Paraguay
		Uruguay	Peru	El Salvador	
			El Salvador	Uruguay	
			Venezuela		
	high	*Type 2*	*Type 4*	*Type 2*	*Type 4*
		Colombia	Argentina	Brazil	Argentina
		Mexico	Brazil	Mexico	Bolivia
				Venezuela	
				Colombia →	

Source: Daughters and Harper (2007), Filc and Scartascini (2007)

countries appeared to be responding to spending pressures from line ministries and the legislature by increasing government expenditure, leading to a deterioration in fiscal results when economic growth and revenue slumped.

In both countries, subnational fiscal indiscipline appears to have contributed to overall fiscal instability. With the transition to democracy came the legislative decision in the late 1980s/ early 1990s to delegate more fiscal authority to lower levels of government, inviting subnational CPR problems. Unconstrained local budget actors were faced with strong incentives to increase spending on local public goods, and thus to improve their own re-election chances, while the costs of local spending increases were passed on to the general tax payer. To finance increasing levels of local public goods, subnational governments put pressure on the federal government to increase transfers and/or turn a blind eye to increasing subnational borrowing. There are accounts of such political pressure in Brazil between the first bailout for the states in 1989 and the third bailout in 1997, and it appears that the federal government found no means of ending the growth in subnational expenditure and debt accumulation up to the point of the third subnational bailout. At that turning point, however, the central government for the first time used its financial leverage over even the most powerful states to force them to accept tough fiscal conditions, woven into their respective debt contracts. However, going beyond explanations that rely purely on the establishment of hard budget constraints, I would argue that changing established patterns of fiscal indiscipline at the state level only became possible after a strong policy signal from central government about its commitment to stay on a path of fiscal consolidation, visible in the government's resolve to strengthen the national-level budget process.

In Argentina, federally imposed budget constraints (deficit and expenditure limits) in the framework of the two fiscal pacts in 1992 and 1993 at first seemed to help solve the existing subnational CPR problem. As shown in Chapter 6, subnational-level fiscal variables improved during the first few years following the implementation of the fiscal pacts. But their success was not to last for long. Under the economic recession, triggered by the Mexican Peso crisis in 1994–1995, the federal government gave in to provincial pressures, tolerating growing local expenditure and once more turning a blind eye to the imprudent (external) borrowing activities of the provinces. In the following years, with the next economic recession triggered by Brazil's devaluation in 1999, subnational-level – as well as national-level – fiscal discipline became ever more difficult to sustain. Given the decreased competitiveness of the Argentine economy, the drop in economic growth and hence in tax revenue and the parallel rise in debt-financing costs, the federal government had little choice but to put an end to the rigid exchange rate regime and to aim for a reduction in its – rapidly accumulated – outstanding debt towards the end of 2001.

Given the lack of viable and sustainable institutional and political instruments to implement austerity, a reduction in the debt ratio by means of reaching a sizeable primary balance adjustment seemed unlikely to begin with. Under the deteriorating economic circumstances and given investor panic and the withdrawal of foreign capital in 2001, the announced sovereign default during the last few days of that year finally came as no surprise to many observers of the Argentine economy. All in all, fiscal instability and concerns over public debt in Argentina, almost throughout the entire period studied above (1990–2006), evolved in stark contrast to the situation in Brazil, which took a series of institutional reform steps, allowing for successful fiscal and, eventually, debt consolidation following the reform years of 1996/97.

In Chapter 5, I showed how the implementation of particular budgetary institutional 'instruments' in Brazil helped the president to implement a fiscal consolidation plan that, to the surprise of many observers, allowed the government to turn around primary fiscal deficits despite the economic downturn in 1998 and to achieve strong and growing surpluses over the next few years. The effective crisis management in 1998, predated by institutional reforms between 1996 and 1997, served the president in regaining confidence among investors and international organizations. But more importantly, over the course of several years, successful structural reform helped to boost confidence in the effectiveness of Brazil's institutions. Although it may have taken international creditors a (long) time to finally build trust in the robustness of Brazil's institutional reforms, they finally seemed to have acknowledged the efforts, after 2003, expressed in a radical decrease in country risk after the first few months of the Lula da Silva administration. In sum, it seems important to acknowledge that a fundamental change in subnational fiscal behavior in Brazil was only achieved after the federal government, based on a broad political coalition in favor of fiscal consolidation, had decided to implement fundamental changes in the rules of the fiscal game.

8.2.2 Searching for Institutional Patterns

Introducing a new argument on the relationship of different fiscal institutions and actual fiscal behavior in emerging market nations, I make several theoretical claims (Chapter 3), which are later discussed in light of my empirical findings (chapters 4–7). Going beyond existing theories on the determinants of fiscal imbalance, I propose in Chapter 3 that national-level budgetary institutions interact with fiscal behavior at lower levels of government. Depending on how structured and transparent the national budget process appears to be, subnational budget actors would seem more (or less) likely to make fiscally irresponsible decisions, putting overall fiscal stability at risk. Sending a strong signal from the central level to lower tiers of government about fiscal consolidation as an over-arching, long-term goal was thought to alter subnational fiscal behavior.

My initial prediction (hypothesis 3, summarized in Table 3.2) was that countries largely fall into four different categories, depending on their respective degrees of horizontal (or national-level budgetary institutional) and of vertical fiscal decentralization (e.g. expenditure decentralization). The first two types are characterized by a strong centralization of budgetary institutions and transparency of the budget process and are therefore thought to carry little risk of fiscal imbalance. The type 1 and type 2 cases differ in their degree of vertical fiscal decentralization. Based on the second hypothesis (Chapter 3, summarized in Table 3.1), we would expect the more vertically decentralized cases to face a higher risk of incurring overall fiscal imbalance, due to the assumed added effect of national-level institutional weakness and the risk stemming from higher vertical decentralization. But based on hypothesis 3, I argued that the potential negative effect of vertical decentralization may be mitigated by strong central-level budgetary institutions. Seen from this perspective, even highly vertically decentralized countries are not necessarily exposed to higher fiscal risk. Two main factors may help to explain this: the first is based on the assumption that under a more centralized budgetary institutional set-up, the central government generally possesses the means to intervene in subnational fiscal decisions. Having the institutional means to punish and reward subnational governments might be seen as the crucial explanation for fiscal discipline on the subnational level. I therefore expected a lower risk that expenditure decentralization would translate into overall government fiscal instability. Second, going beyond central-level threats to sanction subnational fiscal indiscipline, I argue that strengthening national-level budget institutions fulfills an important signaling function. Accordingly, subnational governments are more likely to join a 'coalition' for fiscal consolidation when they observe a change in national-level institutions, changing incentives for the central government and budgetary veto players in a more substantial way. In contrast, I expected the risk of fiscal imbalance to be significantly higher in cases that fall into the two loosely structured categories of national-level budget process and lack of transparency. For type 3 cases, those that show a high degree of national-level budget process decentralization, albeit a low degree of vertical fiscal decentralization, I predicted a high likelihood of fiscal deficits and over-borrowing due to national-level dynamics. Finally, the odds for fiscal imbalance were found to rise significantly for type 4 cases, where subnational governments are granted large expenditure autonomy and where central-level budgetary institutions indicate uncoordinated budget decisions, lacking transparency. In those cases, I expect the interaction of loose fiscal constraints on the national level and fiscal strategies on subnational levels of government to lead to the worst imaginable outcomes, with profoundly negative effects on fiscal stability going beyond what we would expect from adding problems at different levels of government.

Table 8.1 summarizes where the Latin American countries analyzed in chapters 4–6 may be situated, applying the above-described categorization scheme. Over time, institutional reform allowed some countries to move out of the 'danger zone' with the highest risk of fiscal imbalance. A good example is Ecuador where a significant increase in central-level institutional control helped to accommodate an increase in vertical fiscal decentralization. Even though vertical fiscal decentralization (according to data from the IADB) in Ecuador has more than doubled since 1996, budgetary institutional reform after the 1999 sovereign debt crisis apparently served to rein in subnational and central-level fiscal deficits and debt. Between 1996 and 2006, the country managed to turn an overall fiscal deficit of close to 3 percent of GDP in 1996 into a budget surplus of more than 3 percent in 2006. Without doubt, budget improvement in an oil-exporting country like Ecuador and, similarly in other export-oriented countries including Peru, El Salvador, Venezuela and Brazil over the 2000s, has to be evaluated in light of strong, externally driven economic growth. Nevertheless, for governments such as that in Brazil and, to a lesser extent, Venezuela, that maintain a high degree of vertical decentralization, fiscal stability is likely to depend on more than the inflow of revenue. What counts, particularly during periods of continued economic downturn, and particularly so for the emerging market nations at hand, will be the capacity to control expenditure and implement fiscal adjustments, even under extreme macroeconomic pressure. As evidence from the analysis and the case studies presented in previous chapters underlines, type 2 cases generally have a larger chance of safeguarding fiscal stability compared to type 4 cases. In type 4 countries like Argentina, and increasingly Bolivia, the combination of vertically decentralized fiscal authority and weak central-level institutions suggests that governments are much more likely to fail trying to stabilize budgets, particularly in adverse economic conditions.

In the sample at hand, small and highly centralized countries like Costa Rica and Panama count among the most fiscally stable in the region. Furthermore, we find that cases like Chile and Uruguay fall into the category with the smallest risk of experiencing fiscal crisis. Although Uruguay was forced into a sovereign default under very exceptional circumstances in 2001, following Brazil's devaluation and the subsequent financial distress in Argentina, the small country's institutional strength helped Uruguay to get back on its feet in no time. After Uruguay was forced to restructure its debt in 2001, following the lead of finance minister Alejandro Atchugarry, the government implemented a strict fiscal adjustment program. Within one year of the default, the government had turned a primary deficit of −0.86 percent of GDP into a 0.44 percent primary surplus and continued to steadily increase its primary surplus afterwards, reaching more than 4 percent in the third year after default.[2] Paraguay constitutes a case that suffered from similar problems as Uruguay, following the financial meltdown and economic crisis in Argentina. Nevertheless, the government was able to secure a budget surplus in 2006.

Given the limitations of the data, it remains difficult to come up with a statistical analysis that shows that subnational fiscal behavior under vertical fiscal decentralization indeed plays out differently at lower degrees of horizontal decentralization as compared to higher degrees of national-level institutional centralization. Clearly, what is needed is further analysis, relying on data for subnational and national fiscal outcomes, to clarify the assumed relationships. However, evidence from the case studies on

Argentina and Brazil seems to support my claim that vertical decentralization effects turn out differently, depending on the degree of central-level institutional coordination, the establishment of sanctioning mechanisms and, as a precondition of the former, the degree of budget process transparency. If these findings were confirmed in subsequent quantitative analyses, it could open up a new avenue for research on the delegation of fiscal rights and responsibilities in federal unions.

8.3 POLICY OUTLOOK

In the introductory chapter, I explained my focus on fiscal stability, recognizing that it comes at the cost of leaving two other, crucial functions of fiscal policy out of the picture, i.e. allocation effectiveness and redistribution. Indeed, it seems very likely that the degree of vertical fiscal decentralization in a country beyond its relevance for fiscal stability is connected to these two functions of fiscal policy. To begin with, many would argue that allocation effectiveness and fiscal decentralization are connected. In fact, most analysts of federal systems would agree that more of the latter is likely to improve the former. As pointed out by Oates (1972) in his 'decentralization theorem', vertical decentralization may improve allocation efficiency because subnational governments are better able to match the tastes of their constituencies and public goods provision. A real-life example helps to understand this relationship: take the system of distributing publicly guaranteed childcare places in Germany's capital Berlin and a number of other cities. Parents in Berlin are in the lucky position of being able to choose whatever publicly run or private, registered childcare institution they find most suitable for their offspring. Places are paid for through a system of vouchers, provided to parents by the district of residence. Judging by the success of the Berlin voucher system, most people would agree that the decentralized spending of public resources is indeed the best option to match local tastes with tax resources in a place characterized by diverse living conceptions and a plurality of preferences with regard to early education.

As for redistribution, it appears equally evident that it should be affected by fiscal decentralization. However, as many would agree, its relationship with decentralization seems more likely to run in the opposite direction. For example, where the state is called to act upon a grave inequality in living conditions between different regions, municipalities and even city districts, what people generally have in mind is some sort of mechanism that allows higher levels of government to intervene in the fiscal matters of lower levels of government, precisely with the aim of redistributing fiscal resources. Depending on the country and type of fiscal framework, redistribution will take place from the center to local units of government, between different subnational units, or combining aspects of both types of redistribution. In each of these redistributive schemes, however, the fiscal autonomy of subnational units will have to be constrained. Higher levels of government will rein in local fiscal decision-making authority.

There are, of course, many cultural and historical reasons for which aiming for a higher degree of vertical (fiscal) decentralization may seem a legitimate goal of government, despite potential drawbacks, both for fiscal stability and redistribution. History provides numerous examples teaching us to be doubtful of unconstrained political centralization. This includes episodes in which politicians decide to de-politicize certain areas of political decision making by delegating it to 'apolitical' or 'neutral' governing bodies. Keeping these political risks in mind, how can we accommodate all three crucial functions of fiscal policy – stability, allocation efficiency and redistribution – over longer time frames? Institutional models such as the one implemented in Brazil in the late 1990s serve as a case in point that the virtues of vertical decentralization and fiscal and political autonomy of subnational levels of government can indeed be made compatible with overall stability. However, as anyone familiar with the standard of living and economic progress in Brazil would agree, achieving equal living conditions remains a huge challenge. Trying to fit the third crucial function, redistribution, into the equation will be a huge challenge for political economists and institutional economists for years to come.

In this book, I offer a much narrower perspective. Focusing only on the institutional effects of fiscal stability lowers the bar for finding positive examples of successful institutional reform. They include the budgetary institutional reforms of the 1920s in the USA, discussed in the introductory chapter, and the establishment of the 'Copper Stabilization Fund' and accompanying legislation in Chile at the end of the 1980s.[3] These examples generally support the view that budgetary institutions can indeed play an important role in achieving fiscal stability. Beyond them, more detailed empirical evidence on reforms, implementation processes and their (partial) economic success presented in previous chapters of this book equally support that view. That being said, as a social scientist, one is clearly always well advised not to generalize too easily from an analysis of only 15 countries, all situated in the same region, as was done above. With this caveat in mind, based on the existing institutional literature and my own analysis on Latin American countries, I derive several factors that seem to be crucial for successful fiscal stabilization. The points listed below appeared to be relevant for reform in nearly all the cases that I looked at. These are factors that should be taken into account for the design of a regulatory framework trying to strike a balance between decentralized fiscal decision making – for the benefits of local constituencies – and the fiscal stability of the whole:

- A single budget authority needs to have oversight and control over the budget process at the central level, holding veto powers over other budgetary actors.
- Budget decisions of the central budget authority have to be taken on the grounds of ex ante fiscal rules that have been ratified by the majority decision of a representative body (legislature), reflecting the will of the people (constituency) most affected by the budgetary decisions of the executive.
- To guarantee that budget rules will be fulfilled, minimum transparency standards (e.g. a ban on off-budgeting procedures) need to be guaranteed.
- Ex ante rules need to be flexible enough to safeguard the executive's ability to react to extreme economic shocks.
- To be credible constraints, legislative acts establishing fiscal rules have to identify a sanctioning mechanism that extends to central-level and subcentral budgetary actors. Ideally, legislators define ex ante what sanctions apply to both government agencies and individuals at different levels of government if they transgress fiscal rules.
- Acceptance of new fiscal rules is often achieved in a process, rather than by a single legislative act (see the example of Brazil). At the central and subcentral levels, support from political players for institutional reforms has been shown to be of crucial importance. Support from key political actors is needed to win both political majorities for fiscal responsibility legislation and political consensus that the new rules are binding over long time frames. Often, such political support is achieved through side-payments to the relevant political actors or interest groups. Historical examples show that the subcenters are more likely to accept fundamental institutional changes, reducing their (fiscal) sovereignty, under the condition of a crisis. This will lower the costs for the center to strike a deal with the subcenter, providing it with the necessary leverage to implement budgetary institutional reforms beyond the immediate crisis.
- 'Market discipline' under the condition of a credible no-bailout commitment of the center should be seen as an alternative solution to maintaining fiscal stability after a transition phase of central regulation.
- Legislative control of the policy decisions taken by the executive should under no circumstances be abandoned.

After all, fiscal stability remains only one – although an essential one – of the three major functions of fiscal government identified by Musgrave (1959) and others. Central control, through a strong regulatory framework, seems to be a sufficient way of achieving that goal, particularly in the context of an emerging market economy where market distortions are prevalent. Nevertheless, history has taught us that democratic government requires a balance between all three goals – stability, allocation efficiency and redistribution. Otherwise, given the apparent lack of political credibility, fiscal 'super-government' is doomed to fail.

NOTES

1. The potential for central governments to constrain subnational budget actors has to some extent been acknowledged in research by the IADB (Alesina et al. 1999, Filc and Scartascini 2007; see also Panizza 1999 and Stein 1999).
2. Based on its quick response to the debt crisis and the passing of fiscal adjustment measures, Uruguay achieved primary fiscal surpluses (3.13 percent of GDP in 2003, 4.13 percent in 2004) in excess of what was expected by the IMF in return for its financial assistance. The primary budget surplus stood at almost 4 percent in 2006, with the nominal budget almost balanced after years of financial hardship.
3. Chile established its Copper Stabilization Fund in 1985, becoming fully operational in 1987. Designed to smooth out the impact of copper price fluctuations on the economy, particularly on the real exchange rate and on government revenue, the fund's effectiveness was really tested for the first time in 2004. In that year, copper prices were boosted and Chile's GDP growth reached 6.1 percent, yielding an 18.8 percent increase in government revenue in inflation-adjusted terms. The government of President Ricardo Lagos (2000–2006) maintained its commitment to the role of the Copper Fund as a stabilization fund when limiting its real spending growth to 5.3 percent, despite the high incoming revenue. As a consequence, the government achieved a nominal (primary) fiscal surplus of 2.2 percent (1 percent) of GDP. The high copper-related revenue of 2004 allowed a further reduction in the public sector debt, which was already low by international standards. The public debt ratio dropped by more than half, from 13 percent of GDP in 2003 to 5.3 percent in 2006.

Appendix A

PART 1: CONTINUOUS FEDERAL BAILOUTS FOR THE BRAZILIAN STATES (1989, 1993, 1997)

Subnational fiscal instability in Brazil was linked until the late 1990s, to a great extent, to *moral hazard* in relations between the states and their private external creditors. Financial markets read the government's previous two bailouts for the states as a guarantee that the nation would step in whenever subnational debtors were in trouble. As a consequence, private creditors continued lending, substantially under-pricing the real underlying risk. By bailing out the states twice in only four years, the federal government signaled soft budget constraints to subnational budget actors, sending the erroneous message that they could continue to increase their expenditure on local public goods, passing on the bill to the general public.

The first subnational bailout occurred in late 1989, extending into 1990. Hence, the first bailout took place in a year that was characterized, among other things, by a sharp increase in the average annual consumer price inflation to 1430 percent, up from an already high inflation rate of 228 percent in 1987. Subnational governments had previously been increasingly gaining access to international financing. States had been borrowing both from the World Bank and the IADB, as well as from international private creditors. Dillinger and Webb (1999) note that borrowing from official lenders demanded federal guarantees whereas private borrowing did not, explaining the expansion in the latter category. By the end of the 1980s, when they came under greater financing difficulties – given the remaining high financing costs as a consequence of the yet unresolved debt moratorium declared by Brazil in 1987 – several states had stopped servicing their foreign debt. This move led the federal government to take on the states' liabilities and to incorporate all federally guaranteed debts of the states into the long-term debt of the federal treasury.[1] After the fiscal crisis in late 1989 and early 1990, the newly elected Collor de Mello administration implemented a stabilization program aimed at reducing inflation, which peaked in that year at an average of 2948 percent – topped only by the inflation rate in Argentina a year earlier (3079.8 percent). The government program had some short-term success, bringing down average inflation to 433 percent in 1991, but it then started to accelerate shortly after. By mid-1991 it had increased again, reaching more than 950 percent in 1992.

Although short in nature, the temporal success of the anti-inflation measures affected the policy game between the federal and subnational governments. Under high inflation, the states could continue to increase their deficit spending, given that they were able to 'inflate away' any outstanding liabilities. The reduction in inflation changed the incentives for subnational governments. When inflation decreased, the states' demand for debt renegotiation with the federal government suddenly increased. The federal government assumed those debts in exchange for fiscal conditionality, to be implemented through new legislation (Law 8388). However, when inflation accelerated again, after the collapse of the second Collor Plan in mid-1991, the pressure on the states to refinance their debts was reduced. As their demand for debt relief decreased, so did the federal government's influence on state-level fiscal decisions through conditionality.

Additionally, there were two measures that reduced the pressure on state governments. In February 1991, Central Bank Resolution 1789 allowed the exchange of Central Bank bonds for state bonds, which was effectively a rollover of state bonds in the domestic financial market. Also, the Central Bank fostered the demand for states' debt instruments by authorizing the operation of mutual funds with state and municipal bonds in their portfolios. Bevilaqua (2002, p. 14) notes that, as a result, bonds became the main source of financing for Brazilian states and the net debt of subnational governments increased from an already relatively high level of 7.5 percent of GDP in 1990 to 9.3 percent in 1991.[2] The growth speed of subnational government bonded debt, at a real growth rate of 40 percent between 1990 and 1991, according to Bevilaqua (2002, p. 14), brought the federal government, in the plan which focused on amending the 1988 constitution, to constrain state-level bond issuance.[3] Disaggregated data on bond issuance shows that states in the industrially more developed south of Brazil – Sao Paulo, Minas Gerais, Rio de Janeiro and Rio Grande do Sul – held the largest shares in total state bond issuance (Bevilaqua 2000, 2002). Apparently, the borrowing activity in the richest states was the highest.[4] Given the level of their economic and financial development, they enjoyed better access to capital markets.

Subnational debt accumulation turned into a severe problem again in 1992 because publicly owned state banks were faced with increasing difficulties in placing their bonds with private institutions. Creditor concerns about the political risks of their investments had been growing throughout 1992, a year marked by severe political gridlock and turmoil around the impeachment of President Collor de Mello at the end of December of that year. In reaction to their financing difficulties in the private markets, the states turned to the federal government, requesting debt renegotiations of their non-bonded debts with the nation. Their requests were finally met in November 1993 by the successor government of President Itamar Franco, which decided to bail out those state banks that were holding state bonds through a Central Bank Resolution (2081), sanctioned in June 1994. Additionally, before the bailout took place, the government succeeded in passing new legislation (Law 8727) that spelled out the fiscal conditions that the states were asked to comply with in return for financial assistance. The agreement with central government included a rescheduling of non-bonded debt for 20 years and extending to all debts of state governments and their enterprises. Furthermore, the Central Bank, which had by the end of 1993 not been holding any such bonds, assumed the majority of state bonds. In the course of the restructuring, the Central Bank intervened in the two largest state banks – BANESPA of Sao Paulo and BANERJ of Rio de Janeiro – on December 31, 1994 to take care of both banks' substantial liquidity problems (see Appendix A: Part 2 for details). The 1993/94 bailout included up-front debt relief and a reduction in interest on state debts, which were restructured for 30 years in most cases.

Constitutional Amendment No. 3 introduced a ban on the issuance of new state bonds up to December 1999, with the exception of those bonds financing the payment of judicial claims existing in 1988. The rollover operations of existing bonds were not affected, which – unwillingly or unconsciously – made the federal government's plan in 1993 a driver of further increases in bond financing. Bevilaqua (2002, p. 21) argues that the bailout eliminated the fiscal discipline that the financial markets were starting to impose on the states by refusing to hold their bonds, and concludes that it was an important driver of deficit spending and over-borrowing afterwards. Indeed, subnational expenditure continued to grow, which has been attributed to the 1988 constitution prescribing large central government responsibilities for public wage bill expenditure.

After a successful price stabilization, as a consequence of the Real Plan in 1994, payroll and other expenditure put severe financing pressure on subnational governments and the federal government alike. Given the high debt-financing costs – the average real interest rate stood at 21.6 percent throughout the first term of President Fernando Henrique Cardoso (1995–2003), peaking at 38 percent at the end of 1995 – the next subnational fiscal crisis in 1997 came as no great surprise to many observers. As the data impressively show, the accumulation of interest put a great burden on subnational finances in the mid-1990s, next to the budget behavior of the states. However, commenting on the order of relevance of the two explanations, Bevilaqua (2002, p. 39) notes that although 'high real interest rates made debt service unbearable, the evolution of states' debt was probably not sustainable otherwise'.[5] Both factors, continued deficit financing through borrowing and high real interest rates, led to serious fiscal difficulties in 1995, putting pressure on central government to develop yet another debt restructuring plan. Growth in subnational debt had been fostered by two main factors that the federal government was now aiming to control. The first was the extensive use of revenue anticipation loans (AROs) as collateral in short-term debt contracts, by the states to re-finance long-term debt. Second, subnational governments had been accruing large arrears, which were essentially hidden debts. For instance, state governments went into arrears on payments to suppliers and public employees and on loans to state-owned banks.

In November 1995, the federal government called for a comprehensive rescue operation, carried out by the National Monetary Council – the organ that sets the exchange rate for the Central Bank, consisting of the finance minister, the planning minister and the governor of the Central Bank. By decision of the Council (Vote 162/95), the Caixa Econômica Federal (CEF) was authorized to provide emergency credit lines to the states for three specific purposes: the payment of wages and other outstanding arrears, the financing of voluntary retirement programs, and the refinancing of outstanding AROs. In exchange, the states were required to reduce payroll expenditure to 60 percent of net revenue by 1998, to privatize state assets and to increase the efficiency of state-level tax administration. This initiative, however, failed, largely due to the states' refusal to accept the conditions of the federal government. As many observers have argued, that first government approach to restructuring state debts may have been doomed to fail because the target of cutting state spending on the public payroll to 60 percent of current revenue was too ambitious. It was not until September 1997 that the federal government successfully negotiated a comprehensive restructuring with the states (Law 9496 discussed above), combined with a final bailout, putting emphasis on states' obligation to adjust in return for rescue financing.

PART 2: BRAZIL'S PROGRAM TO REDUCE STATE INVOLVEMENT IN BANKING ACTIVITY (PROES), 1995–1997

Brazil began reforming the state banking sector in 1995. Until the crisis of 1995, state-owned banks had been a driving force behind the growing subnational debt. The restructuring and privatization program for state-owned banks became an important pillar of the broader federal government intervention in state finances and fiscal policies, finally implemented in 1997/98. In December 1995, following the breakdown of Sao Paulo's state bank BANESPA, the federal government offered the governor of Sao Paulo a bailout and restructuring of the bank's debt. The offer included the transfer of the majority of (nonperforming) state bonds to the federal level. Shortly after the offer was made to Sao Paulo, the governor of the Amazonas state publically noted his concern that smaller and poorer states were treated unfairly. President Cardoso reacted by calling a meeting of governors in late April 1996 where he promised equal treatment for all states willing to accept a bank restructuring and fiscal adjustment in exchange for the provision of federal rescue funds. At the meeting, Cardoso first declared that any fiscal adjustment would be negotiated with a finance ministry team on a case-by-case basis. He made it clear that rescue loans would be conditional on the privatization of state assets. In August 1996, the federal government announced the creation of a comprehensive framework aimed at restructuring the entire (state) banking sector. Under the program to reduce state involvement in banking activity – the so-called PROES initiative – the government offered the states financing to restructure their banks and prepare them for privatization or to transform them into non-financial development agencies. The PROES introduced a ceiling of 50 percent of federal financing of required resources to restructure state banks and prohibited the use of any federal funds in case a state wanted to keep a bank as a public financial institution. As an additional carrot for the states, the National Monetary Council offered a 90-day rollover of interest on loans from federal financial institutions for states signing off on PROES.

At first, with the large debtor states of Minas Gerais and Rio Grande do Sul aboard, the chances looked good for the president putting a quick end to the subnational imbalances. However, only days before municipal-level elections were held in mid-September 1996, a power struggle between several state governors and the president over the terms of the restructuring agreements caused a hold-up in the implementation of PROES. In October 1996, the federal government received a strong blow from 19 governors convening in Sao Paulo to announce that they were abandoning negotiations with the federal finance ministry team and were requesting a renegotiation of the 1993 debt contracts with the federal government. Governors requested a lengthening of the maturities in states' debt contracts with the nation (initially set to 20 years in the 1993 bailout) and a lowering of ceilings on the share of debt servicing in states' current revenue. State leaders were also requesting larger federal compensation for the revenue losses on exports following from the 1996

Kandir Law. A crucial moment in the governors' 'fiscal revolt' came with the decision of Sao Paulo's governor, a member of Cardoso's party and the leader of the most highly indebted state, to join ranks with the other protesters. The central government remained unyielding about keeping minimal adjustment requirements in the PROES, and in December 1997 it finally triumphed over the revolting states when Sao Paulo, as the first of the four biggest debtor states, signed a binding agreement with the nation.

In the agreement, the federal government took on all of Sao Paulo's bonded debt and debt to BANESPA (in the equivalent of US$50 billion). Of this, US$40 billion was to be refinanced as a loan to the state government, with 30 years to maturity and a real interest rate of 6 percent, which was below market rates. Another $6.2 billion (12.5 percent) was amortized immediately through the transfer of stock in state enterprises (including BANESPA, two large power companies and the state railroad). Additionally, the deal included a federal debt relief of the remaining $3.8 billion (7.5 percent). The first restructuring contract, signed with the state of Sao Paulo, included provisions that would make debt servicing for the state government agreeable. Specifically, that meant that a debt-service ceiling was installed, guaranteeing that debt service would be no higher than 13 percent of net current revenue. Furthermore, the debt-service ceiling was back-loaded, remaining in practice as low as 6.7 percent of current revenue, increasing gradually to 13 percent in 2000. After Sao Paulo, Minas Gerais signed a similar agreement in February 1998, leading the federal government to assume 11.8 billion real of that state's debt. About 78 percent of this debt was refinanced for 30 years at an interest rate of 7.5 percent, another 7.9 percent of the debt was to be amortized immediately through the transfer of assets (mainly receipts from the privatization of two state banks) and the remaining 14.1 percent of the restructured amount was to be forgiven. Like Sao Paulo, Minas Gerais was granted a back-loading debt-service ceiling, set at 6.7 percent of current revenue in 1998 and raised to 13 percent in 2000. But in the agreement with Minas Gerais, the federal government, for the first time, made its financial assistance conditional on the state ending the risky financial activities of its two major banks. As part of the debt agreement, the state was required to recognize the losses accumulated by two state banks and to borrow 4.1 billion real from the federal government to pay off its net liabilities. This was included in the total package of debt to be refinanced, raising the total to 15.9 billion real. However, the debt service was slowed by lowering the ratio of debt service to current revenue in the first few years. In March and April 1998, the last two of the four largest bond-issuing states, Rio Grande do Sul and Rio de Janeiro, followed suit, signing debt-restructuring contracts on similar terms. In the end, the same refinancing terms were applied to all remaining states in Brazil, including those that had been servicing their debt before.

By mid-1999, 24 out of the 27 state governments had restructured their debt under the PROES. All in all, the new restructuring agreement with the federal government meant only minor increases in federal expenditure on the part of the states. At the time, some critics of the PROES initiative argued that the federal government should have gone further in making federal aid conditional on more detailed adjustment plans, requesting from the states precise strategies, including the naming of areas for expenditure cuts and revenue increases. In contrast, others were more worried that the debt relief for the states was too small. Indeed, states were left with relatively high debt stocks afterwards (see Figure 5.5).

NOTES

1. The federal government's decision to restructure subnational debt came after a large-scale default on external private debt in 1987. At the time, former President José Sarney (1985–1990) declared a unilateral moratorium on Brazil's outstanding debt, causing turmoil among investors who fled the country as a consequence, resulting in a sharp drop in foreign investments. Under political pressure from the US government, President Sarnay later, in 1988, declared that the moratorium was a mistake. Yet, the external debt problem remained a major problem for Brazilian governments until a final deal with international private creditors was signed in 1994. The moratorium of 1987 is widely perceived among Brazilian politicians and economic experts as a traumatic experience, which – for all its bad consequences – led at least to a common denominator, valid across party lines, that no government should ever follow a similar strategy again.
2. To compare, consolidated provincial debt in Argentina ranged between 3 and 5 percent for most of the 1990s, before soaring to 6 percent in 2000, and finally jumping to 11 percent of GDP in 2001.
3. The surge in subnational bonded debt came as a consequence of Central Bank Resolution 1789 of February 1991, allowing the exchange of Central Bank bonds for state bonds, which was effectively a rollover of state bonds in the domestic financial market. Furthermore, the Central Bank authorized the inclusion of state and municipal bonds in portfolio operations of mutual funds.
4. According to data presented in Bevilaqua (2000, 2002), the shares of the Brazilian states in total bonded debt were as follows in 1989 (values for 1996 in parentheses) Sao Paulo, 37 (42) percent; Minas Gerais, 23 (20) percent; Rio Grande do Sul, 15 (14) percent; Rio de Janeiro, 18 (13) percent; Other, 7 (11) percent.
5. Commenting on their order of relevance, Bevilaqua (2002, p. 39) notes that although 'high real interest rates made debt service unbearable, the evolution of states' debt was probably not sustainable otherwise'.

Appendix B: List of research interviews

DISCLAIMER

In the spring of 2007 and 2008, I interviewed the list of politicians, policy experts and economists below in a series of semi-structured research interviews. I am grateful to everyone who agreed to share his or her crisis experience with me and thus contributed significantly to the success of my research project. In accordance with the interviewees, I agreed to draw on the interviews as a source of background information. Only in the (exceptional) case that an interview partner agreed to being quoted directly, including his or her name, did I make use of direct quotes in the main text.

BRAZIL

Fernando Henrique Cardoso, President of Brazil (1995–2002); Minister of Finance (1993–1994); Minister of External Relations (1992–1993), interviewed in February 2008, Sao Paulo, Brazil

Arminio Fraga Neto, Brazilian Central Bank, President (1999–2002), Gavea Investimentos Ltda., Co-Founder, Chief Investment Officer, Chairman, interviewed in February 2008, Rio de Janeiro, Brazil

Amaury Bier, Deputy Minister of Finance (1999–2002), Secretary for Economic Policy (1998–1999); Ministry of Planning, Chief Economist (1996–1998); Gavea Investimentos Ltda., CEO, past: World Bank, Executive Director (2002–2004), interviewed in February 2008, Rio de Janeiro, Brazil

Ilan Goldfajn, Brazilian Central Bank, Director of Economic Policy (2000–2003); ITAU Unibanco Bance commercial, Chief Economist, past: IMF, Economist (1996–1999), interviewed in February 2008, Rio de Janeiro, Brazil

Amir Khair, State of Sao Paulo, Secretary of Finance (1989–1992); Brazilian Development Bank (BNDES), Fiscal Policy Advisor, interviewed in February 2008, Sao Paulo, Brazil

Paulo Batista Nogueira, IMF, Executive Director for Brazil (2007–); Ministry of Planning, Undersecretary of Economic Affairs (1985–1986);

Ministry of Finance, Advisor to the Minister of Finance on External Debt (1986–1987), interviewed in May 2008, Washington, DC

Paulo Mansur Levy, Ipea-Instituto de Pesquina Economicy Aplicada, Head of Research, interviewed in February 2008, Rio de Janeiro, Brazil

ARGENTINA

Domingo Cavallo, Argentine Minister of the Economy (1991–1996, 03-12/2001); Minister of Foreign Affairs (1989–1991); President of the Central Bank (07-08/1982), Yale University, Jackson Institute for Global Affairs, Senior Fellow, interviewed in March 2008, Buenos Aires, Argentina

Daniel Marx, Economy Ministry of Argentina, Secretary of Finance (1999–2001); Special Financial Representative/Assistant Secretary at the Economy Ministry (1988–1993), Quantum Financas, Executive Director, interviewed in March 2008, Buenos Aires, Argentina

Miguel Kiguel, Economy Ministry of Argentina, Undersecretary of Finance/Chief Advisor (1996–1999); Central Bank of Argentina, Deputy General Manager for Economics and Finance (1994–1996), Econ Views, Executive Director, interviewed in March 2008, Buenos Aires, Argentina

Javier Alvaredo, Economy Ministry of Argentina, Secretary of Finance (12/2000–8/2002), Private Sector/Financial Services, interviewed in March 2008, Buenos Aires, Argentina

Juan Carlos Barboza, Economy Ministry of Argentina, Undersecretary of Finance (2007–2008), Central Bank of Argentina, Principal Director of Reserves Administration (2008–2011), ITAU Unibanco Argentina, Chief Economist, past: Advisor to the Superintendent of Financial/ Currency Exchange Entities (2008–2010), interviewed in March 2008, Buenos Aires, Argentina

Daniel Artana, FIEL (Fundación de Investigaciones Económicas Latinoamericanas), Chief Economist, interviewed in March 2008, Buenos Aires, Argentina

Juan Luis Bour, FIEL, Chief Economist (1977–); Economonitor, Analyst, interviewed in March 2008, Buenos Aires, Argentina

Ludovico Videla, Fundación Bunge y Born, Executive Director, interviewed in March 2008, Buenos Aires, Argentina

INTERNATIONAL ORGANIZATIONS

Brian Pinto, World Bank, Lead Economist, interviewed in March 2007, Washington, DC

Punam Chuhan, World Bank, Senior Advisor, interviewed in March 2007, Washington, DC

Charles Blitzer, IFC, Senior Advisor, past IMF Ass. Director, Monetary and Capital Markets Department, interviewed in March 2007, Washington, DC

Eduardo Borensztein, IMF, Advisor/IADB Regional Advisor, interviewed in March 2007, Washington, DC

Jeromin Zettelmeyer, German Ministry of the Economy, economist, past: IMF, EBRD, Deputy Chief Economist/Director of Research, Deputy Head of Regional Studies, Western Hemisphere Department, interviewed in March 2007, Washington, DC

Jochen Andritzky, German Council of Economic Experts, Secretary General, formerly at IMF, Economist, interviewed in March 2007, Washington, DC

PRIVATE SECTOR/LEGAL EXPERTS

Walter Molano, Bcp Securities LLC, Managing Partner, interviewed in May 2008, Newark, NJ

Lee Buchheit, Cleary, Gottlieb LLP, Lawyer and Sovereign Debt Negotiator, interviewed in March 2007, New York

Lex Rieffel, Brookings Institution, Senior Fellow, Global Economy and Development; US Treasury, Economist and Institute of International Finance (IIF), Senior Executive (1975–1992), interviewed in March 2007, Washington, DC

Sabine Miltner, Deutsche Bank, Managing Director, Group Sustainability Officer, formerly at the Institute of International Finance (IIF), Director of Emerging Markets Policy Department, interviewed in March 2007, Washington, DC

Bibliography

Abuelafia, E., S. Berenztein, M. Braun and L. di Gresia (2009) 'Who Decides on Public Expenditure? The Importance of the Informal Budget Process in Argentina', in *Who Decides the Budget: A Political Economy Analysis of the Budget Process in Latin America*, ed. by M. Hallerberg, C. Scartascini and E. Stein, Washington and Cambridge, MA: Inter-American Development Bank and Harvard University Press.

Alesina, A. and A. Drazen (1991) 'Why are Stabilizations Delayed?', *American Economic Review*, 81, 1170–1188.

Alesina, A., R. Hausmann, R. Hommes and E. Stein (1996) 'Budget Institutions and Fiscal Performance in Latin America', Working Paper 5586, Cambridge, MA: National Bureau of Economic Research (NBER).

Alesina, A., R. Hausmann, R. Hommes and E. Stein (1999) 'Budget Institutions and Fiscal Performance in Latin America', *Journal of Development Economics*, 59, 253–273.

Alston, L., M. Melo, B. Mueller and C. Pereira (2009) 'Presidential Power, Fiscal Responsibility Laws, and the Allocation of Spending: The Case of Brazil', in *Who Decides the Budget? A Political Economy Analysis of the Budget Process in Latin America*, ed. by M. Hallerberg, C. Scartascini, and E. Stein, Washington, DC and Cambridge, MA: Inter-American Development Bank and Harvard University Press.

Alt, J.E. and D.D. Lassen (2006) 'Fiscal Transparency, Political Parties, and Debt in OECD Countries', *European Economic Review*, 50, 1403–1439.

Angrist, J. and J.-S. Pirschke (2008) *Mostly Harmless Econometrics: An Empiricist's Companion*, Princeton, NJ: Princeton University Press.

Anselin, L. (1995) 'Local Indicators of Spatial Association: LISA', *Geographical Analysis*, 27, 93–115.

Artana, D. (2007) 'Are Latin-American Countries Decentralized?', *Documento de Trabajo* 92, Buenos Aires: Fundación de Investigaciones Económicas Latinoamericanas (FIEL).

Artana, D., S. Auguste, M. Cristini, C. Moskovits and I. Templado (2012) 'Sub-National Revenue Mobilization in Latin American and Caribbean Countries: The Case of Argentina', IDB Working Paper Series No. IDB-WP-297, Washington, DC: Inter-American Development Bank.

Bahl, R.W. and J.F. Linn (1992) *Urban Public Finance in Developing Countries*, Oxford: Oxford University Press.

Bank, I.-A. D. (1997) 'Fiscal Decision Making in Decentralized Democracies', in *Latin America after a Decade of Reforms: Economic and Social Progress in Latin America*, Washington, DC: Johns Hopkins Press.

Bearce, D.H. (2009) 'EMU: The Last Stand for the Policy Convergence Hypothesis', *Journal of European Public Policy*, 16, 582–600.

Beck, T., P.K.G. Clarke, A. Groff and P. Walsh (2001) 'New Tools in Comparative Political Economy: The Database of Political Institutions', *World Bank Economic Review*, 15, 165–176.

Beers, D. and J. Chambers (2006) 'Default Study: Sovereign Defaults at 26-Year Low, to Show Little Changes in 2007', Report, New York: Standard and Poor's.

Beetsma, R., M. Giuliodori and P. Wierts (2009) 'Planning to Cheat: EU Fiscal Policy in Real Time', *Economic Policy*, 24, 753–804.

Beramandi, P. (2007) 'Inequality and the Territorial Fragmentation of Solidarity', *International Organization*, 61, 783–820.

Berman, L. (1979) *The Office of Management and Budget and the Presidency, 1921–1979*, Princeton, NJ: Princeton University Press.

Bevilaqua, A.S. (2000) 'State Government Bailouts in Brazil', *Texto Para Discussao* 421, Rio de Janeiro: PUC-Rio Departemento de Economia.

Bevilaqua, A.S. (2002) 'State Government Bailouts in Brazil', Research Network Working Paper No. R-441, Washington, DC: Inter-American Development Bank.

Bird, R. and F. Vaillancourt (1998) *Fiscal Decentralization in Developing Countries*, Cambridge: Cambridge University Press.

Blanchard, O. and A. Shleifer (2001) 'Federalism With and Without Political Centralization: China versus Russia', *IMF Staff Papers*, 48, Special Issue.

Blanchard, O.J. and F. Giavazzi (2004) 'Improving the SGP through a Proper Accounting of Public Investment', CEPR Discussion Papers 4220, Washington, DC: Centre for Economic Policy Research (CEPR).

Bleher, M.L. and A. Cheasty (1991) 'Analytical and Methodological Issues in the Measurement of the Fiscal Deficit', *Journal of Economic Literature*, 29, 1644–1678.

Block, S. and P.M. Vaaler (2004) 'The Price of Democracy: Sovereign Risk Ratings, Bond Spreads and Political Business Cycles in Developing Countries', *Journal of International Money and Finance*, 23, 917–946.

Bomfim, A. and A. Shah (1994) 'Macroeconomic Management and the Division of Powers in Brazil: Perspectives for the 1990s', *World Development*, 22, 535–542.

Bonvecchi, A. (2010) 'The Political Economy of Fiscal Reform in Latin America: The Case of Argentina', IDB Working Paper No. 175, Washington, DC: Inter-American Development Bank.

Bonvecchi, A. and G. Lodola (2010) 'The Dual Logic of Intergovernmental Transfers: Presidents, Governors, and the Politics of Coalition-Building in Argentina', *Publius*, 41, 179–206.

Borensztein, E., B. Eichengreen and U. Panizza (2006) 'In the New Millenium: New Markets and New Opportunities', Prepared for the annual meetings of the board of governors, Inter-American Development and Inter-American Investment Corporation, Belo Horizonte, Brazil, Washington, DC: Inter-American Development Bank.

Braun, M. (2006) 'The Political Economy of Debt in Argentina, or Why History Repeats Itself', Buenos Aires, AR: CIPPEC. Paper prepared for the World Bank Study 'Sovereign Debt and Development: Market Access Countries', under the coordination of Brian Pinto.

Brender, A. and A. Drazen (2005) 'How Do Budget Deficits and Economic Growth Affect Reelection Prospects? Evidence from a Large Cross-Section of Countries', Working Paper 11862, Cambridge, MA: NBER.

Brennan, G. and J. Buchanan (1977) 'Towards a Tax Constitution for Leviathan', *Journal of Public Economics*, 8, 255–273.

Brennan, G. and J.M. Buchanan (1980) *The Power to Tax: Analytical Foundations of a Fiscal Constitution*, Cambridge, MA: Cambridge University Press.

Brooks, S. (2007) 'Globalization and Pension Reform in Latin America', *Latin American Politics and Society*, 49(4), 31–62.

Broz, L. (2010) 'Partisan Financial Cycles', Paper prepared for 'Politics in Hard Times: The Great Recession and Contemporary Politics', A Conference in Honor of Peter A. Gourevitch. University of California, San Diego, 23–24 April.

Buchanan, J.M. and R. Wagner (1977) *Democracy in Deficit: The Political Legacy of Lord Keynes*, New York: Academic Press.

Burki, S.J., G.E. Perry and W.R. Dillinger (1999) *Beyond the Center: Decentralizing the State*, Washington, DC: World Bank.

Buti, M., S.C.W. Eijffinger and D. Franco (2003) 'Revisiting the Stability and Growth Pact: Grand Design or Internal Adjustment', Discussion Paper 3692, Washington, DC: Centre for Economic Policy Research (CEPR).

Calvo, G.A., A. Izquierdo and E. Talvi (2003) 'Sudden Stops, the Real Exchange Rate and Fiscal Sustainability: Argentina's Lessons', Working Paper 9828, Cambridge, MA: National Bureau of Economic Research (NBER).

Campello, D. (2008) 'Between Votes and Capital: Democracy and Financial

Integration in the Developing World', PhD thesis, Department of Political Science, University of California Los Angeles.

Campello, D. (2015) *The Politics of Market Discipline in Latin America: Globalization and Democracy*, Cambridge: Cambridge University Press.

Carey, J.M. and M.S. Shugart (1995) 'Incentives to Cultivate a Personal Vote: A Rank Ordering of Electoral Formulas', *Electoral Studies*, 14, 417–439.

Clark, W.R. and M. Hallerberg (2000) 'Strategic Interaction between Monetary and Fiscal Actors under Full Capital Mobility', *American Political Science Review*, 94, 323–346.

Cline, W. (1995) *International Debt Reexamined*, Washington, DC: Peterson Institute.

Congleton, R. (2006) 'Asymmetric Federalism and the Political Economy of Decentralization', in *Handbook of Fiscal Federalism*, ed. by E. Ahmad and G. Brossio, Cheltenham: Edward Elgar.

Corsetti, G. and N. Roubini (1992) 'Tax Smoothing Discretion Versus Balanced Budget Rules in the Presence of Politically Motivated Fiscal Deficits: The Design of Optimal Fiscal Rules for Europe after 1992', Discussion Paper 682, London: CEPR.

Creel, J. and F. Saraceno (2010) 'European Fiscal Rules after the Crisis', *Journal of Innovation Economics*, 2, 95–122.

Daughters, R. and L. Harper (2007) 'Fiscal and Political Decentralization Reforms', in *The State of State Reform in Latin America*, ed. by E. Lora, Washington, DC: Inter-American Development Bank, Chap. 7, 213–261.

de Haan, J. and J.-E. Sturm (1997) 'Political and Economic Determinants of OECD Budget Deficits and Government Expenditure: A Reinvestigation', *European Journal of Political Economy*, 13(4), 739–750.

de la Torre, A., E.L. Yeyati and E. Schmukler (2003) 'Living and Dying with Hard Pegs', *Economia*, 5(2), 43–99.

de Mello, L.J. (2000) 'Fiscal Decentralization and Intergovernmental Fiscal Relations: A Cross-Country Analysis', *World Development*, 28, 365–380.

de Tocqueville, A. (2004) *Democracy in America* (trans. by A. Goldhammer), New York: Library of America.

Diaz-Cayeros, A. (2006) *Federalism, Fiscal Authority, and Centralization in Latin America*, New York: Cambridge University Press.

Dillinger, W. and S.B. Webb (1999) 'Fiscal Management in Federal Democracies: Argentina and Brazil', World Bank Policy Research Working Paper 2121, Washington, DC: World Bank.

Dornbusch, R. (1995) 'Progress Report on Argentina', in *Reform, Recovery, and Growth: Latin America and the Middle East*, ed. by R. Dornbusch and S. Edwards, Chicago, IL: University of Chicago Press.

Drazen, A. (2000) 'The Political Business Cycle after 25 Years', *NBER Macroeconomic Annual*, 15.

Easterly, W., C. Rodriguez and K. Schmidt-Hebbel (1994) *Public Sector Deficits and Macroeconomic Performance*, New York: Oxford University Press.

Eaton, K. and T. Dickovick (2004) 'The Politics of Re-Centralization in Argentina and Brazil', *Latin American Research Review*, 39, 90–122.

ECLAC (2009) *Social Panorama of Latin America*. Santiago de Chile: Economic Commission for Latin America and the Caribbean (ECLAC), United Nations Publications.

Eichengreen, B. (1990) 'One Money for Europe? Lessons from the US Currency Union', *Economic Policy*, 5, 117–187.

Eichengreen, B. (2007) 'The Breakup of the Euro Area', Working Paper 13393, Cambridge, MA: National Bureau of Economic Research (NBER).

Eichengreen, B. and T. Bayoumi (1994) 'The Political Economy of Fiscal Restrictions: Implications for Europe from the United States', *European Economic Review*, 38, 783–791.

Eichengreen, B. and J. von Hagen (1996) 'Fiscal Restrictions and Monetary Union: Rationales, Repercussions, Reforms', *Empirica*, 23, 3–23.

Eichengreen, B., R. Hausmann and J. von Hagen (1999) 'Reforming Budgetary Institutions in Latin America: The Case for a National Fiscal Council', *Open Economics Review*, 10, 415–442.

Enderlein, H. (2009) *Solving the Trilemma of Multi-Layered Fiscal Frameworks in Industrialized Countries*, Berlin: Hertie School of Governance.

Facchini, G. and C. Testa (2008) 'Fiscal Decentralization, Regional Inequality and Bail-Outs: Lessons from Brazil's Debt Crisis', *Quarterly Review of Economics and Finance*, 48, 333–344.

Fedelino, A. and T. Ter-Minassian (2010) 'Making Fiscal Decentralization Work: Cross-Country Experiences', Occasional Paper 271, Washington, DC: IMF.

Feldstein, M. (2002) 'Argentina's Fall: Lessons from the Latest Financial Crisis', *Foreign Affairs*, 81, 8–14.

Filc, G. and C. Scartascini (2004) 'Budget Institutions and Fiscal Outcomes: Ten Years of Inquiry on Fiscal Matters at the Research Department', Technical report, Washington, DC: IADB. Proceedings of the Inter-American Development Bank (IADB), Research Department, 10-Year Anniversary Conference.

Filc, G. and C. Scartascini (2007) 'Budgetary Institutions', in *The State of State Reform in Latin America*, ed. by E. Lora, Stanford, CA: Stanford University Press, 157–184.

Fitoussi, J.-P. and J. Creel (2002) 'How to Reform the European Central Bank', Working Paper, London: Centre for European Reform.

Fornisari, S., F. Webb and H.-F. Zou (1998) *Decentralized Spending and Central Government Deficits: International Evidence*, Washington, DC: World Bank.

Franzese, R. (2010) 'The Multiple Effects of Multiple Policymakers: Veto Actors Bargaining in Common Pools', *Rivista Italiana di Scienza Politica*, 40, 341–369.

Franzese, R.J.J. (2002) *Macroeconomic Policies of Developed Democracies*, Ann Arbor, MI: University of Michigan Press.

Franzese, R.J.J. and K.L. Jusko (2006) 'Political-Economic Cycles', in *Oxford Handbook of Political Economy*, ed. by D. Wittman and B. Weingast, New York: Oxford University Press, 545–564.

Gaetani, F. and B. Heredia (2002) 'The Political Economy of Civil Service Reform in Brazil: The Cardoso Years', Technical report, Washington, DC: IADB.

Garrett, G. (2000) 'Capital Mobility, Exchange Rates and Fiscal Policy in the Global Economy', *Review of International Political Economy*, 7, 153–170.

Giambiagi, F. (2007) 'Dezessete Anos de Política Fiscal No Brasil: 1991–2007', Texto Para Discussao 1309, Rio de Janeiro: Instituto de Pesquisa Economica Aplicada (IPEA).

Giambiagi, F. and M. Ronci (2004) 'Fiscal Policy and Debt Sustainability: Cardoso's Brazil, 1995–2002', Working Paper 04/156, Washington, DC: IMF.

Gleich, H. (2003) 'Budget Institutions and Fiscal Performance in Central and Eastern European Countries', Working Paper 215, Frankfurt, a.M.: European Central Bank (ECB).

Griliches, Z. and J.A. Hausman (1986) 'Errors in Variables in Panel Data', *Journal of Econometrics*, 31(1), 93–118.

Grossman, P.J. (1989) 'Fiscal Decentralization and Government Size: An Extension', *Public Choice*, 62(1), 63–69.

Hallerberg, M. (2004) *Domestic Budgets in a United Europe: Fiscal Governance from the End of Bretton Woods to EMU*, Ithaca, NY: Cornell University Press.

Hallerberg, M. and P. Marier (2004) 'Executive Authority, the Personal Vote, and Budget Discipline in Latin American and Caribbean Countries', *American Journal of Political Science*, 48, 571–587.

Hallerberg, M., C. Scartascini and E. Stein, eds. (2009a) *Who Decides the Budget?*, Washington, DC and Cambridge, MA: Inter-American Development Bank and Harvard University Press.

Hallerberg, M., R. Strauch and J. von Hagen (2009b) *Forms of Fiscal*

Governance: Evidence from Europe, New York: Cambridge University Press.
Hallerberg, M. and J. von Hagen (1999) 'Electoral Institutions, Cabinet Negotiations, and Budget Deficits in the European Union', in *Fiscal Institutions and Fiscal Performance*, ed. by J.M. Poterba and J. von Hagen, Chicago, IL: University of Chicago Press, 209–232.
Hallerberg, M. and G.B. Wolff (2008) 'Fiscal Institutions, Fiscal Policy and Sovereign Risk Premia in EMU', *Public Choice*, 136, 379–396.
Hallerberg, M. and S. Ylaeoutinen (2010) 'Political Power, Fiscal Institutions and Budgetary Outcomes in Central and Eastern Europe', *Journal of Public Policy*, 30, 45–62.
Hauptmeier, S., J.S. Fuentes and L. Schuknecht (2010) 'Towards Expenditure Rules and Fiscal Sanity in the Euro Area', Working Paper No. 1266, Frankfurt, a.M.: European Central Bank.
Helleiner, E. (1994) *States and the Reemergence of Global Finance: From Bretton Woods to the 1990s*, Ithaca, NY: Cornell University Press.
Henisz, W.J. (2000) 'The Institutional Environment for Economic Growth', *Economics and Politics*, 12, 1–31.
Hibbs, D.A. (1977) 'Political Parties and Macroeconomic Policy', *American Political Science Review*, 71, 1467–1487.
IMF (1996a) *Argentina Provincial Finances Study: Selected Issues in Fiscal Federalism* (in two vols) – *Vol. 1: The Main Report 15487-AR*, Washington, DC: IMF.
IMF (1996b) *Argentina Provincial Finances Study: Selected Issues in Fiscal Federalism* (in two vols) – *Vol. 2*, Washington, DC: IMF.
Ize, A. (1991) 'Measurement of Fiscal Performance in IMF-Supported Programs: Some Methodological Issues', in *How to Measure the Fiscal Deficit: Analytical and Methodological Issues*, ed. by M.L. Bleher, Washington, DC: IMF.
Izquierdo, A., R. Romero and E. Talvi (2008) 'Booms and Busts in Latin America: The Role of External Factors', Research Department Working Paper Series 631, Washington, DC: Inter-American Development Bank.
Jin, J. and H.-f. Zou (2002) 'How does Fiscal Decentralization affect Aggregate, National, and Subnational Government Size?', *Journal of Urban Economics*, 52, 270–293.
Johnson, C.L. and K.A. Kriz (2005) 'Fiscal Institutions, Credit Ratings, and Borrowing Costs', *Public Budgeting and Finance*, 25, 84–103.
Joumard, I., P.M. Kongsrud, Y.-S. Nam and R. Price (2005) 'Enhancing the Effectiveness of Public Spending: Experience in OECD Countries', OECD Economics Department Working Paper 380, Paris: OECD.
Kaminsky, G.L. and C.M. Reinhart (1999) 'The Twin Crises: The Causes

of Banking and Balance-of-Payments Problems', *American Economic Review*, 89, 473–500.

Kaplan, S.B. (2009) 'From Spendthrifts to Misers: Globalization and Latin American Politicians', PhD thesis, Department of Political Science, Yale University.

Kaplan, S.B. (2013) *Globalization and Austerity Politics in Latin America*, Cambridge: Cambridge University Press.

Kiewiet, D.R. and M.D. McCubbins (1991) *The Logic of Delegation: Congressional Parties and the Appropriations Process*, Chicago, IL: University of Chicago Press.

Kim, J.J. (2012) 'Constrained Unilateralism: Politics of Necessity and Urgency Decree in Argentina', Ponoma, CA: California State Polytechnic University, Department of Political Science.

Kontopoulos, Y. and R. Perotti (1999) 'Government Fragmentation and Fiscal Policy Outcomes: Evidence from OECD Countries', in *Fiscal Institutions and Fiscal Performance*, ed. by J.M. Poterba and J. von Hagen, Chicago, IL: University of Chicago Press, 81–102.

Kopits, G. and S. Symansky (1998) 'Fiscal Policy Rules', IMF Occasional Paper 162, Washington, DC: IMF.

Laeven, L. and F. Valencia (2008) 'Systemic Banking Crises: A New Database', Working Paper WP/08/224, Washington, DC: IMF.

Lao-Araya, K. (1998) 'The Fiscal Constitution of a Developing Country: The Case of Thailand', PhD thesis, Bloomington, IN: Indiana University.

Leblang, D.A. (2002) 'The Political Economy of Speculative Attacks in the Developing World', *International Studies Quarterly*, 46, 69–91.

Leblang, D.A. and W. Bernhard (2000) 'The Political Economy of Speculative Attacks in Industrial Democracies', *International Organization*, 54, 291–324.

Lieberman, E. (2005) 'Nested Analysis as a Mixed-Method Strategy for Comparative Research', *American Political Science Review*, 99, 435–452.

Manasse, P. (2005) 'Deficit Limits, Budget Rules, and Fiscal Policy', IMF Working Paper WP/05/120, Washington, DC: IMF.

Marlow, M.L. (1988) 'Fiscal Decentralization and Government Size', *Public Choice*, 56, 259–269.

Martínez, J. and J. Santiso (2003) 'Financial Markets and Politics: The Confidence Game in Latin American Emerging Economies', *International Political Science Review*, 24, 363–395.

Milesi-Feretti, G.M. (2003) 'Good, Bad or Ugly? On the Effects of Fiscal Rules with Creative Accounting', *Journal of Public Economics*, 88, 377–394.

Mora, M. and R. Varsano (2001) 'Fiscal Decentralization and Subnational

Fiscal Autonomy in Brazil: Some Facts of the Nineties', Texto para discussao 854, Rio de Janeiro: IPEA.
Moser, C. (2008) 'The Impact of Political Risk on Sovereign Bond Spreads: Evidence from Latin America', PhD thesis, Department of Economics, University of Mainz.
Mosley, L. (2000) 'Room to Move: International Financial Markets and National Welfare States', *International Organization*, 54, 737–773.
Mosley, L. (2003) *Global Capital and National Governments*, New York: Cambridge University Press.
Musgrave, R.A. (1959) *The Theory of Public Finance: A Study in Public Economy*, New York: McGraw-Hill.
Mussa, M. (2002) *Argentina and the Fund: From Triumph to Tragedy*, Washington, DC: Institute for International Economics.
Nieto-Parra, S. and J. Santiso (2009) 'Revisiting Political Budget Cycles in Latin America', Working Paper 281, Paris: OECD Development Centre.
Nordhaus, W.D. (1975) 'The Political Business Cycle', *The Review of Economic Studies*, 42, 169–190.
Oates, W. (1972) *Fiscal Federalism*, New York: Harcourt Brace Jovanovich.
Oates, W. (1985) 'Searching for Leviathan: An Empirical Study', *American Economic Review*, 75, 748–757.
Oates, W. (1989) 'Searching for Leviathan: A Reply and Some Further Reflections', *American Economic Review*, 79, 578–583.
Oates, W. (2005) 'Toward a Second-Generation Theory of Fiscal Federalism', *International Tax and Public Finance*, 12, 349–373.
Panizza, U. (1999) 'On the Determinants of Fiscal Centralization: Theory and Evidence', *Journal of Public Economics*, 74, 97–139.
Pauly, M.V. (1973) 'Income Redistribution as a Local Public Good', *Journal of Public Economics*, 2, 35–58.
Persson, T. and G. Tabellini (2000) *Political Economics: Explaining Economic Policy*, Cambridge, MA: MIT Press.
Persson, T. and G. Tabellini (2003) *The Economic Effects of Constitutions*, Cambridge, MA: MIT Press.
Plekhanov, A. and R. Singh (2007) 'How Should Subnational Government Borrowing Be Regulated? Some Cross-Country Empirical Evidence', *IMF Staff Papers*, 53, 426–452.
Pop-Eleches, G. (2009) *From Economic Crisis to Reform: IMF Programs in Latin America and Eastern Europe*, Princeton, NJ: Princeton University Press.
Poterba, J.M. and K.S. Rueben (2001) 'Fiscal News, State Budget Rules, and Tax-Exempt Bond Yields', *Journal of Urban Economics*, 50, 537–562.
Poterba, J.M. and J. von Hagen, eds. (1999) *Fiscal Institutions and Fiscal Performance*, Chicago, IL: University of Chicago Press.

Powell, A. (2002) 'The Argentina Crisis: Bad Luck, Bad Management, Bad Politics, Bad Advice', Business School Working Paper No. 24, Universidad Torcuato Di Tella.

Prohl, S. and F. Schneider (2009) 'Does Decentralization Reduce Government Size? A Quantitative Study of the Decentralization Hypothesis', *Public Finance Review*, 37, 639–664.

Prud'homme, R. (1995) 'The Dangers of Decentralization', *The World Bank Research Observer*, 10, 201–220.

Qian, Y. and B.R. Weingast (1995) 'Federalism as a Commitment to Preserving Market Incentives', *Journal of Economic Perspectives*, 11, 83–92.

Reinhart, C.M. and K. Rogoff (2009) *This Time is Different: Eight Centuries of Financial Folly*, Princeton, NJ: Princeton University Press.

Reinhart, C.M. and K.S. Rogoff (2011) 'From Financial Crash to Debt Crisis', *American Economic Review*, 101, 1676–1706.

Reinhart, C.M., K.S. Rogoff and M. Savastano (2003) 'Debt Intolerance', Brookings Papers on Economic Activity No. 34, Cambridge, MA: NBER.

Remmer, K. (2007) 'The Political Economy of Patronage Expenditure Patterns in the Argentine Provinces, 1983–2003', *Journal of Politics*, 69(2), 363–377.

Remmer, K.L. and E. Wibbels (2000) 'The Subnational Politics of Economic Adjustment: Provincial Politics and Fiscal Performance in Argentina', *Comparative Political Studies*, 33, 419–451.

Rodden, J.A. (2002) 'The Dilemma of Fiscal Federalism: Grants and Fiscal Performance around the World', *American Journal of Political Science*, 46, 670–687.

Rodden, J.A. (2003) 'Reviving Leviathan: Fiscal Federalism and the Growth of Government', *International Organization*, 57, 695–729.

Rodden, J.A. (2004) 'Comparative Federalism and Decentralization: On Meaning and Measurement', *Comparative Politics*, 36, 481–500.

Rodden, J.A. (2006) *Hamilton's Paradox: The Promise and Peril of Fiscal Federalism*, New York: Cambridge University Press.

Rodden, J.A. and G. Eskeland (2003) 'Lessons and Conclusions', in *Fiscal Decentralization and the Challenge of Hard Budget Constraints*, ed. by J.A. Rodden, G. Eskeland and J. Eskeland, Cambridge, MA: MIT Press, 431–466.

Rodden, J.A. and E. Wibbels (2002) 'Beyond the Fiction of Federalism: Macroeconomic Management in Multitiered Systems', *World Politics*, 54, 494–531.

Rodden, J.A., G. Eskeland and J. Litvack (2003) *Fiscal Decentralization and the Challenge of Hard Budget Constraints*, Cambridge, MA: MIT Press.

Roubini, N. and J.D. Sachs (1989a) 'Political and Economic Determinants of Budget Deficits in the Industrial Democracies', *European Economic Review*, 33, 903–934.

Roubini, N. and J.D. Sachs (1989b) 'Government Spending and Budget Deficits in the Industrial Countries', *Economic Policy*, 4, 99–132.

Roubini, N. and B. Setser (2004) *Bailouts or Bail-Ins: Responding to Financial Crises in Emerging Markets*, New York: Peterson Institute.

Samuels, D. (2002) 'Pork Barreling is Not Credit Claiming or Advertising: Campaign Finance and the Sources of the Personal Vote in Brazil', *Journal of Politics*, 64, 845–863.

Sanguinetti, P.J. (1994) 'Intergovernmental Transfers and Public Sector Expenditures: A Game-Theoretic Approach', *Estudios de Economia*, 21(2). Working Paper Series of the Department of Economics, University of Chile.

Scharpf, F. (1979) 'Die Theorie der Politikverflechtung. Ein kurzgefaßter Leitfaden', in *Politikverflechtung im föderativen Staat*, ed. by J.J. Hesse, Baden-Baden: Nomos, 21–31.

Scharpf, F. (1988) 'The Joint-Decision Trap: Lessons from German Federalism and European Integration', *Public Administration*, 66, 239–278.

Schuknecht, L., J. von Hagen and G. Wolswijk (2007) 'Government Risk Premiums in the Bond Market: EMU and Canada', CEPR Discussion Paper, Washington, DC: CEPR.

Shadbegian, R.J. (1999) 'Fiscal Federalism, Collusion, and Government Size: Evidence from the States', *Public Finance Review*, 27, 262–281.

Shambough, J.C. (2004) 'The Effects of Fixed Exchange Rates on Monetary Policy', *Quarterly Journal of Economics*, 119, 310–352.

Souza, S.S.d. (2008) 'Por Que a Fria Austeridade Das Regras Fiscais Nao Resiste ao Calo dasUrnas', PhD thesis, Universidade Federal de Pernambuco, Centro de Filosofia e Ciencas Humanas.

Stein, E. (1999) 'Fiscal Decentralization and Government Size in Latin America', *Journal of Applied Economics*, 2, 357–391.

Sturzenegger, F. and J. Zettelmeyer (2006) *Debt Defaults and Lessons from a Decade of Crises*, Cambridge, MA: MIT Press.

Tanzi, V. (1996) 'Fiscal Federalism and Decentralization: A Review of some Efficiency and Macroeconomic Aspects', in Annual World Bank Conference on Development Economics, Washington, DC: World Bank, 295–316.

Tanzi, V. and L. Schuknecht (2000) *Public Spending in the 20th Century: A Global Perspective*, Cambridge: Cambridge University Press.

Ter-Minassian, T., ed. (1997a) *Fiscal Federalism in Theory and Practice*, Washington, DC: IMF.

Ter-Minassian, T. (1997b) 'Intergovernmental Fiscal Relations in a Macroeconomic Perspective: An Overview', in *Fiscal Federalism in Theory and Practice*, ed. by T. Ter-Minassian, Washington, DC: IMF, 156–172.

Ter-Minassian, T. and J. Craig (1997) 'Control of Subnational Government Borrowing', in *Fiscal Federalism in Theory and Practice*, Washington, DC: IMF, 156–172.

Tiebout, C. (1956) 'A Pure Theory of Local Expenditure', *Journal of Political Economy*, 64, 416–424.

Tommasi, M. (2006) 'Federalism in Argentina and the Reforms of the 1990s', in *Federalism and Economic Reform: International Perspectives*, ed. by J. Wallack and T. Srinivasan, New York: Cambridge University Press, 25–84.

Treisman, D.S. (2000) 'Decentralization and Inflation: Commitment, Collective Action, or Continuity', *American Political Science Review*, 94, 837–857.

Treisman, D.S. (2004) 'Stabilization Tactics in Latin America: Menem, Cardoso, and the Politics of Low Inflation', *Comparative Politics*, 36, 399–419.

Treisman, D.S. (2007) *The Architecture of Government: Rethinking Political Decentralization*, New York: Cambridge University Press.

Tsebelis, G. (1995) 'Decision Making in Political Systems: Veto Players in Presidentialism, Parliamentarism, Multicameralism and Multipartyism', *British Journal of Political Science*, 25, 289–325.

Tsebelis, G. (2002) *Veto Players: How Political Institutions Work*, Princeton, NJ: Princeton University Press.

Tufte, E.R. (1978) *Political Control of the Economy*, Princeton, NJ: Princeton University Press.

United Nations Development Program (UNDP) (2005) *Fiscal Decentralization and Poverty Reduction*, New York: UNDP.

Vaaler, P.M., B.N. Schrage and S.A. Block (2006) 'Elections, Opportunism, Partisanship and Sovereign Ratings in Developing Countries', *Review of Development Economics*, 10, 154–170.

von Hagen, J. (1991) 'A Note on the Empirical Effectiveness of Formal Fiscal Restraints', *Journal of Public Economics*, 44, 199–210.

von Hagen, J. (1992) 'Budgeting Procedures and Fiscal Performance in the European Communities', Economic Papers No. 96. Luxembourg: EC.

von Hagen, J., M. Bordignon, M. Dahlberg, B.S. Grewal, P. Petterson and H. Seitz (2000) 'Subnational Government Bailouts in OECD Countries: Four Case Studies', Research Network Working Paper R-399, Washington, DC: Inter-American Development Bank.

von Hagen, J. and B. Eichengreen (1996) 'Federalism, Fiscal Restraints, and European Monetary Union', *American Economic Review*, 86, 134–138.

von Hagen, J. and I.J. Harden (1995) 'Budget Processes and Commitment to Fiscal Discipline', *European Economic Review*, 39, 771–779.

von Hagen, J. and G.B. Wolff (2008) 'What do Deficits tell us about Debt? Empirical Evidence on Creative Accounting with Fiscal Rules in the EU', *Journal of Banking and Finance*, 30, 3259–3279.

Wallis, J.J. (1991) 'The Political Economy of New Deal Fiscal Federalism', *Economic Inquiry*, 29, 510–524.

Webb, S.B. (2003) 'Argentina: Hardening the Provincial Budget Constraint', in *Fiscal Decentralization and the Challenge of Hard Budget Constraints*, ed. by J. Rodden, G. Eskeland and J. Litvack, Cambridge, MA: MIT Press, 189–212.

Webb, S.B. and C.Y. Gonzales (2004) 'Bargaining for a New Fiscal Pact in Mexico', World Bank Policy Research Working Paper 3284, Washington, DC: World Bank.

Wehner, J. (2010) 'Institutional Constraints on Profligate Politicians: The Conditional Effect of Partisan Fragmentation on Budget Deficits', *Comparative Political Studies*, 43, 208–229.

Wehner, J. (2011) 'Electoral Budget Cycles in the EMU: A Challenge to Context Conditionality', Department of Government, London School of Economics and Political Science.

Weingast, B.R. (1995) 'The Economic Role of Political Institutions: Market-Preserving Federalism and Economic Development', *Journal of Law, Economics and Organization*, 11, 1–31.

Weingast, B.R., K.A. Shepsle and C. Johnson (1981) 'The Political Economy of Benefits and Costs: A Neoclassical Approach to Distributive Politics', *The Journal of Political Economy*, 89, 642–664.

Wibbels, E. (2000) 'Federalism and the Politics of Macroeconomic Policy and Performance', *American Journal of Political Science*, 44, 687–702.

Wibbels, E. (2004) 'Decentralization, Democracy, and Market Reform: On the Difficulty of Killing Two Birds With One Stone', in *Decentralization and Democracy in Latin America: Causes and Consequences*, ed. by D. Samuels and A. Montero, Notre Dame, IN: University of Notre Dame Press.

Wierts, P. (2008) 'How do Expenditure Rules Affect Fiscal Behaviour?', Working Paper No. 166/2008, Amsterdam, NL: De Nederlandsche Bank.

Wildasin, D. (1997) 'Externalities and Bailouts: Hard and Soft Budget Constraints in Intergovernmental Fiscal Relations', Policy Research Working Paper No. 1843, Washington, DC: World Bank.

Wildavsky, A.B. (1975) *Budgeting: A Comparative Theory of Budgetary Processes*, Boston, MA: Little, Brown and Co.
World Bank (2000) 'Entering the 21st Century', World Development Report 1999/2000, Washington, DC: World Bank.
Ylaeoutinen, S. (2004) 'The Role of Electoral and Party Systems in the Development of Fiscal Institutions in the Central and Eastern European Countries', ZEI Working Paper B13-2004, Bonn: University of Bonn.

Index